MW01094356

THE LEGIBLE ELEMENT

THE LEGIBLE ELEMENT

essays

≈

RALPH SNEEDEN

The Legible Element
Ralph Sneeden

© 2023
All Rights Reseved.

ESSAYS
ISBN 978-1-958094-28-0

BOOK & COVER DESIGN ≈ EK LARKEN

Cover image ≈ "Eaton's Neck, Long Island"
by John Frederick Kensett, 1872

Author photo ≈ Deirdre Caldarone

EastOver Press encourages the use of our publications in educational settings.
For questions about educational discounts, contact us online:
www.EastOverPress.com or info@EastOverPress.com.

≈≈≈

PUBLISHED IN THE UNITED STATES OF AMERICA BY

EASTOVER
— PRESS —
ROCHESTER, MASSACHUSETTS
www.EastOverPress.com

For Gwen — the anchor, the sail
And for my sisters, Pati and Ev

In memory of my grandfather,
Ralph Aloysius Sneeden (1895–1976)

[handwritten annotations at top:]
questions
— thread — how do you find this thread?
— theme before or after? You start
— what moments are important?
— what order?
— Vocabulary? diff rhythm?
— humor?

CONTENTS

≈≈≈

[handwritten at bottom:]
responsibility
   ↳ danger/adventure

writing about water

As one who hangs down-bending from the side
Of a slow-moving boat upon the breast
Of a still water, solacing himself
With such discoveries as his eye can make
Beneath him in the bottom of the deeps,
Sees many beauteous sights (weeds, fishes, flowers,
Grots, pebbles, roots of trees) and fancies more,
Yet often is perplexed and cannot part
The shadow from the substance—rocks and sky,
Mountains and clouds, from that which is indeed
The region, and things which there abide
In their true dwelling—now is crossed by a gleam
Of his own image, by a sunbeam now,
And motions that are sent he knows not whence,
Impediments that make his task more sweet;
Such pleasant office have we long pursued
Incumbent o'er the surface of past time
With like success. Nor have we often looked
On more alluring shows (to me, at least),
More soft, or less ambiguously descried,
Than those which now have been passing by,
And where we are still lingering . . . .

— William Wordsworth

THE BLUE HOLE: A PREFACE

> . . . as if themselves calling back to the call of the
> waves.
>
> — *Edward Thomas*

In the shadow of the bulkhead where my grand-parents' backyard dropped into Wooley Pond, the rowboat was tethered to a half-buried cinder block. This kept it from drifting away when the tide was in. Normally, I'd be lugging the boat toward the water, swinging a leg over its gunwale, cinching the small outboard motor to the transom, or snugging the oars in their locks, pushing off. On this day, however, I untied the green, slimy rope knotted to the block itself and dragged the battered aluminum skiff in the opposite direction, past the jetsam, farther up onto dry ground. Then I tossed my towel over the prow. After rocking the cinder block free from the wet sand, I hefted it in front of my hips and carried it out into the cove, striding carefully until the water rose above my mouth and nostrils, sand turned to pebbles, pebbles to broken shells and mud. And then I kept going.

My grandfather had picked me up at the ferry from New London that morning, the beginning of my first day of summer vacation on Long Island. I'd unpacked, had lunch, changed into shorts, and wanted to get in the water as soon as I could. I had my reasons. Throughout that final month of my eighth-grade year, I'd been developing in the darkroom of my brain an image of myself sitting cross-legged on the bottom of Wooley Pond with that hunk of concrete in my lap.

I was, for the time being, an engaged student, a year or two just shy of having to crawl through my parents' gauntlet of accountability for deplorable grades. Getting out of New England to spend July and August with my grandparents wasn't yet tainted by shame or the parental threats of summer school echoing in my ears as I fled town with guns blazing. The deserved verbal beatings and new strictures would come soon enough after I was swallowed in the disconnection and chaos of the '70s public high school "shopping mall" curriculum. That junior high year, however, I had the good sense to refrain from self-immolating and warded off threats to the oasis by actually doing my work. But I remember that I was *just* beginning to hate school enough, or at least becoming bored with it, to resent not being able to spend as much time outdoors as I was accustomed.

Once I was deep enough and the grit turned to pudding underfoot, the pressure began to build in my ears. Keeping my promise to perform the scene I'd already envisioned, I settled down in the silt for as long as my breath held and the diamondback terrapins, sea robins, or toadfish would keep their distance. At this point, the key to the game was to deliberately picture myself installed in that row of classroom desks while I was crouching on the floor of the cove, *escape* fully submerged in the greenish, salty murk of Wooley Pond. It had nothing to do with endurance training. It was simply my imagination's way of reversing the charges, taking revenge, constructing a succession of mirror images that canceled or balanced the agonizing plight of being trapped indoors at school. *Outdoor person*

In one strong, steady exhalation, I released my anchor and rose to the surface, transported, cleansed, unburdened. And, to hide the event from my grandfather's microscopic administration of any tools, accessories, or waterborne vehicles on his property, I reminded myself to retrieve and reattach the skiff's anchor at low tide when the water would be below my collarbones. *not supposed to do this / under boat*

Benjamin Braddock's situation in the film *The Graduate* doesn't quite provide the ideal corollary: that image of the self-alienated hero alone at the bottom of the pool, withdrawn from the community that he reviles but that also created and enabled him. At least Dustin Hoffman's character had the luxury of a scuba apparatus. I was given a pretty long leash back then and didn't feel domestically suffocated at all; breaking away from family was not really on my radar, identity and purpose not part of my search. I just wanted to be in the water instead of hunkering behind a flip-top desk with the teacher's voice blowing past my ears as I listened to the humming of the overhead projector's little fan and pretended to ponder the equations on the screen.

The gravity that was pulling at me was something much bigger than the bright ego of my own solar system. This exercise was neither misanthropic nor a death wish, nor a sinister celebration of independence. In my habitual daydreams during the school year, I was always wading close to a fringe of eel grass netting shrimp with a friend, or anchored in the middle of the bay, stacking folds of squid up the shaft of a long hook. Or on my knees in sand at low tide chasing the siphons of soft-shell clams retreating between marooned periwinkles. Or riding my bike past the potato fields along Mecox Bay on my way to Flying Point, fins and towel lashed to the rack, anticipating the moment when I could spot the lone battle standard of the lifeguards' red flag flickering just above the dune grass, and I knew there would be waves.

But there is one character's rebellion I recognize as my own. Where does Truffaut's juvenile delinquent in *The 400 Blows* wind up in the film's final scene after he escapes from reform school? His jog to the sea through farmland, along fences and clotheslines, is one of the most moving long shots I know and hits very close to home with its pulse of flight and liberation. It's hard to misinterpret his fully clothed steps into the wash of low tide at Honfleur, his turning to face the camera accompanied by the decelerating pizzicato of the soundtrack's violins. We know that something has changed, a line has been crossed, even though his immersion is only ankle deep and, possibly, fraught with perplexity in the face of this frontier and its stunning novelty. His fate seems to have led him there almost *without* his knowing, whereas I knew exactly where to go during all my adolescent escapes. Still, I retain his example because of its purity, though the life behind Jean-Pierre Léaud's character (derived from Truffaut's own childhood) has gravitas, a tragic poignancy absent from my own situation and its predictable — if not privileged — mild, ritual traumas.

When I got my driver's license and took my father's 1974 Dodge Ramcharger for my first solo run, I peeled out neither for the wooded backroads nor toward the hangout in front of the Cumberland Farms convenience store, nor to the school parking lot. Instead, after picking up a friend, I raced up Route 95 to Newburyport, then to the north end of Plum Island where the barrier beach meets the inlet of the Merrimack River. I drove onto the beach near the jetty, out toward the point and straight down to the water where I buried both axles in the loose, wet sand near the tide line. Luckily, the tide was on its way out.

In his tender and elusive novel *So Long, See You Tomorrow,* William Maxwell got as close as any writer to nailing the emotional infrastructure of my childhood survival:

With the help of these and other commonplace objects — with the help also of the two big elm trees that shaded the house from the heat of the sun, and the trumpet vine by the window, and the white lilac bush by the dining room window, and the comfortable wicker porch furniture a nd the porch swing that contributed its creak . . . creak . . . to the sounds of the summer night — I got by from one day to the next.

Increments in my own would include the chokecherry tree in my grandparents' backyard, the aforementioned rowboat snugged or bobbing in the spartina, the corroded eel and minnow traps hanging from their designated nails on the garage wall. But for me, setting overruled objects in the long run, and I can confess now that I "got by from one day to the next" by thinking about water or the markers surrounding it — anything that I might associate with being in it, on it, or at least within striking distance, doing something near its shore. A cocktail of shameless physical self-gratification, play, curiosity, exploration, and, of course, the chase (for example, waves, clams, fish).

W. G. Sebald's narrator in *The Rings of Saturn* describes a couple of fishermen on the beach, facing the ocean, engrossed in their wait: "They just want to be in a place where they have the world behind them, and before them nothing but emptiness." And it's true; when we are overwhelmed by the din of the mainland, those of us cursed with any of the competing manias of wave riding, diving, fishing, sailing, or swimming might contemplate, brood on the ocean's flat horizon. Perusal of the void, however, the search for "nothing but emptiness," doesn't sit well. Observation is not enough for me, and it's the fullness I've always been after.

I remember being at an outdoor restaurant for lunch in Montauk with my parents, sisters, and aunt when I was about ten. Though I was excited to be eating on a pier studying the bustle of charter and commercial fishing boats, especially the bloody gills of a large mako shark hanging by its tail from a chain, I was a *spectator.* And it was torture. I kept peering through the boards at the glowing, lime-green water beneath our table. Walking to the restroom, I craned over the rail of the gangway trying to follow the schools of big shiners in their elliptical circuits around the pylons. It was a hot sunny day. I had on a button-down shirt, long pants, sneakers, socks, and I wanted to tear it all off and leap from the railing in my underwear. I wondered if the other people on that crowded deck felt the same way. They seemed content with eating and talking, enveloped in scenery, neither being distracted by it nor, I imagined, fighting any urge to swim. If they were mesmerized by what surrounded them, they weren't letting on. I felt sorry for them but also self-satisfied about what probably separated us, a benign arrogance that I doubt had anything to do with immaturity or with being a twitchy preadolescent boy. I would feel the exact same way today: wanting to connect with the water in some tactile, bodily manner because of how it *looks* at a certain moment.

In Massachusetts during the summer after my senior year of college, I answered a classified ad for a handyman in the *Gloucester Daily Times*. I got the job, and the house turned out to be a gothic, stately, but tired old place on the outskirts of Rockport, built in the late nineteenth century, I eventually learned, by the officer who had commanded the 7th Cavalry at the Wounded Knee Massacre. I mowed the lawn, weeded the gardens, split and stacked wood, and ended up painting the entire interior of the house (absurdly high ceilings, ornate moldings, mullions, miles of banisters and balustrades). The owner was a fussy retiree — a former State Department employee at a consulate in South Asia and distant relative of the aforementioned "Indian fighter" — who supervised and editorialized every one of my brushstrokes and shovel thrusts. I recall many things from that summer, but the lunch breaks especially, not only because they were respite from the tyrant, but because I was able to swim.

After a few weeks, my "boss" realized that his checklist of chores was an ambitious burden for a single worker, so he gave me permission to hire an "assistant" (hierarchy figured prominently in his worldview). Chris, a recently laid-off English teacher at Beverly High School, was about five years older and toying with the process of applying to graduate schools when he had answered my ad. We warmed up to each other quickly, not only because we both read, but especially after we realized that we shared a love for esoteric jazz and a common revulsion toward the person who was paying us and who became the target of our private, comedic mockery for the rest of the summer. We relished our status as local yahoos, lug-heads in cutoff jeans and fatigues, paint-spattered high-top sneakers and construction boots. Our overseer was given to reminding us that both his children had followed the family path from esteemed boarding school to Ivy League pinnacle—partially old-school white snobbery with a touch of the disorienting insecurity and purposelessness that can consume the recently pensioned, especially when they've held some position of importance and are used to giving orders. I think he was actually worried about us in his own tenderly perverse, paternal way, stymied because he couldn't fathom what sort of legitimacy, success, or status we could ever hope to secure given our academic histories and alma maters.

We were polite cowards, nodding obsequiously as he read a list of unnecessarily overwritten tasks for the day, glaring over his bifocals between increments to make sure we understood. We bristled silently when he grumbled some outrageous epithet about a Black deliveryman who'd just handed him a package. Because we sensed that he had us slotted as a couple of public school, state-educated lummoxes, we conspired to throw his summation off balance. When he stood over us, awkward and silent at the corner of the garage watching us stir cans of primer, we talked about the opening scene of Ellison's *Invisible Man*, Kafka's and Keats's tuberculosis, the politics behind Gogol's story "The Nose," the funky interplay in Keith Jarrett's European quartet, or Jack DeJohnette's fluid drumming on Ralph Towner's "Oceanus." We might as well have been speaking a lost Magyar dialect. Gradually, he left us alone, but I credit his mean tediousness as the reason why our lunches "off campus" began to stretch from thirty minutes to more than an hour. The destination was a short drive from the house, out along Marmion Way, past Straitsmouth Island to an untrammeled (at that time) headland at the end of a dirt road.

Emerson Point was one of the greatest hits on my list of scuba diving spots for going after lobster, a knob of granite between Loblolly Cove, Pebble and Cape Hedge Beaches, and the general area known as Land's End. I knew the bathymetry pretty well: reefy, relatively shallow nooks that had identifiable landmarks of angular shelves and the floors of miniature canyons where fluke skimmed, pollock hid in the waving bladder wrack, and the tidal current picked up steam between the mainland and the twin lighthouses of Thatcher's Island.

Below a particularly sheer fifteen-foot cliff was a deep, almost cylindrical shaft, ideal for jumping or diving into, keyhole-shaped because of a narrow gulley radiating seaward between submerged boulders. Like an underwater hallway, that weedy corridor beyond the round "hole" offered a perfect exit for the swimmer before he even broke the surface after a surgical plunge. Aiming for it wasn't too difficult because there was a rare patch of white sand at the center. Looking at it through twelve feet of clear, cold ocean revealed an explicit sapphire target, like a blue hole. It was the first thing I'd check every time we clambered over the rocks to the edge with our lunch bags. Even though I knew that swimming down to it and touching it would remind me what it really was, from above it was a reassuring passage to a parallel reality.

The summer was complicated. I watched Chris carefully, already launched on his professional trajectory as a teacher and academic. He was fiercely literary, eloquent, knew what he wanted to do, yet here he was, encountering workaday hardship, winding up back at square one: cleaning pine needles from gutters, weeding around rose bushes, and taking guff from a racist, unimaginative, pretentious former bureaucrat. Chris's situation, sandwiched in the strata of history and cultural juxtaposition piled around us in that coastal suburb, made me start to wonder what I was going to do with *my* life. Our time at that small mansion was both confusing and provocative with its weird composite, its legacies of violence and diplomacy, noblesse oblige, and exclusivity. Along with our own jackass bohemian presence grinding against it all. For a few months after graduation, I'd been floating in that liminal post-Humanities B.A. fog, no "real" job in sight, comfortable with a summer gig on the coast, though I could hear the start of a new school year *without* my participation sharpening its tongs. All I really understood about my identity and what drove me through life was that everything I did was in the interim: academics, prospective careers — all of it was just biding time until I could screw around in the water again. And, of course, to find accomplices who appreciated that obsession and proclivity.

Why water?

To name that summer as a confluence of the things that were shaping me intellectually, emotionally, morally, artistically, and professionally is easier to appreciate now. The dependability of the blue hole at Emerson Point, though finding it stemmed from the rebellion of our hedonistic shirking, seems to be bound more inextricably to that intersection than I had understood. In some aqueous way, it seems a symbol closer to the *aleph* in Borges's famous story of the same title: "one of the points in space that contains all other points."

I'd swum and bodysurfed for most of my early adolescence, but those lunch breaks were religious. Chris and I hadn't planned on jumping in, but the afternoon we initiated what would become, for me, a perennial desire that could be channeled, if you will, to other places, other swimming holes, other phases of my life when the grind needed to be held accountable, put in its place, or its definition overhauled. I was beginning to perceive the breath of Responsibility fogging the window that looked out on my *playing*, how it demanded apologies and explanations as it peered jealously into that frivolous world meant only for weekends and vacations. It was also when I realized that compromise was inevitable. The social and economic footwork

difficult

required to maintain a water-centric lifestyle wouldn't be easy (prohibitively expensive real estate aside). It wasn't something I was going to grow out of; rather, it would become my principal means of emotional recalibration and attitude adjustment. I'd also begun to realize that the people about whom I cared the most tended to feel similarly.

⌐ not alone

Emerson Point became an even more holy place when Gwen and I reconnected after college, and I started taking her out there. We'd drifted apart during my senior year when she went to France for a year abroad, but mostly because my immaturity had spurred me into a panicked, reckless flight in the middle of my first serious relationship. When we learned that we were both teaching within a few miles of each other on the North Shore, I got a second chance. And that coast figured ~~prominently~~ in repairing what my insecurity and fear had sabotaged. *who* -

My parents were poised to move from Rockport to Cape Cod, but Gwen and I still made the commute to Cape Ann from Beverly and Hamilton where we were living, respectively. We'd often go to Emerson Point at dusk after picking up sandwiches at a deli in Essex. Once we'd eaten and finished batting away mosquitoes for their five-minute crescendo, we'd watch the moon rise in back of Thatcher's Island. We talked for hours, learning more about each other's life, working out our understanding of exactly where things might be going between us. We'd wake up to the Atlantic's soughing, the moon's absence replaced by starlight liberated from all the North Shore's ambient light. It was a strange, exhilarating time for me, having to merge the worlds of human and outdoor love. Divulging such sanctuaries to another person was my entrance into a corridor of intimacy for which I'd been practicing subconsciously (almost like my scheme with the cinder block) but had never applied to reality.

Gwen's reaction to these forays was, I think, one of the most important factors in our joining forces. Once that door had opened, we began forging our way through my own list of watery *Heimaten* (homelands) starting with pilgrimages to the South Fork of Long Island and the Little Peconic Bay. Reciprocity figured into it, too, because she had skin in the game. Duxbury, Massachusetts, where she'd grown up, had its own trove of personal layers, storied coastal pockets to which she would eventually initiate me and which we would explore further with an evolving sequence of small sailboats. We've been married for thirty-eight years. These water-based transactions have driven the spiritual economics behind the most meaningful relationships in my life. Before leaving the North Shore for good in the early '90s, I remember taking a few friends and eventually our own kids out to Emerson Point, introducing them to it as if we owned it.

For half of the twentieth century and the first quarter of the twenty-first, my own family developed—as a result of squabbles and various preventable behaviors—a terrible habit of surrendering homes with immediate access to the water. Though geographically spoiled, I've also been conditioned to expect the worst, leapfrogging each tragic sale like a parasite across three modest but spectacularly situated properties, preparing for the next loss. Ultimately, it forces you to be more creative; you don't need a house on the water to have a life in or on the water. Between Gwen's intact childhood home and my own parents' migrations, we managed to sustain this privileged lifestyle for as long as we could, while putting our own three kids on the fast track, giving them a generous taste, at least, of what mattered most to us in our own lives, what we couldn't live without.

Renting a place in Montauk during the second pandemic winter, my daughter and her husband drove across the South Fork of Long Island to see for themselves my grandparents' three-bedroom bungalow on Wooley Pond, the one my kids had been hearing about since they were born. It was for sale for just under four million, even though it hadn't changed much and was still starkly modest for the Hamptons. And sort of recognizable. They sent me pictures, which of course broke my heart. And we laughed at the outrageous cost. Then the other night, a year later during the holidays, they Googled it to see if it had sold yet. It hadn't, but now was just *over* four million, a suspect, counterintuitive increase. This time we learned that it was being unloaded by a famously disgraced news anchor who'd been taken down by the #MeToo movement, and who owned a few (much more extravagant) properties between the bays and the ocean.

This was a moment when I felt a steel door shutting, partitioning my current life from a room in my past that had always seemed intact, open. The house has been out of my family for almost forty years, changed hands a few times, but, until my daughter's research, had always felt accessible, still robust in its active collusion with my imagination and memory. I'm not sure why her news changed everything for me. Perhaps it was the description attached to the ad, the realtor's overwritten evocation of the massive theoretical house that would replace my grandparents' cottage, in effect razing the monument to the origins of my own enduring tryst with water. I know the owner could never be attached to it the way I am, and that he would probably never live in it, only interested in sacrificing it to mounting legal fees. But I can't resist picturing the scoundrel, if he ever decides for some desperate reason to keep the property for himself: he's at the sink, alone, gazing at Wooley Pond over the stone countertops of his "chef's kitchen," clueless about the potency of the scene before him. His ignorance is excusable, of course, but in my scenario nevertheless seems bent on eliding from human history the apparition I'm trying to conjure right now: those ripples around a boy out there in a different century. A boy who, I'm beginning to appreciate, might have been more interested in the water itself than the house.

In high school chemistry and through under-graduate biology I had persistent trouble distinguishing between *hydrophylic* and *hydrophobic* properties of molecules. I kept wrestling with the idea that a "love of water," when it comes to physics and chemistry, means that a substance, because it is better equipped to bond with hydrogen, dissolves more easily. The hydrophobic molecule, however, repels water and so is better suited for materials used in boat building or the prevention of erosion. An object that is committed to maintaining a partition between itself and surrounding water stands a better chance of floating, not becoming part of the water. So, antithetically, surfers, swimmers, or sailors rely on hydro*phobic* construction to do what they love the most. And this has never made sense to me: the fear of water in my own molecular composition guaranteeing my love for it.

Trying to set this down, to give it shape with language, might seem a domestication or formalization of something that should remain mysterious, feral, nonverbal. But the impulse to *write* about it, I've found, can be as irresistible as diving in or wading out—with or without a chunk of cement. The expansion of my spiritual range, the intense awareness of life transformed by contact with water, despite the risk, have made me a better human, so why wouldn't I probe the depths? If I were to fixate on my fear of perishing in it—a concern that rears up even in my relatively tame inshore

29

experiences — I wouldn't be as inspired to shove off into the currents borne by the hydrophobic but leaky hull of my own prose.

Though a boat viewed from the beach appears to be hauling its wake behind like a white shawl, the truth is that you are watching the bow and propeller cut a gash that the ocean, in its adherence to the laws of physical science, smooths and reabsorbs. A life permeated by water has trailed me in a similar way, can't be wrung out or shaken loose no matter how many years go by, even though paradoxically whatever I did *in* it just stays right where it happened as if it never happened at all. Likewise, that sensorily undeniable set of waves that took my breath away a few hours ago, so raw in that recent experience, leaves no trace. So it's writing that ultimately needs to rip its own temporary swath, churn the surface of memory into something that seems more permanent or, at the very least, remains visible long enough to be appreciated by others — a fabricated wake articulating itself as time closes around it and someone tries to read it.

(covered up by the water

write to serve what happens in the water)

There is an undeniable and tenuous sanctuary in the act of prowling knee-deep through sun-shot water inside a perimeter of North Atlantic marsh grass, crab net at the ready, avoiding with each careful step the *punji* sticks of dead razor clams. That experience shares a porous border with the solace of sitting on a surfboard in the equivocating fringe of a Southern California fogbank, alone. Though only a

(vivid / disorienting / specific)

hundred yards and a quick paddle away, those essential glimpses and gaps — the intermittent evidence of land — are like memories and years in the process of being erased or jumbled by some insidious disease. We depend on them, nevertheless, for our bearings, those reminders of the other dimension. Water switches on a jolt of perspective that permits outright danger and euphoric sublimity some strange commerce in the cramped quarters of time and space. When riding a wave, paddling for one, or trying to get over and behind another to open water, I can think of *nothing* else. Writing or playing an instrument is like this for some of us, looking up after an hour or two or three, wondering where we've been. That's the hoped for — easy — part, the supremely selfish but self-obliterating phase of the journey, the throes of the experience. But the hiatuses — the times between those full engagements — are trickiest to negotiate. I'm beginning to wonder if what I was doing on Long Island as a child, imagining myself carrying that weight out into the cove, then actually doing it, then trying to conjure it in memory for the purpose of understanding it, lending it some form, was practice of some sort, my own way of respecting the artistic process that has propelled me before I was even aware of it. Sitting here, high and dry, poised to write, willing my entry into that lost world is precarious, especially avoiding the riptides or thumping closeouts of nostalgia.

Today's session at Sunset Cliffs is still vibrating under my skin. And because other experiences intrude, conflation is inevitable. *The Little Peconic Bay, Plum Island Sound, Punta Mesco, Emerson Point, Santorini, Atascadero, Black's Beach* . . . . The challenge is to keep all of these from intermingling, sloshing into one body of water. I'm trying to focus on that pulse of smaller sets that arrived out of nowhere, hypnotic, lifting and depositing me where I'd been waiting, where the possibility of texture had been inconceivable, until it was suddenly rifling in a muted explosion along the invisible cliff face in back of me. Suddenly, bigger waves advanced with lips snarling and teeth bared.

If I was going to hitch a ride, I had to stop thinking or being distracted by the circling grebe keeping one red eye on me after it shattered the surface, beak scissoring into a shoal of grunion or smelt. I needed to scramble a little farther outside the reef to avoid getting buried, to paddle farther into the disorienting gray, the opposite direction of home. *Home*: where this very evening, when my feet are still trying to rekindle the warmth stolen by the Pacific, I feel even more powerfully the obligation to describe the day in words, to imagine myself out there again.

— Point Loma Heights, San Diego

PART I

STEPPING OFF: CONFESSIONS FROM THE LITTORAL ZONE

And we went on living it, like a wave, that doesn't
know it is at every moment different water.

— *Alan Williamson*

hooly!

In 1967, age six and a half, <u>I almost drowned</u>
when I wandered into a deep cleft between
sandbars. That particular summer on the Jersey
Shore my older sisters had taken to riding what
seemed to be kind, propellant waves with the rafts
our mother had rented near the boardwalk. They
were the heavy-duty canvas sort you couldn't
buy in a store. I wasn't a confident swimmer yet,
so my mother wouldn't even let me near one,
which made no sense; the rafts were oversized
life preservers after all. Instead, I'd pace ankle-
deep, consigned to chasing the almond-sized mole
crabs before they burrowed back into the loose,
aqueous sand, occasionally gazing out to catch
one of my sisters bouncing, skimming toward
me with the rictus of astonished play carved into
her face. Her white knuckles gripped the raft's

haha

yellow rubberized prow while a wreath of foam exploded around her shoulders. I knew she wasn't taunting me, performing for my land-locked benefit; she was in another world.

We were on our family's annual pilgrimage from Bergen County to visit my grandmother's place in Seaside Heights, a white clapboard two-family beach shack she had owned since the 1940s, the above-ground portion of which had been surrendered to renters for the season. We bunked with her in the cramped basement apartment, sprawled on couches or doubled up in the big, musty bed that filled the entire guest room, emerging each morning to the sidewalk as if from a bunker, into the salty August daylight on our way to the beach. Day after day we'd say goodbye to her, and I used to wonder why she never accompanied us, how one could live so close to the ocean and want absolutely nothing do with it. Her interest was focused on administering the terrestrial concerns of the parking lot she owned next door. A car would pull off Franklin Avenue onto her patch of beige gravel, and she'd be on it like a moray eel shooting after a hapless shrimp, her apron bulging, swinging with quarters and rubber-banded cylinders of dollar bills.

We were lucky to get her distracted blessing before beginning our trek up the sidewalk, a tangle of rattling beach chairs and towels around our necks, cooler suspended between us like a wounded comrade. As we ploughed through the smells of creosote, tar, and sausages and peppers, the morning sun revved its punctual rejuvenation of bungled frozen custards, gobs of taffy, and pizza slices painted on concrete, their being rinsed by a downpour long overdue. But ascending the boardwalk ramp, I felt my nose dilate with the subtle fizz of recently broken surf. It cut through the sweet, rancid carnival fog, charged the wires of my imagination, quickened my pace, but also sent a throb of alarm through my groin, that same ghost organ that might quiver to life if you were gazing down from the flimsy scaffolding of an abandoned fire tower or lighthouse railing. Or, in this case, when you're hovering in that pocket of liminal disorientation where Seaside Heights' predictable kaleidoscopic decadence butts against the majestic but alarming natural power of a swell that has arrived mysteriously overnight.

Bruce Brown's *The Endless Summer*, touted to be civilization's first mainstream surf documentary, had finally landed at the Shore in 1967, a year after its release. My sisters took me to see it, and like millions of other people I was caught in that film's undertow. While recounting our favorite images at Maruca's Pizza afterward, I settled on what I realize now must have been the Waimea sequence: clips of Greg Noll and others rocketing down the jacking faces of the film's biggest waves, their freefalls and pile-driving wipeouts. That same night, the adrenal residue of the movie fueled my stroll along "the boards" with my family, where I spied the fluorescent black-light version of the movie poster in one of the stalls and began hoarding my allotted pinball money for the rest of the summer. That casual silhouette with the white-cuffed board shorts was me, the head with balanced surfboard my own. I had never been within arm's reach of a surfboard, and yet I could feel the bulk of balsa or fiberglassed foam pressing on my scalp, the heat of that enormous, almost nuclear sun on my neck.

Seaside had its surf culture before that movie, however. I'd watched the local practitioners bobbing in the lineup off Casino Pier as if they were a pod of rare, migrating mammals. My sisters told me stories about surfers grabbing the dorsal fins of dolphins and being towed to sea. Once, flying a kite with my father on a stormy day, I'd watched two surfers paddle out and disappear into a hundred yards of froth, then weave back miraculously *beneath* the pier, whose pilings were slicing the slate-colored swells like a barnacled mandolin. This danger was almost as swashbuckling as my mother's stories of German U-boats out there twenty-five years earlier, how they exploited the gaudy lights to silhouette freighters and torpedo them. Eventually, the length of the boardwalk was shrouded with precautionary blackout curtains behind which she and my grandmother worked the wheels of chance, calling numbers, doling out cigarettes to winners, sweeping nickels from the painted counter.

The morning after seeing the movie, I was still riding the goofy voice-over of *The Endless*

Summer, which now resonated through my very real proximity to surf, conveying me down the ramp past the booth where our hands were stamped with waterproof fluorescent ink. Descending to the sand itself, I must have decided that this would be the day of communion. I made for the water before we had even popped the umbrella, skimming under my mother's radar while she was working suntan lotion into my blonde middle sister's permanently scorched shoulders. My dad wasn't with us this time; his vacation rarely meshed with our trips to The Shore.

Venturing out to the sandbar was like moonwalking, striding and letting the buoyancy suspend me in a protracted antigravity leap, keeping my chin above the water, springing each time my toes met the sand. I loved the feeling of walking out to sea where it should have been getting deeper, only to arrive at the thigh-deep sanctuary. It felt illicit. There were plenty of people around, but I had not considered that most of them were at least twice my height and were, perhaps, swimming. Strutting around on my new stage, I braced myself as the leftovers of bigger sets rolled through, briefly buoyant in the swirling whitewater. One of these waves must have carried me, because when it passed and I expected to be set down again, bottom never came. I sank, immediately chugging what seemed like a pint as my feet searched for purchase on an invisible staircase; a few yards in any direction probably would have delivered me to another merciful platform. I remember bobbing once to take a sputtering breath, my face a floating, contorted mask. It was like emerging from those disappointing dreams of flying; in your sleep one prong of consciousness is still engaged, needling your dream-belief that flapping will keep you aloft, until you wake and understand that the element through which your limbs are pumping is, of course, not capable of doing what you thought.

disappointing

I went down again and took in more water, contemplating the bright sun through its effervescence. And then, suddenly, I was locked in two copper-red arms, staring up into the pissed-off face of a lifeguard. "OK. OK. You're all right. I've got you," he murmured, standing chest-deep, slinging me onto his hip and lugging me to shore as I spat and belched, squirming like a greased monkey. I hadn't even heard the high-pitched staccato of his whistle, the warning signal that someone was in distress. It was a scene I had heard and watched transpire dozens of times as lifeguards leapt from their chairs and sprinted into the breakers collared with the tethers of rescue buoys, butterflying out to some poor idiot. I worshipped them, a sucker for the brand of heroism that radiated from their ranks, whether in teams pulling the oars of surf dories out and over the crests, or solitary, high in their white perches, blond crew cuts shrouded in their red hooded sweatshirts, identity no more than a nose glazed with zinc oxide, the glint of sun off

in too much distress

of aviator glasses. They were soldiers, *lifers,* not high school kids who'd taken summer jobs.

I still marvel at the quickness of his having spotted me among so many, dropping from his post and getting to me before I disappeared. To say there were a thousand people would not have been an exaggeration. He could have been looking the other way for a second, simply rubbing an eye that was stinging with Coppertone or checking out some bikinied coed. But something illuminated me in his peripheral vision, and he had flown to scoop me up before my mother realized what was going on. When he returned me to her, she hadn't even known I was the one at the heart of the commotion. He was not kind to her. It was my own fault, yet I let him go up one side of her and down the other, standing there dripping in his official white trunks and red, numbered tank top, barking a critique of her parenting skills as she shrank before him, glancing down at me, beginning to grasp the situation.

I've been teaching high school for more than thirty years now, at a boarding school in New Hampshire for more than twenty of them. It's a sweet deal if you can survive the ten years of mandatory dormitory duty, living among forty-eight adolescent boys in a perpetual state of wondering what nascent tragedy or potential lawsuit is brewing on your watch. It was a lot of fun, a few blissful years sailing by on banter, manageable whiffs of dope smoke in the corridor, curable homesickness, tame roommate disputes, easily stifled whining. But in the first third of one particular year, I decided unequivocally that the time to pull the chute had arrived. We had taken the entire dorm on its annual trip south to the beach in Massachusetts for a "bonding" day, and one of the students was swept out to sea.

My family had moved from New Jersey to Massachusetts in the late '60s, and sailing a small boat with my father had acquainted me intimately with the estuaries and coves around Cape Ann and the North Shore. The mythic power of that tidal current rifling Plum Island Sound was the first thing I had described to the boys as I stood at the front of the bus, imploring them to stay in sight if they were going to dip so much as a toe, then finishing with the perennial mandate to pick up their trash. It was an achingly beautiful late September morning, a weekday, and with the combination of summer's having ended and the workweek having reabsorbed its toilers, we had the place to ourselves.

The boys had dispersed into pods of activity: a brutal, misnamed version of touch football, awkward commerce between respectable and severely challenged Frisbee tossers, the solemn circle of overachievers blowing sand out of their calculators, and the predictable neck-deep burials. No one was interested in swimming. The faculty relaxed; a couple of them embarked on a walk. I chatted with the dean of students, who had volunteered to come along with us on the *rhetorical questions*

excursion. Who wouldn't trade a school day for a morning at the end of a protected coastal National Wildlife Refuge? The south end of Plum Island is one of the rare, protected barrier beaches north of Cape Cod, a long strand that hadn't been devastated by development in the middle of the past century like the beleaguered coasts of New Hampshire and southern Maine. We were all the way out, past the last parking lot where the spit reverts to the State. A few disheveled surf casters flanked us, preparing to pack it in, installed before sunrise, their lanterns doused.

Barely thirty minutes had passed before one of my colleagues came motoring back toward us, his legs grinding the sand as he sprinted around the point's obstacle course of rocks. Panting, almost in tears, he explained that one of the boys was now thrashing in the standing waves of the current. "Where?" we asked, concerned but still cool, thinking we'd had them all in our sight. "How far from shore?" Armored and numbed by dorm experience against knee-jerk alarm, we let it sink in.

"He is gone. He is *out* there," came the gasping reply. Doubled over, my colleague explained that another teacher was still around the point trying to raise the Ipswich police on his phone. *Sic* The dean and I looked at each other and began running toward the carpet of glitter the sun was laying across the channel. The absence of any boats, which had been an element of serenity, now transformed the panorama to a wasteland. When I rounded the point and faced south, the

43

glare grew even more intense. I could barely focus on the water. "Where is he?" shouted the dean. "Can you see him?"

Cupping my hand over my brow allowed me to make out the tiny dot of a head more than two hundred yards out. It was as insignificant as trash, a detached mooring buoy or a bucket blown from a dock, flotsam disappearing behind swells and reappearing, conveyed east as if on a haywire factory belt. There would be no whistles, no trained paramilitary professional to the rescue, just a few teachers, paralyzed, pacing frantically. No one was going in that water. No one was going to let anyone else go in. One of us made a tepid gesture of wading out, but the others shouted him back.

The head went under, popped up, the arms making an almost sleepy effort to swim as the temperature of the water began its cruel drain. Sometimes, because of the glare, we'd lose him completely for a few excruciating seconds, and my heart would accelerate with disbelief that it was over, that it had happened at all, the consequences descending like a curtain of galvanized chains. While the teacher who had remained at the scene continued shouting into his phone, two people we had previously not seen arrived: a fisherman, who had taken it all in from the point, and a sunbather, who had heard the shouting from where he was tucked back in the dunes, out of the wind. Both had placed calls to the Coast Guard up in Newburyport and to the Essex police. The little head, however, was already another hundred yards away.

From that distance the mouth of the Ipswich River is camouflaged, the jetty at the end of Steep Hill Beach the only indicator of a breach, and on its north side the cottage-peppered headland of Little Neck. That's where I spotted the orange rescue boat emerging tantalizingly slowly from a fold in the marsh. No mistake. We pointed at it, shouted, waved, but even if they could have seen us, they would have written us off as a bunch of dancing maniacs. Then the tame wake burst into a rooster tail and the boat was on a wire for the drowning kid.

When they brought him to us, he was wrapped in a gray blanket, shivering, incongruous among the Harbor Patrol team in their orange survival suits. The boat idled across the current into the beach where I stood thigh-deep, *lucky* arms crossed. It was a fluke that they were out there to begin with, the only reason being a *training run,* breaking in the town of Ipswich's new toy. When they got the call, they happened to be just inside the estuary, putting the engine through its paces, so unfamiliar with its operation that as they approached the shallows I had to grab the gunwale to show them the hydraulic lift switch on the throttle, instruction that distracted me briefly from wanting to reach up, grab the boy by his hypothermic throat, rip him from the deck, and pummel him senseless. This child who had been seconds away from drowning, whom the water had taken like a train.

flushhm

In a photo from 1979, in Cayucos, on the Central Coast of California, the dry hills wrinkle into themselves behind my sister and me as we pose in front of an oleander's constellations. We are in wetsuits, holding a pair of her boyfriend's surfboards: Gerry Lopez Lightning Bolts, just over seven feet, a white pintail and a purple swallowtail. The pin, especially, is for experienced surfers and bigger waves, and arguably among the least appropriate board for novices.

Evie had been teaching elementary school out there for about five years, and I'd flown from Massachusetts to visit her for the summer after my freshman year in college, my first time back in California since the early 1960s. I had been born in Los Angeles after my parents relocated there in the mid-1950s from Long Island. They returned East when I was a toddler. Only in recent decades, after my rededication to surfing (thanks to my son's persistent nagging) have I wondered what trajectory my life would have taken if my family had stayed put in the San Fernando Valley and its quick drive over the mountains, through Topanga Canyon, to the Pacific. As it was, the return to my first coast to visit my sister was not so much a homecoming as another condition for the ongoing cycle of initiation.

Throughout the 1970s, any velocity-curious kid in the country had his own private, vicarious Southern California experience through the medium of *Skateboarder* magazine. But I had also subscribed to *Surfer* magazine not because I actually surfed, but because I wanted to. Against all rational wariness from nearly succumbing to the ocean in New Jersey when I was six, I was still fixated on the idea of riding waves. I had rolled my way back to it through skateboarding, when the urethane wheel, in all its glowing, amber beauty, began to appear on the shelves of bike stores on the North Shore of Massachusetts. This is when the allure of California had begun to tug at my aesthetic and imagination even more powerfully; before adolescence I'd denied my origins in the West, because they were framed by such a narrow window in my family's migrations. But now I was getting close to the age at which I could actually go there on my own if I wanted to.

Skateboarding came at a time when I was almost burnt out on hockey, which I had been playing year-round since the age of nine. Team sports and coaches had worn some of my gang down, eventually, as politics intensified and the stakes rose with our ages. Some of us just wanted something different after being ground through the mill of town and high school football/soccer/ hockey/baseball leagues for ten years, and pond hockey was more fun than the organized version. My friends and I turned to things like Frisbee. We snorkeled in the murky local lakes, terrorizing frogs, pickerel, and sunfish with hardware-store spears. We golfed illegally on our swampy, mosquito-infested public courses. But skateboarding, especially, began to quench

escape from hockey politics

the need for action — and danger, perhaps — that hockey had satisfied throughout my childhood. My parents, however — like the seniors at my high school — thought skateboarding was childish, considering the cumulative money and time they had invested in hockey, driving me to rinks all over Essex and Middlesex counties and into the heart of Boston on subzero weekend mornings.

My new sport conjured the reputation of an outsider, a persona to which I was not entirely opposed at age sixteen. Afternoons and weekends, my friends and I cruised our four-town radius looking for places to skate, like thieves casing prospective bank targets or convenience stores. There was the slick asphalt of new developments such as Pye Brook Lane in Boxford, alongside and beneath which we had fished for trout each spring. There was the tiered, steep labyrinth of the Ipswich General Cemetery, which we, in our gothic athleticism, called "Death Row." But these sites always led to confrontations with groundskeepers, police, mourners, or mothers — not unlike our own — who were simply trying to get to the grocery store without crushing beneath their station wagon tires the limbs and skulls of any number of skateboarding teenagers trussed and armored in knee and elbow pads, work gloves, and hockey or motorcycle helmets.

The culture of skateboarding, or even a subtle whiff of its outlaw promise, had come to me from the place where I was born, and yet I don't remember being bitter about the life that *could have been.* Even as I pored over the photos of headbanded, horizontal blond hipsters smacking the tiled lips of drained swimming pools in my magazines, I never cursed my parents for leaving California. If there had been yearning, I tamed it. I had been deprived of coming of age in the epicenter of that revolution, but I was happy where I was in New England, and part of that was because we seemed to be doing something no one else was. — *different*

My friends and I drove to Boston one day after we'd heard that an indoor skatepark (the city's first) called Zero Gravity had opened on Lansdowne Street. It was the beginning of the end, the day when my love affair with skateboarding began to sputter for two reasons: you had to pay, and you had to do it indoors in a competitive pit with judgmental strangers. For us, it was not supposed to be about community. Most surfers are on the hunt for empty lineups, and most fly fishers flee from having to share, elbow to elbow, a gravel bar or stream bank. In this new, complicated frontier, we were suddenly transported to a realm not unlike the teeming weekend ski slopes of New Hampshire, jostling in the lift lines with people who had better equipment, who reminded us that we were part wanted to be different? of a mob, of something popular, *normal.* At the tops of the skatepark's torturous wooden structures, we stood self-consciously in the queue as if on a gallows, outsiders in a new hierarchy of local kids who could rip like the dudes in

Skateboarder, ruled the place, and seemed to have nothing but scorn for anyone they didn't recognize. Clad in our improvised gear, we predated *Ghostbuster* impersonators. The world whizzed around us like a National Geographic nature special, a storm of posturing, wheeled baboons scrapping for alpha dominance in a coliseum of curved plywood ramps. Our opponents seemed to ignore the artifice of that built environment, a maze that mimicked the contours of water. But it wasn't water. Pulling up at a break where clean waves are firing inflicts an irrepressible excitement that freshly rolled pavement or elaborate skateparks could never match. I've come close to yanking the zipper (or arm) right off my wetsuit trying to gear up in frenzied anticipation.

A few years later, I brought my prized skateboard, a deep red Gordon and Smith Fibreflex, to college with me. I rode it to class a few times before relegating it to various apartment closets under the rubble of shoes. At my first teaching job, I filed it on my office bookshelf like a knick-knack. It was stolen soon after that.

Throughout my adolescence, the memory of almost drowning did not loom as a prohibitive dream; rather, it became a foundational experience that fueled a desire to be more comfortable—and not stupid—in surf. Skateboarding, with its requisite road rash and sprained wrists, showed me a relatively safe and logical route back to the breakers. And when I began to spend summers with my father's parents on the South Fork of Long Island, I was rebaptized by a love affair with bodysurfing at Flying Point Beach. I had learned not only to swim but to be comfortable spending time beneath the surface, too, to roll with whatever the waves demanded if I couldn't dodge them. I knew that sandbars were rugs waiting to be pulled out from under any wader. In a tight swarm, towel-capes flapping from our shoulders, swim fins and lunch bags lashed to our ten-speeds, my new friends and I raced through the town of Water Mill, then along the potato fields, toward the dunes and the promise of waves peeling across the bars. When we were old enough to drive there, I got my first literal taste of surfing by floundering on a borrowed board. After a few hours in sand-pounding beach break, I walked away spitting the grit from my teeth, frustrated, disillusioned, my bruises and scrapes suspiciously similar to what the asphalt had dealt.

The day my sister's boyfriend had taken the preposterous photo of us in California, we'd climbed down a ladder from a restaurant on the Embarcadero and paddled across the harbor at Morro Bay. Weaving between otters and the rank hulls of fishing and abalone boats at their moorings, he led us out to the Strand and the jetty south of the imposing helmet of Morro Rock. This was to be the first time I'd tried to surf *with* anyone, a tutor who was an ally, a local resource, who yelled, "Paddle!" and "Pop *UP*, Raoul!" in a West Coast drawl that made his new French nickname for me even cooler by butchering it. Real-time instruction focused on timing is what will nudge a beginner over the hump, but it was also his presence in the water that made me blot out the potential nightmare of those chest-high, sloppy summer waves shearing along the boulders, which seemed enormous now that I was among them.

He had arrived on the Central Coast having fled the vortex of drugs, general self-destruction, and overrun beaches South of L.A. where he'd grown up. When my sister met him, he'd been landscaping in and around Cayucos, just north of San Luis Obispo, while studying the nascent science of hydroponics at Cal Poly. Renting a house high above the town, he could wake up, grab the binoculars, and analyze the arriving swell all the way from Atascadero north to Estero Bay. In retrospect I admire how casual he was in his responsibility for my sister and me out there, while he managed to catch a few waves himself. The new perspective of being at eye level — not on the beach — behind a good surfer as he drops and trims was transformative. Straddling my board, so engrossed in watching his light brown hair rise above the crest thirty yards down the line, or the burst of spray as he spun into a cutback, I was repeatedly flushed to shore by the bigger sets.

I scratched my way back outside, caught my breath, and waited, having already botched my first dozen attempts. When the right train arrived, climbing aboard didn't seem like a landmark event. I paddled, recognized from

bodysurfing the moment when you can transfer
the source of thrust to the wave itself, and stood
up on the deck, balance and control a state to
which my body adjusted before I had a chance
to think. The residual gift of skateboarding.
My sister, standing next to her board in the
shallows, howled and pumped the air with her
fist. She told me later that in my initial crouch,
long arms dragging the surface, I reminded her
of a gibbon. And this is the image I haven't been
able to shake on subsequent trips back West to
surf with a nephew who was living in Santa
Barbara and with friends at Hollister Ranch,
west of Gaviota: an aging primate caught in
some perverse, inverted evolutionary phase,
gliding across the water's surface instead of
army crawling from it to higher ground.

California hadn't made me cocky, but it
gave me permission, that following winter in
1980, to try my luck in Massachusetts at Good
Harbor Beach in Gloucester, not far from where
my parents had moved the year before. In my
possession was a permanent loaner, a Natural
Art shortboard one of my friends had picked
up in Florida. He'd lost interest in it after a
year, moved away, and never asked for it back.

I arrived at the desolate, snowbanked parking lot already wedged into the restrictive
scuba-diving wetsuit I'd rented. This is what
probably tipped off the two guys out there that
I was a "kook"—a clueless poser. I paddled out
between the north end of the beach and a miniature East Coast version of Morro Rock called

Salt Island, where the beefy, overhead, post-nor'easter swells were wrapping around the point. The two surfers already in the lineup were hunched in collusion, the noses of their boards almost touching. Snow had begun to fall, drifting among us from the leaden sky like ash from a distant volcano. As I wobbled past them, trying to push a little farther outside the break to play it safe, they didn't waste a second. "HEY!!" one shouted, without any intonation of snide humor. "If you get in trouble out here, we're not saving you. You're gonna fuckin' drown."

I forget what my response was, but I remember despising them for years, even as my surfing progressed in fits and starts until I decided to put it on hold. The loaner haunted me from various basements and garages, its presence in each crypt calling like a premature burial victim as my wife and I began the scramble through our young marriage from apartment to apartment. Selling it (was it even ours to sell?) is probably what preserved our relationship and allowed me to focus on family and career instead of becoming another surfing cliché: the domestic casualty. Everyone has to begin somewhere, but permission can be hard to come by, given the edgy tolerance of the aspiring by the anointed as we bumble through our early stages. But now, when I see some twenty-first-century incarnation of my novice persona thrashing through my personal surfing space on a dangerous midwinter day, I look back on those two dudes in Gloucester with some affinity and respect. They hadn't told me, "Get the fuck out of here. Go back to shore, or *we'll* drown you." They simply evaluated my level of skill and told me they wouldn't be responsible, wouldn't be able to rescue me from myself.

Two years ago, when my twenty-three-year-old son phoned from Dakar to tell us he'd blown out his ACL for the third time, I wondered what sort of father I was, encouraging him to surf in Senegal while studying there. A few years before Africa, when he was eighteen, he had gone to Samoa—alone—having socked away two summers' wages from landscaping and crewing on a lobster boat. He called us after surfing his first offshore reef. "It was huge," he'd emailed. "Double overhead, steep, and fast. But Dad, I knew I could do it." And then he went on to describe the drop, trimming along the concave wall, mesmerized by the jagged coral passing by through that warped blue storefront like a wicked skyline, the suburbs just outside an even shallower reef surfers call "the surgeon's table." Jake is famous for injuring himself, always finding a way to lacerate a finger, crush a hand, or dislocate a shoulder, not to mention the repeated assaults on his right knee. In his former coaches' words: spirit and ambition exceed skill.

I know I can do it. . . . This is how we persuade ourselves when confronting the ocean in its more complicated moods. The water either invites or repels, the latter being the easiest to recognize; but when you read its face and decide you're *going in*, enraptured by what it looks like at that moment, it's easy to forgo the contingencies. Whatever seduces you must piggyback a chemical more subtle and insidious than adrenaline, which gives you only a strength you never thought you had, not a trippy sort of confidence. I'm talking about something more hedonistic, deliberately selfish, the accompanying interior monologue something like: *This is going to be fun: my wetsuit makes me float. My board floats, too, and is attached to my ankle by a leash. Therefore, I am safe.* You tend to forget there might be someone at home waiting for you.

At twelve, Jake synced my return to surfing with his own introduction to the sport when he badgered me into buying and "sharing" a board with him. I remember distinctly watching him trip on the leash as he wrestled the seven-foot WRV down the shore into the benign moil of Narragansett Town Beach in Rhode Island. And when he emerged after half an hour, I read in his brows and the shape of his mouth an ecstasy that was tinged with dismay. He had scared himself. Just what I'd hoped.

My children have an enduring obsession with *Into the Wild*. The parent in me likes to think that Jon Krakauer's parable about Christopher McCandless's dead-end example in the Alaskan wild tempers their indulgences with hesitation because of the tragic hero's unmitigated recklessness. Whenever he is mentioned in our household, my wife's reaction is swift and usually spliced to a hefty rope of expletives. My kids always take her on, their empathy rational because it acknowledges the darkness behind any romantic gauze around the book or Emile Hirsch's character in the movie; they're thinking abstractly about independence and rebellion against societal expectations, saying *no* to the college/career conveyor belt. For them, it was less about adventure than about principles that never crossed my mind as I sat open-mouthed, aspirating *The Endless Summer.* I wanted *in.* And I suppose I always have, craving immersion or buoyancy whenever I gaze into or across a body of water, whereas my children's intellectualization has, in the long run, been healthy. Even Jake, with all his physical mishaps, seems to have tempered his experiences or aspirations with wisdom and perspective that eluded his father. Surfing with him over the past two decades has also forced me to mature in my own relationship with the waves, trapping me in the confusing dual role of parent/protector and accomplice. When he takes off on a gorgeous wave and I lose sight of him, I am exhilarated and proud, but I am counting the seconds until I see him kick out safely and paddle back out to me. When we watch slick, music-injected surf documentaries, I am becalmed when our sighs and groans are harmonized, as we react to images of monster waves we have no interest in riding.

But today's surfing flicks are so extreme in their conditions they make Bruce Brown's seem safe. That's why I didn't get too worked up when a reprint of that movie poster appeared affixed to my middle daughter's closet door when she was in middle school. One surfing memorabilia website has my original black-light version selling for $594. What did ever happen to that thing? Streaked with the triage of yellowing Scotch tape, its manically tacked corners looking as if they'd been blasted with buckshot, it probably just disintegrated.

This past summer, after surfing all morning, my son and I pulled into the local shop because he needed a few things. I waited in the broiling car until he returned, a teetering stack of surf wax balanced in the crook of his elbow and a sheepish smirk on his face. He leaned conspiratorially into the driver's-side window. "Better go in," he said. "Robert *August* is in there." I was fried. My ribs and lats felt as if they'd been through a dirty boxing match. I just wanted to get home and take a shower, rehydrate. Then I contemplated the significance of this convergence, that I might actually get a glimpse of one of *The Endless Summer's* stars, who was making an appearance at the surf shop because they sold his company's longboards. "Come on, Dad. You *have* to," Jake said, so I climbed out, assenting to a quick hit-and-run tourist gawk at a celebrity. But on my way in the door, Dave, the owner of the shop, who'd become a friend over the years, greeted me with a handshake and shepherded me directly to August, who was standing alone near a rack of bikinis, holding a license plate that said *Ask Me About Free Naked Surf Lessons.* Dave made the introductions, and as I shook the

humor

sixty-eight-year-old August's tanned hand, we laughed about the plate and how it just might keep him from getting mobbed.

We had a brief conversation that now seems more like hallucination than memory or belief. So many things I could have asked him and didn't, about the impetus for the purported "longboard renaissance," or how much he surfed nowadays and where. He seemed healthy and normal, but had he paid a price for his lifestyle? And what good would it have done to perpetuate the clichéd ejaculation "I had the poster when I was a kid!" which he must have tolerated in a million chats with folks from my generation? It was enough of an existential struggle to get my mind around his being three-dimensional, human, gray-haired with wire-rimmed glasses. So I stuttered my way through, drowning in the heat of self-consciousness before the substantiation of an image: that stylized black profile on my bedroom wall through which I felt I could have reached into another dimension forty-six years earlier.

Because I've received flak for disappearing at any hour of the day for a surf, I've taken to leaving notes to inform my eighteen-year-old where I'll be putting in, signing them, "James Franco." When I return—after dark sometimes—frozen, dripping, Eliza sighs nervously at my allusion to *127 Hours,* Danny Boyle's 2011 survival film about a rock climber's appalling blunder of not letting anyone know where he has

59

gone. It's a tentative laughter that ensues. Before he'd left the nest, my son/accomplice had been a dependable shock absorber for family admonishment. But now I had to take it on the chin, alone. At home *and in the water*. My wife loves to swim and dabbles in bodysurfing but has no interest in standing up on a board. Both of my daughters had caught the bug and secured used boards of their own but were also extremely conservative about getting them wet, breaking them out — cagily — when the conditions were small, sunny, absolutely safe. And when the rest of the family was either watching from the beach or in the lineup with them.

Even after Jake had called from Samoa, reassuring us that everything was fine, and that he wasn't surfing alone, I didn't sleep for months as he made his way to Fiji, New Zealand, and ultimately Australia. Where is the threshold to proficiency, the border of that realm where experience earns exemption from being overconfident, or inoculation from delusion? All I could do was train my telescope on the foggy DMZ between being a partner-in-crime and being his dad, dialing in on some conjured image of my son, exhilarated, vaulting out of a skiff with other surfers to push it scraping over a shallow reef, hoisting his brown shoulders back over the transom, forging on to deeper water where a pulse of formidable beauty is rearing up, taking shape.

His emails kept appearing, but I decided not

to brag about one adventure I'd had without him. I did not offer the spirited narrative about how in early October I had ripped my meniscus in a particularly gorgeous, gigantic (for New Hampshire standards) swell. He was in surf paradise, and why would I bore him with pedestrian anecdotes? On that particular day I'd stood tentatively on the granite blocks dumped below the concrete ramparts, waiting with board under my arm for a lull in a species of wave that usually sprawled across the double pages of my upscale "surf porn" magazine. It occurred to me that this was the best the North Atlantic could offer, comparatively, in the face of Jake's depictions of the Pacific. Even more shocking than the quality of the surf was the absence of fellow suicides in the peak I had been scouting. Instead, they were clustered like a flotilla of anxious ducks about an eighth of a mile north. The storm was so far out to sea that the sun was blazing, the air warm, and the sets seemed more than a few minutes apart from each other. A single purple-faced surfer was making his exit, scrambling up the rocks, exhausted. As he mounted the stairs and passed me, he could only shake his head and spit out, "All yours. Had it to myself two hours."

But it's so much easier to fling yourself into the ocean when you know you're going to meet up with someone on the other side of those sizeable waves. Especially if that person is your son. Before he left, we'd made it our business to go out in anything. Now, we've grown more selective, snobby, laughing at the memory of particularly insane forays into storm surf that offered nothing rideable — what patient and discerning practitioners call "victory at sea" conditions and usually avoid. Throughout his high school and college years, Jake and I had fallen into a pattern of expeditions that depend- ed on mutual support. We knew when to cheer the other into commitment, helped each other identify the waves to take but also when to shout, "No!! Let it go!" over the roar of a closeout.

team

The guy who'd just come out was dumping a jug of fresh water over his head, the top half of his suit peeled down to his waist. He gave me a "What are you waiting for?" look, so I descend- ed and began the lonely, dry-headed paddle out that delivered me more than a hundred yards from the seawall.

Such leisurely passages are scarce in "decent" New Hampshire beach-break surf, the lulls between sets an extravagant gift in the last gasp of summer — not to mention the potential reward of a long, clean ride. The size of the waves is easier to take, too, because the water isn't thirty-eight degrees. In winter, every wave you can't beat is an aluminum bat to the forehead. During those sessions, if your wetsuit hood slips back or fills after a wipeout, the cold makes you want to vomit. Indian-summer hurricane swell is different; a middle-aged person can almost sustain his relationship with the sport without the usual punishment of punching through oncoming waves, repeated duck-diving, turtle- rolling, or other evasive maneuvers, including the last-ditch board-fling to avoid being speared by it.

But just when wallowing in all that early autumn luxury (i.e., not being winded or frozen) almost made me forget why I was there, I'd see it coming, the distinct corrugation an eighth of a mile out. And once the set was upon me, I knew the swell was different, being catapulted from some distant and exotic kingdom in the same ocean.

It took a while, but when I'd finally roped one of these fast-moving behemoths by dropping into it a little later than usual, acceleration was a revelation. The feel of the board chattering down the wave-face, behaving more like a water ski, was disconcerting. And I'd never known my thighs to burn before, to be locked-on for such a duration to the task of muscling the board's rail over into the pocket of energy that would keep me a step ahead of the avalanche. In that zone, when the wave seems on your team, pushing instead of hunting, your speed allows you to do more, to play instead of focusing on staying alive. You spend some time leaning back, pelvis angled forward, savoring the elegant speed of the high line, or you head down to the trough in a crouch, then spring back to the lip. You drag your fingertips along the glossy wall as you might admiringly the flank of a newly waxed sports car. The memory of these — in my case, brief — transcendent episodes is what keeps me coming back. On that October day, however, being held down once the wave closed

63

out taught me a new paradox. Pinned against the sand by that volume of boiling, angry water, you understand pretty quickly that *not* trying to swim is what will save you. You have to wait until it lets you go. When I surfaced, I understood that my leash had snapped and watched my board sporadically rocketing like a hooked tarpon out of the barreling plain of foam before it sailed up into the rocks. I was so worried about how much I'd have to spend on ding repair that I didn't acknowledge the stiffness in my fluid-filled knee until I climbed into bed that night. But my deepest regret after such sessions isn't injury to board or body; rather, it's that Jake has been absent from the equation, either to weigh in on my embarrassing decisions, hoot at my foibles, or see me at the apex of my limited game.

misses
his
son

Hampton Beach, New Hampshire, and all its honky-tonk, isn't suspended precariously over the Atlantic on a wooden platform, but it is not unlike Seaside Heights, New Jersey. A good time to consider the boon and risk of what I do is after I've paddled back out alone on winter days—when it's still huge and ugly, just before the ragged sets are aligned by offshore winds sweeping up in the wake of a nor'easter's rampage past New England. More than a year and a half after Hurricane Sandy whacked the Jersey Shore, the *New York Times* and the *New Yorker* were still churning out articles along with aerial shots of the frayed and ravaged boardwalk at Seaside. People say we're crazy, but the individual surfer adrift stands a better chance of surviving the North Atlantic's tantrums than a suspended road of planks. The iconic image of the dislodged, half-submerged roller coaster at Casino Pier, though an affront to my childhood, is also a reminder of scale: the erasure and ephemerality of an anchored community and its cultural history compared to the absorption of one person and his flirtations with adaptability, timing and exploiting the physics of waves for his own pleasure. For me, it's harder to stay out of the water and gaze from a dry jetty and deliberate about mortality. And that's how you learn: by stepping off. Survival, however, does not provide you with a choice; you emerge absolutely content to watch it from a distance, or you resign yourself to the thrill of having a chance to drown over and over again. I sometimes wonder whether, as he matured, the student whom the Ipswich Harbor Patrol had rescued and delivered ever ventured back into what probably should have killed him. Once my son got a taste, I sensed there was probably nothing I could do to keep him from it, only pray that the more time he spent out there, his acute joy might be refuted by the sort of fear the poet Stephen Dunn describes in "A Primer for Swimming at Black Point," a fear that we should be "happy for," because it reminds us that the water doesn't care about us.

Sitting back on my board, I start imagining what everyone else near the coast of New Hampshire might be doing in their parallel universe: choosing a program on a treadmill, commuting, bagging the dog's poop on the sidewalk, pounding nails around a new bay window, or deleting email. I catch my breath and let the fire in my arms and shoulders subside, with nothing to face but the resolute mystery of the advancing swells, a thousand increments of smoke and violet in their turbid reflection of clearing skies, spattered and streaked with foam, growing. With the reversed wind ratcheting up and grooming it all, the texture begins to lose its spiked chop in favor of mossy velour. I know I'll have to pivot the nose and engage at some point; the quick ride is why I fought my way to this place, after all, only to lie down again and stroke into the negotiations of exhilaration and dread. But the battle is over, temporarily. Because I've taken my beating on the inside, made it past the whitewater of the detonation district, I can pretend to relax as I wait for the right one, watching gulls wheel nervously at warp speed along the faces, how they eject in sudden jerks when the waves' crests convulse with definition and the shadows of deepening troughs darken their wings.

specific concrete moment [handwritten margin note]

What is the point of this essay? effect of humor? [handwritten note]

LOOKING FOR ICE

1.

At the boarding school where I teach, my campus residence bears a plaque with the name of an English teacher who drowned after falling through ice. He had been skating on the river after the year's first deep freeze, which had been followed by a snowstorm. I was told that once his pickup hockey game had ended and the players dispersed, he made the choice to remain behind, to skate upriver, enticed perhaps by the beauty of new snow, to explore the transformed hemlock-banked waterway alone. This happened the winter I was hired, before I started teaching the following fall. Our paths had crossed briefly during a fellowship in New York City and at a cookout in New Hampshire with friends we had in common. I didn't know him well but liked him immediately, and afterwards I felt as if I'd lost a friend, a kindred spirit. I appreciate what he might have felt. The power that could have drawn him onward along that white, unblemished path until it betrayed him.

2.

Some of my wife's most visceral memories of growing up on the South Shore of Massachusetts are associated with skating on the region's cranberry bogs. If flooded for a "wet harvest" in October by the network of feeder streams, the clustered patchwork evolves in winter into the ideal hybrid of natural ice given form by agricultural intention. I become jealous listening to her inspired narratives about hopping the berms with her sisters and friends, playing hockey then exploring the interconnected sluices and waterways for miles through the towns of Duxbury and Pembroke. The shallowness of the bogs quells a skater's fear of the consequences of falling through. In our almost thirty years of married life, the slim luck of weather and temperature intersecting precisely at holiday visits to her parents' home has resulted only once in the opportunity to wander that labyrinth on skates. Now the prospect is even more unlikely because it seems the bogs rarely freeze thoroughly enough. If they do, snow hardened on the surface like a shell of polystyrene foam makes skating impossible.

That single foray on the bogs was as close as I've ever come to realizing my persistent childhood fantasy of ice travel through an engineered landscape. When I was in elementary school on the North Shore of Massachusetts, I was convinced that the most efficient and fun means of mobility was skating. I daydreamed a modern

Hans Brinker–esque world in which all roads, highways, and sidewalks were accompanied by or interlaced with groomed, perpetually frozen canals. You could skate over to your friends' houses, skate to the movies, to school, to the drug store to buy comics, or even a few states away to visit your grandparents in Flushing — without paying tolls. It was safe, fast, and you wouldn't need a license. You'd be outside, conveyed by your own power. But on most winter Sunday mornings, when I had vacuumed the stairs and the rest of my chores were done and time and the world seemed poised, wide open, I was usually slumped in the back seat of our family's forest green Chevy, waiting for the stiff vinyl to warm, on my way to church.

This was the overture for a lifetime of negotiations between obligation, fear, and an electric, undeniable desire that reared up when the elements conspired to deliver perfect conditions. Like many ten-year-olds in the rural swath that still existed in the late 1960s, just beyond the reach of the Boston suburbs and below the New Hampshire border, I resented demands that kept me inside on weekends. Especially in the noxious, incense-fogged interior of St. Mary's, a contemporary brick hangar of a building. My restlessness was especially acute in winter. The intensity of my parents' public religious commitment fluctuated with the seasons, easing up and ultimately evaporating after Easter, but reasserting itself like some tenacious disease when school began again after the summer and light withdrew from our side of the planet. They must have known better during July and August, sensing the potential of an all-out mutiny from my sisters and me if one sweltering day of our vacations were surrendered to the then-popular guitar-propelled "folk masses" at St. Mary's, or the solemn affairs at St. Rose of Lima, her cranky, conservative sister in another neighboring town, whose priest, Father Sczipko (we called him Zipcode), was even crankier. ∟ religious)

In the middle of the winter, however, even the adventurously violent scenes depicting the Stations of the Cross could not distract me from imagining what my friends were doing without me. I began supplanting the gestural, line-drawn images of The Savior (tired hippie in loincloth) and the broom-helmeted centurions roughing him up with my own twisted Currier and Ives–like vignettes of preadolescents soaring over jumps in overloaded toboggans, or rifling snowballs at cars. I filled those artificial sandstone tablets along the aisle with dioramas of hockey players slashing, cross-checking, launching shots from the blue line, pucks whizzing up into a soft pocket just beneath the crossbar, ringing off the posts, swashbuckling breakaways robbed by sprawled goalies.

At night I would pray for blizzards that would thwart our going to church, but even more devoutly for a deep freeze after heavy rain, which could repair the deeply scarred, overskated pond surfaces more flawlessly than a Zamboni. Breath steaming from their laughing faces in the January air, my friends waved sheepishly as our communion-bound tires squeaked past them in the new snow. When we were far enough away and they could still see me craning to keep them in sight through the back window, the little band of atheists gave me the finger with the synchronized precision of a military salute.

3.

When we still lived in California, my being an infant, then a toddler, did not stop my parents from being shameless tourists. They explored the state, sniffing out the necessary attractions, since they knew they would eventually make their way back East to family. During our five years on the West Coast, we worked our way from Marineland of the Pacific, the San Diego Zoo and Mission San Juan Capistrano up to Disneyland, Knott's Berry Farm, Yosemite, ascending the trail of other Missions and beaches to the cable cars of San Francisco before veering out to Gold Country, Lake Tahoe, and finally to Palisades Tahoe (formerly known as Squaw Valley) where the VIII Olympic Winter Games had been held the year before in 1960. And where I had my first experience on ice.

The accompanying home movie proves that my father was not merely holding me, the infant, like a football or loaf of bread; rather, his expression of excited generosity as he looked down into my bewildered, ruddy face then back to the rink revealed intention. He seemed to know that it was a moment of passage.

When I review that film, it's even clearer to me that he wasn't the most steady skater, which lends an air of danger — or even recklessness — to the scene as he navigates carefully along the boards, among narcissistic rogue figure skaters obliviously spinning within arm's length, families falling in a heap, laughing, and one older gent, arms held up in surrender, whose terrified eyes and brow loom suddenly in the lens. I am swaddled within an inch of my life, bareheaded, locked in the crook of my father's elbows as he carefully pushes and glides his way proudly toward the camera jouncing in my mother's hands.

After we'd moved back East to New Jersey, my parents bought me a pair of "open" green plastic sandal-like skates with double runners that strapped over my boots. These enabled me to stand in the middle of the town pond watching my father in envy as he crunched into a turn in his ancient leather, single-bladed, size-thirteen war canoes. I was five, could barely stay upright, but there was something mesmerizing about his momentum, the sound of those edges biting the soft, trafficked ice as he crossed over, skirting the rim of the pond around all of the other skaters and standers. Skating in northern New Jersey in 1965 was a recreational novelty. Two years later in New England we immediately discovered that winters were longer and colder, but that even if they weren't, the proliferation of state and private rinks guaranteed ice time

Specificity

twelve months a year.

Our migration north to Massachusetts in 1967 deposited us in an intense maelstrom of hockey and a life on ice in general. At the age of seven I sensed that living in New England and not being a Bruins fan was suicidal. Though I understood neither the National Hockey League nor how to talk about it with my friends, I learned quickly. Icons like Bobby Orr made it easy. But following hockey did not provide me with the impetus for learning how to skate. Proficiency on ice was directly proportional to regular, predictable freezes, or "real winters," as we came to say. Our first year in Massachusetts, my parents had bought me a pair of used hockey skates with tattered yellow sneaker laces and ankles as flimsy as sliced bologna. But regardless of quality, they *weren't* figure skates, which would have certainly marked me as a leper among my peers.

One day at Cub Scouts the Den Mothers herded us over to a pond in the neighborhood and let us skate for our "weekly activity" — an alternative to bowling, touring someone's dad's plastics factory, or coaxing tangled nests of gimp into unusable key chains. The pond was tiny, but the banks on one side were domesticated, deliberate: a permanently installed bench, a post with a floodlight for night skating, and the customary ladder and rope for sliding out to anyone who fell through.

That afternoon, as the early darkness fell and the headlights of cars began to flare on the adjacent road, I began to skate. While the mothers

unscrewed the caps from thermoses of hot choc-
olate, hurriedly opened round tins of cookies for
us, and stomped to get the blood flowing in their
underprotected feet, something in my body fell
into sync: an agreement with the gravity necessary for leaning into a turn and trusting a skate's
edge. It was completely liberating, and because
of this I was the last one off the ice, uncharacteristically immune to the lure of snacks that had
drawn the other boys away. Crouching, gaining
speed, I had the ice to myself, counterclockwise,
circle after circle, like a tetherball leashed to its
post without the threat of a diminishing orbit.
Only when the others had taken their skates off
and stuffed their double-socked feet back into
unlaced sneakers or boots, and the shouting
Den Mothers had lost their patience, did I step
reluctantly back to earth.

freedom

in a world of his own similar to water

4.

Collins Pond, the other body of water
where I learned to skate, faced southwest at the
bottom of a hill in our neighborhood. It was
hidden behind a clump of overgrown forsythia
bushes, crabapple, and cherry trees that screened
it from the pasture, the Collins's house and barn
and Kelsey Road beyond. On the other side was
a swampy plain with mounds and hummocks
of deflated marsh grass turned gray and ochre
in winter, and a little sluice at one end where
water flowed out through a culvert under the
road. Beyond, the power lines above the abandoned railroad track bed provided us a way to tell

details specific one clear place the

time as the sun sank incrementally in the western sky. At the southeastern end of the pond was the spring that fed this sanctuary and brought fish, frogs, turtles, and *us* to what should have been no more than a seasonal muddy pocket in a horse paddock. We knew the source was in that dark mossy corner because it rarely froze in winter, and if it had, the ice was thin, and as black as the water beneath. If one of our pucks wandered over there during a game, there was a collective whine as it sped toward the open water, slowing like a roulette ball about to settle on the number you fear most. The game stopped and everybody stood like nervous pylons, sighing or swearing if it teetered and slipped over the brittle edge into the water as ineluctably as a coin deposited in a bank, or frustratingly came to a halt on a skin of ice that could barely support a squirrel.

During the occasional thaw, before the sun rose too high and began to soften the ice, we permitted ourselves a game in short-sleeved shirts, until willowy, polite Mrs. Collins would wander down from her house. Standing there on the bank with her hands in her coat pockets, she asked, smiling (probably terrified of a lawsuit), if we weren't tempting fate by skating in such balmy weather.

It was a regular party on those days, our lunch breaks long and boisterous, nothing like the days of hurriedly unwrapping and wolfing down a frozen sandwich while standing. Instead of swaddling our cans of soda in sweaters or jackets and burying them in our bags so they wouldn't freeze solid, we would nestle them in the snow. We took our time lacing skates, sitting together on a dry patch of grass in the feeble but decadent winter sun, our bags, helmets, and pads scattered in a careless pile. Together, we'd brought so much equipment, food, and clothing I now wonder what Mrs. Collins really thought of the noisy refugee camp that materialized every weekend in that corner of her yard when she'd look out her kitchen window. On premature spring days like these, even the ticks would reemerge, and we'd marvel as one of us would pluck a specimen of these normally detested insects from his hockey sock along with a few burrs.

But even when the late-January-early-February deep freeze was locked confidently around us, there was still evidence of the seasons we could then only imagine. After particularly lengthy cold spells the water above the spring would freeze and I army-crawled out to the black window for a look. The strata left by thawing, freezing, snowfalls, dustings, frozen rain, and sleet combined with the violent engravings of skate blades made the surface opaque with history; the fleeting gift of black ice strong enough to hold a boy was something not to be wasted. Lying there until the heat of my body welded my jeans and hockey shirt to the surface, I felt I was permitted a glimpse into a world both dangerous and forbidden in its unlikely beauty. It was just mud, rocks, and decomposing leaves, after all, filtered through the tannin lens of a swampy farm pond. But to glimpse the wandering turtle who had somehow dislodged himself into a confused, sleepy foray, the translucent minnow or fluttering pectoral fins of the rare bluegill suspended just below your face, or other unnameable, hearty water insects going about their business like delivery trucks was breathtaking.

We had learned to forget what we had lost to this portal. But if I focused hard enough, I could catch peeking from the silt of the monochrome terrain an orange *Cooper* logo, or the resigned and tragic profile of the Chicago Blackhawks brave on one of our coveted souvenir pucks. For a few minutes the pond became an oversized glass-bottom boat. Other than miniature galaxies of frozen bubble streams (methane? some poor, oblivious, hibernating amphibian's arrested exhalations?) or the occasional immobilized leaf, there was nothing to impede your view of the pond's bottom six feet below. Just a still, brown world a degree or two away from annihilation.

In the summer, when we returned for frogs and pickerel, I stood on the bank, bamboo pole in hand, looking out to that spot in the dark corner patrolled by dragonflies and textured with scum and lily pads, imagining the impossibility of my other heavily clothed self, spread-eagle, facedown, hands cupped around temples, floating in winter.

5.

Usually, if we chose to skate on one of the bigger, deeper ponds or lakes, one of our fathers had to swing by and stab a crowbar through the ice to check its thickness. We waited on shore in a muttering, pensive crescent, poised to drop our equipment and begin suiting up or kicking at the snow in disappointment, swearing as much as we could until the adult shuffled back to us apologetically shaking his head. One of these, Stevens Pond, was rumored to be bottomless. We actually believed the tale about a team of researchers from the University of Massachusetts who'd tried to sound its depths without success. I thought about this every time I glided out to its center with my family or a troop of friends, imagining a water-filled space of endless darkness beneath the skin of ice, an existential pang that I soon forgot once the skating began.

bluntness

After my sister's first boyfriend fell through and died at the Mill Pond, everything changed. It was a warm day in late winter, but the ice seemed stubborn, enduring, as if it would never melt, even though the snow was gone and the quality of light was changing and the earthy, evaporative moistness of spring hung in the air. Burgundy oak leaves frozen to the ice since late autumn were probably melting hand-like shapes into the slushy, pooling surface. Who wouldn't want to seize the opportunity of milking one more session from that pond in the balmy hinge between the seasons?

Mill Pond had a rope swing knotted to a big

oak that leaned over the water on a particularly precipitous slope. On any given warm day in late spring, before the pond was clogged with weeds and lily pads, you would find a queue of impatient wet kids gripping the slick, muddy incline with their toes. Each successive moron launched himself more ambitiously than the last, climbing higher into the oak, grabbing a higher knot, emitting an even more tortured Tarzan yodel, and finally doing something more contorted after he let go and sailed out to the center with a flailing splash. My sisters took me there with them, but the thrill of danger was palpable, snarling from the teeth of the rusting circular blade you could just see through the rotting boards of the abandoned sawmill. The history of this place suggested it was more of a risk to be there in the *warm* seasons, so the news of a boy's death in late winter seemed to come from nowhere that afternoon as we sat around the kitchen table in disbelief and my sister sobbed in her bedroom.

Once a pond or lake, or even a certain ocean cove or point, claims a life, it seems to change the nature of the element itself. Even if we understand that the cycle ultimately evaporates and replaces all of it, or the tide sweeps in to flush out the water's memory of tragedy. Regardless of the season, I couldn't bike past the Mill Pond without replaying the short film of what I imagine might have happened: one boy lying on the ice reaching with a hockey stick as the one in the water tries to grab again and again the slippery rim of the hole to hoist himself out.

6.

The risks were real, but packaged among them like glass ornaments were the experiences that harbored the motives for returning again and again to natural ice and farther away from the relative safety of clammy warehouse arenas. I understand now that I was most happy when I was neither chasing a puck nor covering any uniformed peer, but how did I end up playing hockey almost twelve months of the year until I graduated from high school? The culture of the sport and its camaraderie carried me along, and somewhere in that decade a bright space opened when I wasn't conflicted between or even aware of playing indoors or outdoors. This was right before becoming demoralized in the labyrinth of tryouts, confused by the political commerce between town athletic associations, vindictive coaches, and meddling parents. Before the stakes rose, I just played without a chance or reason to think about what I was doing, ricocheting between the hemispheres of town and school teams.

A few years of being in summer leagues and going to hockey camps conveyed me into a realm of precarious comfort, strange instincts. Bewilderment about the technical aspects of the sport gave way to an almost cocky nonchalance. The rinks seemed smaller. The chaos on the ice assumed a form, became more predictable, and the game began to make sense. Before then, I was simply a hustler who every so often connected a decent pass, but who skated *all the time* during his shift. One coach identified my role perfectly as the team buzz saw: a force of brainless, blind energy. On our rides home from games and practices my father had lectured me about my ironic spaciness, how I'd dart and loop all over the ice, intensely engaged, but completely out of position. My triumphs were accidents. Once in a while I'd derail somebody whose break-away goal had seemed a foregone conclusion, materializing out of nowhere and stripping him because my erratic ellipse just happened to intersect with his deliberate line.

Early in high school I was playing a lot: on the school's JV team and in two night leagues, along with the rare pickup pond game. And in that descending window just before I burned out, I burned for the ice between shifts, counting the seconds before flying over the boards back into the game with determination instead of terror. After I'd broken an ankle in seventh grade, I counted on my skating skills to hover and dance safely around the action, always look-ing over my shoulder or waiting outside a fray for the puck to be spat out, the last to burrow into the corners after it. But suddenly my abiding fear of being hit evaporated; my purpose wasn't just survival anymore. I was small but stockier, so my game became aggressive; I didn't wait to be checked, didn't draw that panicked deep breath before venturing toward the boards. Grappling while digging the puck out from in back of the net didn't faze me, neither did tangling others' legs with my own, lifting or prying their sticks, or simply dropping my shoulder to blast them off the play. It was a new dimension that I understood to be the essence of the game, access to and possession of an energy that bridged time and space and guaranteed I wouldn't be a scavenger or bystander. I was good at getting there first. *—good skater*

But the game and its environment had always been secondary, an external organism that yammered for attention while I marveled at my own improving dexterity, grace, and speed. Rusty beams, puck holes and dimples in insulation panels, the torn net installed to prevent them, plexiglass smudged with black tape marks of flailing sticks, the shattered lights of pockmarked scoreboards, disintegrating banners in the rafters, bleachers spattered with cocoa and ketchup, those globs of drying mucus on the rubber mat inside the bench. Real players, the hardcore acolytes, might wax nostalgic for all of these or, possibly, transcend them. Rinks belong to a dimension different from the lake you labor across pushing a loaded, bending shovel in the Sisyphean effort to keep up with a blizzard. Or the surreal treadmill belt of reflected clouds or stars scrolling beneath your feet. In the measured confines of glycol-injected concrete or sand, lost in the fumes of the pachydermal, concentric pen of the Zamboni, it seems paradoxically that you have no coordinates, no point of reference.

After college (where I did not play hockey)

I taught Latin at a small high school north of Boston, and because it was a private school and they knew I'd played hockey, I was expected to coach. Which I ended up doing for almost a decade. Inhaling that stale rink air again for months on end seemed to expunge whatever bitterness I'd harbored for overdosing on the sport as a kid. But no matter how much fun my players were having, or how proud of their sportsmanship I was, regardless of what spectacle or barn burner might be unfolding on the ice, I began to realize I'd fallen out of love with the immutable indoors. I'd had my fill of screaming myself hoarse from the bench or dodging the frequent stray slapshots, plastic whistle clenched between my teeth, and I was able to stop feeling guilty about why I'd put the singular athletic purpose of my childhood on mothballs.

In each of the sweaty, pimpled, sparsely bearded faces of my charges, I recognized the superimposed ghosts of the boys who'd skated with me when I was young. Sometimes I was caught off guard by a jolt of nostalgia that brought me close to tears when I noticed how deeply they were enjoying each other's company, the tilt at hand, or even their coaches possibly. They were *in* it, and I, of all people, was helping to guide them through.

It took a while for me to admit that I was expending too much psychic energy in a charade, pretending to be as passionate as they were. All I really wanted was to protect them from whatever might diminish the fragile grace or abandon they'd brought along from the ponds of their childhood, what had been slowly slipping away from me. Most of them did love the game more than I, and that was all right. So I quit coaching hockey, relinquished the last official role I'd have on indoor ice. Sure, I flirted with the sport, playing in disorganized lunchtime pickup games at the school where I teach now (which has two rinks), once with a group that had a few ex-Bruins in the lineup (they moved and connected passes so fast, I felt that I was standing still). But that was less about love, more about ego, proving to myself I could still do it.

Before her early morning commute made it unsustainable, my wife was playing with a women's team every Monday night. Once in a while she'd ask me some question about being offside, the responsibilities of back-checking, or what to do about people who were hackers. I was surprised by how easily I cranked the answers up out of that well.

7.

Whenever I visit Grasmere, in the Lake District of England, I cannot resist the museum at Dove Cottage and the Wordsworth Trust, not only to have a look at the handwritten manuscripts of some of my favorite poems but to gawk at Wordsworth's skates, which reside in a glass case in dim gallery light. I wrote a poem about those blades once before Seamus Heaney tried them on in a glimmering tribute in his book *District and Circle*. When I read his poem, I wanted to slip into a simmering fit of poet's envy but ended up just being amazed that an Irish Nobel Laureate would care enough about these artifacts to write about them. It was heartening to discover that I was not as sentimental or trivial as I had imagined, that my fixation crossed international borders and wasn't governed by New England aesthetics. That these might be the very skates that provided the experience the poet evokes in *The Prelude* is probably what has rooted me in front of them again and again:

> All shod with steel,
> We hissed along the polished ice in games
> Confederate, imitative of the chase
> And woodland pleasures — the resounding horn,
> The pack loud chiming, and the hunted hare.
> So through the darkness and the cold we flew,
> And not a voice was idle; with the din
> Smitten, the precipices rang aloud.
> The leafless trees and every icy crag
> Tinkled like iron; while far distant hills
> Into the tumult sent an alien sound
> Of melancholy not unnoticed . . . .
>
> Not seldom from the uproar I retired
> Into a silent bay, or sportively
> Glanced sideways, leaving the tumultuous throng,
> To cut across the reflex of a star
> That fled, and, flying still before me, gleamed
> Upon the glassy plain . . . .

Originally, it was the evocation of boyish physicality and the details of place that drew me to this excerpt. But now it is the solace of Wordsworth's "retiring from the uproar" that I have internalized—a goal that has defined my life on frozen water beyond being a setting for play or contest. Like swimming, skating ultimately gave me permission to be alone, buoyed by yet detached from the world to understand the universe better. And to say *buoyed* is not incorrect, because when skating, we ride a thin layer of water formed when our weight is focused on the edges of those metal blades and wherever they make contact with the ice, which in its natural, unmolested state is not slippery.

"Then is not death at watch / Within those secret waters?" asks another British poet, Edmund Blunden, in "The Midnight Skaters," as if responding to Wordsworth's Romantic melancholy. "What wants he but to catch / Earth's heedless sons and daughters?" This is how a survivor of the Great War reads the landscape from the newly frozen, dangerous surface of the twentieth century. Though Blunden's imagination, like his predecessor's, launches upward to acknowledge "thrones / Of stars, sound gulfs of wonder," he is ultimately suspicious on Wordsworth's "glassy plain" and extrapolates downward. "With but a crystal parapet / Between, he has his engines set." What had been cosmic expansion in Wordsworth's narrative, a paean to solitude, becomes an awareness of Death's conspiracy in Blunden's world, framed by the poet's readily available diction and imagery of trench warfare. The "crystal parapet" is neither an architectural feature of some winter fairyland palace nor a euphemism for No Man's Land. The proximity of the enemy is too close, directly underfoot.

When you look into it, the quaint wisdom that two inches of ice can heft a small group of skaters is tainted by an overwhelming number of ambiguities. This is the beauty and horror of natural ice—that it seems to be predictable, that it should obey some of the most rigid natural laws. And yet, by getting involved with surface tension, elasticity, tensile strength, and fickle weather, the pond, lake, or river skater must always be aware of the variables conspiring against him, of being supported by an element upon which he has little "natural" place—a secondary environment whose texture and properties might change with every stride. You can't see where the current is chewing away on the other side, thinning silently a spot that you would trust. In my pedestrian reading about the crystal structure and mathematics of ice, I have come to understand this behavior as *anisotropic*, that ice's properties have different values when measured in different directions. Fish and game departments for many northern and Midwestern states offer a number of variations on ice wisdom, such as, "There is no such thing as safe ice, only safer ice," or the less semantic, "The only safe ice is *no* ice."

When it comes to humans and ice, the question of safety is always hovering nearby. More significant than meteorology, the conditions on which skaters depend are more reminiscent of an official agreement between two countries, an understanding of legal stipulations or the terms of surrender. Through all those years of anguish and exhilaration, team formation and solo flight, proactive risk and submissive boredom, abandoning and seeking, I can't name what kept me safe. To skate despite your awareness of the enemy — that Death is *at watch within those secret waters* — is to ratify an accord. It's a gambler's contract, but one that places a premium on the singular experience; when you are aware of the subsurface threat, like Blunden, the choice to embark on natural ice is pure flirtation, reckless defiance:

> Then on, blood shouts, on, on,
> Twirl, wheel and whip above him,
> Dance on this ball-floor thin and wan,
> Use him as though you love him;
> Court, elude him, reel and pass,
> And let him hate you through the glass.

8.

When my kids were small, we lived on a spring-fed pond in Wenham, Massachusetts. Because the house had been built into a steep hill, we could barely see the road below; it was like living in a treehouse. The kitchen window looked out through the branches of two enormous beeches, and sunlight reflecting from the pond surface through the leaves in summer would shimmer on the white ceiling. Standing at the sink, looking up at the undulating surface, you almost felt you were underwater.

The pond was deep and not many people skated there. But since it was stocked with trout, the few ice fishermen who did show up kept us entertained, wrestling their gas-powered augers out of the openings they had been drilling, then sitting for hours beside them, peering into the orifices as if waiting for an answer from the pond. They were not like the smelt fishermen on the Squamscott River in New Hampshire, where we live now, those squatters who are permitted to slide what look like modified outhouses and garden sheds to the cracked, precarious frozen plates shifting with the tide. They install their lanterns, radios, hibachis, thirty-packs of Bud Light, magazines, and lawn furniture around their little huts like the forlorn character in Raymond Carver's "Why Don't You Dance?" whose yard sale is a mirror image of his home's interior. How many of these structures have I seen neglected late in the season, sinking into the very holes over which they'd been placed as they drifted out to sea?

The fishermen in Wenham, however, were not part of some macho diaspora desperate for a domestic center; rather, they seemed involved in some experiment with religious seclusion. With neither shacks nor suburban paraphernalia, the few that ventured out there left at least thirty yards between their encampments. They surrounded themselves with a perimeter of multiple holes, like a solar clock, each increment with its own baited line and flag waiting to be triggered by whatever was cruising below.

That year, I found myself peering out the kitchen window longing to skate. Whether the frozen surface was black and inscrutable, hidden beneath a swirling quilt of snow or behind a foggy scrim of grim pewter, I surmised it with a familiar twinge of excitement, the desire to be out there, on it. So we laced up one morning after a week of bitter, penetrating cold. The conditions were perfect. No snow, the ice as thick as it could get. Having designated a rink-sized area near the shore below the house, my wife and I spent an hour passing a puck around while the kids contentedly pushed their plastic milk crates (in New England, a young skater's training wheels) back and forth between us, learning to push off, glide, keep their balance without falling, snapping their wrists, bashing their skulls.

Just as my toes started to numb and pinch and I knew it wouldn't be long before we had to retreat to the house, I skated away from them over the deeper water, past some dark ice fishing holes that had resealed, looping into the marshy coves at the far eastern end, batting dead cattails as I passed at high speed, then sweeping back out to the open center crossing over backwards, pivoting forward again and accelerating. Without the contest and its inherent dependencies, its intentional and unintentional collisions, gripped truncheon, fixation on puck, without the penitentiary of boards, you become a different kind of skater. When I returned, they were just standing in their hastily pulled-on boots on the

excellent skate

bank, watching me. As a family, we had tootled around on a local rink during public skates, but now they'd seen me open up. My wife looked at me as if I were a different person.

But a few nights later, I woke up in a sweat having dreamt I was watching my daughter slide from my grip down into a dark watery hole in the ice. The details filched from reality were insidious, right down to the cinched hood, the reaching arms of her familiar pink-and-black jacket.

During that winter living on the pond, there were a few days when I walked across it as a shortcut on my way to teach, pausing in the center to consider the morning sun just beginning to saw through the fringe of pines. I stood there feeling the resonance of sudden pressure cracks beneath my feet, tendrils chiming away almost electronically. When the ice has any degree of translucence, these adjustments reveal with their jagged silvery bands the third dimension, the depth of what has frozen. For a few long seconds the thunderous ripple seems like the lake telling itself to relax. They are sometimes called "safety cracks," after all. At a moment like this, I would think about how I'd explain to my son and daughter the seismic indifference, the danger of ice, without scaring them away from it forever. They'd seen me confidently, comfortably spin away from them on that beautiful cold morning, trying to reclaim something in those arbitrary, improvised loops. But trudging across on my way to school like a lone sapper in a minefield, I wondered if I could translate those cracks, those unraveling white ribbons, <u>into a story of thickness</u>, <u>something that could hold us up</u>.

One morning, not long before early spring had mapped the surface with the tectonic borders of the coming melt, I watched one of those fishermen in his ritual setup, monitored periodically his long wait, perhaps his prayers, beside the slushy indentations. At regular intervals, he'd get up from sitting on his overturned bucket and trudge to his other holes. Right when I was pouring a cup of coffee, he paused and hauled out an enormous trout, writhing as he grabbed it by the gills and drew it from the water I couldn't see. From that distance, it not only seemed as if the creature itself were being excised from the grips of a solid substance but also as if the man were rescuing the fish, delivering it from peril into a realm of air and light, rather than extracting it, <u>once and for all</u>, from its natural habitat.

Years later in New Hampshire, we got up the nerve to take all three of our children and one of my daughter's friends out onto the <u>infamous river where my colleague had drowned</u>. It was in the middle of a three-week deep freeze, the water probably squeezed right down to the gravel and clay by feet of ice. Snowmobile traffic at night sounded like a pack of mobile, untethered chainsaws whose groomed, snaking trail transformed the river deceptively into a recently plowed road. But there were some

connection to beginning .

considerable stretches of glassy, pearl-gray ice that the wind had swept clean, and it was on one of these we dumped our bag of pucks, skated gingerly, hesitantly — an attempt to exorcise the event that swirled persistently in the summer eddies and winter gusts alike. We skated for an hour, but not with abandon. Sometimes my wife and I just stopped what we were doing to watch the kids in their little game of keep-away, or the stiff current of fine, blowing snow as it followed the banks, copying the water's behavior in the other seasons. The surface seemed to be alive.

— the river

why so this?

Purpose?

Why keep coming back with danger?

IMMERSION NOTES;
OR, "THIS AIN'T *SEA HUNT!*"

The knells for my stillborn career as a marine biologist rang during the year I failed zoology as an undergrad and was nearly arrested by a state trooper in rural Virginia. At the time of the latter, I was asleep in the back seat of a late '60s Catalina headed to the Florida Keys with four friends who were also scuba divers. We were on spring break, flooring it straight through from Amherst, Massachusetts, the tail of the giant green car sagging with the freight of our duffels, weight belts, tanks, regulators, masks, fins, and three cases of Moosehead beer, a fourth (open and dwindling) crammed between whoever was in the back seat. The rules: the driver had to commit to a six-hour shift, refrain from reaching back for a beer, and decline any smoldering object that might be passed in his direction, but his right hand permitted an occasional visit to the glove compartment and its baggie of Yellowjackets and Black Beauties. I remember being woken up by a bright flashlight and the drawling command for "you boys" to step out and line up against the car. Whoever was taking his turn at the wheel had gotten off the highway to piss and driven straight through a red light. We stumbled out into the cold March air, and I was immediately smitten by a strange, guilty sense of relief. Mercifully, our expedition to Key Largo might be snuffed before we were barely past the mid-Atlantic states.

The officer was vaguely curious about all that equipment in our trunk, but after his foraging beam settled on the charred nub of a joint in the ashtray, he became fixated on securing the rest of our supply. The deal: give him the weed he knew we had or we'd be posting bail in the morning. Each of us assumed privately that he was just coercing us into incriminating ourselves and that we would be going to jail either way. Then the driver threw caution to the wind (again) and fished half an ounce out of his jacket pocket—a fraction of what he'd packed along. The moment after he handed it over was interminable, the cop opening the baggie, burying his face in it for a big, connoisseur's sniff, then suddenly expertly rolling it up again, slapping it against his thigh, and climbing back into his car. He lowered his window and offered cordially, "Y'all drive more careful, now. And have a good night."

We leaned against the Catalina, breathing the cruiser's lingering exhaust. I had been anxious about the whole trip all along, not only panicked about my meager funds holding out, but also hesitant at the prospect of a serious dive in alien waters. Getting arrested, though humiliating and not without its parental consequences back home, would have been a way out, but I began to hope that I was through the worst, since the trooper was probably twisting up his first spliff of the day. I tried to reassure myself that whatever might transpire in the waters off the Florida Keys could never be as terrifying as this weirdly resolved episode with the law. Southern law. I liked being underwater, but that didn't stop me from regretting the situation and wondering why I, a half-hearted amateur, would volunteer for such a reckless odyssey. There would be no quarter for stoners or posers a hundred feet down.

When I was a kid growing up north of Boston, our family was one of the last in our neighborhood, and perhaps the entire town, to own a color television set. There were many shows that might have benefited from full chromatic translation, but *The Undersea World of Jacques Cousteau* was the most excruciating to watch in gray scale. I followed it religiously, regardless. Each of Cousteau's documentary adventures was usually trumpeted a few weeks earlier by an article in that month's *National Geographic*, and my countdown would begin. As vivid, colorful, and breathtaking as those magazines on our coffee table might have been, they were not animated, so I parked myself in front of the TV, guessing at the sapphire intensity of the empty depths conducted by whale flukes. Jellies undulated, sharks veered, but through a bleak world that seemed in the pall of its overcast winter monochrome a cousin to our New England landscape. My favorite explorer's two-man saucer-shaped submarine had no hint of its dashing yellow. Why submit myself to the torture of that swashbuckling *National Geographic* theme music (admit it, the Copeland-esque score by Elmer Bernstein is coming back to you at this instant) only to be nosed through a school of black and white squid against a backdrop of morbid charcoal that should have been the most ethereal turquoise imaginable? I had no choice but to endure, to let my imagination's palette ink up that confusingly inspiring and grim world, until I hatched a strategy.

At ten, I assumed everyone shared my passion for Cousteau, so it stood to reason that every neighbor would be dialed in when the new episode was aired. In improvised burglar's apparel (navy hooded sweatshirt/jeans) I bolted in a running crouch across the field to the Oppedisanos' house, then slithered up to their basement family room window for a more realistic glimpse of the true element.

Resorting to espionage was the alternative to being too embarrassed to ask my neighborhood friends, the three brothers who lived across the street, if I could watch the program at their house. How often had I been called a nerd or a pansy by them or ridiculed by my own sisters for being interested in anything mildly scientific?

At the time, I understood that a little brother's reputation was directly proportional to his older siblings' who just wanted me to be *cool*. Which meant—at least while we inhabited the same school district—not dressing like an idiot, but also playing sports and entertaining some mild interest in girls, the latter of which was the last thing on my mind. I just wanted to be doing stuff outside, really, and they didn't get it. My oldest sister scolded me point-blank, demanding to know why I was such a "Nature Boy," and why it was that I preferred committing to memory the names of birds and fish rather than cars and sports teams. "Most guys your age know the difference between Corvettes and Camaros," she said. "Instead of . . . chickadees . . . and, and . . . tanagers." Apparently, she had failed to notice the half-built model of "Big Daddy" Don Garlits's drag car strewn across the family room card table and the posters of the Rams' quarterback Roman Gabriel and Vikings' wide receiver Gene Washington above my bed.

Undeterred by this ongoing humiliation, I pressed my face up against the Oppedisano's window. Jackie and Frank were settled on the sofa absorbed in something, only to turn suddenly in confusion at the appearance of my face, hands cupped over brows, straining downward at their massive television cabinet, longing for an explosion of bubbles, Cousteau's wetsuit with its distinct leg stripes, maybe a psychedelic shrimp, or any swarm of gilled iridescence. They were watching a war movie.

I was grounded for a month. Without any television. The collateral damage of my father's mandate included exile from the other two ocean-themed shows to which I was devoted: *Flipper* (what kid didn't crave the main character Bud's coastal lifestyle?) and *Voyage to the Bottom of the Sea* (the frugal genius behind the soundtrack's pervasive sonar bleep!). Soon, I also found myself combating a new reputation as the pervert on our street, a preadolescent Peeping Tom who pathetically cited as his defense that he only wanted to watch Cousteau in color. Even though my family knew me too well, that my evolving marine fixation was genuine, the surrounding neighbors were skeptical for years. Jackie Oppedisano, however, in a gesture of forgiveness and graciousness, invited me over to watch the program anytime I wanted, as long as I stopped lurking in her bushes. Strangely, if I did take her up on it, I don't remember it, perhaps because I was so embarrassed by the whole thing.

In October, my parents brought home a bag with royal blue Cressi snorkeling gear from their anniversary trip to Bermuda. Right there in the kitchen, I pulled the flippers over my sneakers and suctioned to my entire face an oversized mask designed for breathing through both nostrils and mouth without having to grip a mouthpiece in your teeth. To accommodate this double intake, two enormous curved snorkels like antlers or caterpillar antennae sprouted from the top, each equipped with a hinged stopper to prevent chop from pouring in and filling the mask. For the rest of the fall our house became my personal aquarium. With this apparatus affixed to my head, I swam its hallways and stairwells until the challenge of brushing my teeth and my sisters' annoyance compelled me to take it all off and stow it in the basement.

The wait for summer was brutal. When I wasn't at a hockey practice or game, or sledding and skating with my friends after school, I ventured downstairs to worship and fantasize about the adventures nesting in that tangle of blue rubber. It didn't seem right that the masks and fins had been relegated to a morgue-like shelf between the frayed, taped corners of board game boxes.

For the next two years, whether we were canoe camping at Lake George, visiting our grandparents on Long Island, or just slogging to our local beaches on Cape Ann and Plum Island Sound, the equipment came with us. My sisters and I battled each other like wolverines to get our turns with it. The turbid, genital-crushing waters of Ipswich and Gloucester seemed sterile, unpopulated compared to Cousteau's teeming shipwrecks with their shoals of pompano and gnashing lupine snouts of morays. In New England I found the fish to be pathetic, brown at best. Poking around the jetty at the mouth of the Ipswich River, you might be lucky enough to see some desperate crab battling the brisk, particle-fogged current, gripping a barnacled rock face for dear life, or maybe the feelers of a scrawny lobster waving forlornly from beneath an overhang. Other than a few pollock, an embarrassed flounder burying itself in a cloud of sand was the most exotic spectacle I could hope for. In 1970, striped bass were a rare, almost mythic species, something you'd only hear about from serious fishermen who remembered catching them in previous decades before you were born. Bluefish had a reputation of being kin to piranha when they were schooled up and feeding on sand eels, shiners, or bunker; you simply prayed you didn't run into a gang of them. The North Atlantic, in all its gun-metal and olive-drab tyranny squashed any promise of the most subtle evidence of that warm gleam, those pyrotechnics of life and tropical color.

When the big Quasar TV was finally delivered to our house, it was less an aesthetic upgrade than a means of stifling cultural marginalization on our own street. And our whining, too. Even so, the initial thrill of my parents' buckling and buying the appliance lasted only two Cousteau episodes when I began to feel an itch of dissatisfaction. As with surfing movies, you can watch only so many ideal waves being ridden by so many composed, urbane surfers in perfect environments and conditions. Music eradicates any physical threat, transforms a life-or-death situation into a jazz club, or, even more disturbingly, the groove that might settle on your shoulders if you were fondling cashmere sweaters at a chic department store. By the time I was thirteen, it wasn't satiety with Cousteau that drove me away from the screen and deeper into the water, but the vicariousness of it all. My supplication on the red shag carpet in front of the great oculus I had craved for years was another extension of pretending.

In the summer Long Island's blood-warm Peconic Bay, which fed and drained the cove in back of my grandparents' house, offered not only the privilege of staying in the water for more than forty-five seconds but also hosted a prolific menagerie that was somehow a little more dangerous, I imagined, than the usual suspects around Cape Ann. Before her own late adolescence had jostled my next oldest sister against my "square" fascination with nature, we relished together the types of fish and crabs in our backyard. We knew them almost as well as we did the human residents of that tight middle-class summer community — the diminutive, the curmudgeonly, the monstrous, the comedic. When we returned each June, we'd greet whatever might be cruising the shallows: schools of shiners and killifish, the lone pipefish with its nozzle-shaped seahorse face and body of an eel, the grass shrimp flitting backwards along the borders of the marsh. Even though they were new generations, we treated them like old friends, as if time, growth, and the indifference of the natural world were not immutable processes, facts.

Aboard my grandfather's boat, we yanked a lot of species from the bay, battling those stumpy St. Croix rods and corroded Penn spool reels, long-shafted hooks crammed with reeking pleats of squid. Few activities guarantee unpredictability as raw as the essence of boat fishing, to drift in dumb expectancy and boredom over what you can't see. This is, of course, after you've settled the disputes over who gets to use which rod. Whether it was the color of the wrapping on the ferrules and guides, a wooden butt, or cork grip, it seemed that the rod, like a sword or wand, had chosen *you*.

A tentative, electric throb of nibbling or blitz of a big strike is only the beginning. The next increment, as you reel in the mystery, is looking down into water, following the sun's wavering finger of crepuscular light as if it will deliver not only the answer to *What kind of fish?* but a chance to breech another dimension. The sudden belly flash or the haunting, cinematic, crystal-ball appearance of a fish's mottled back is the apex of the thrill; the moment right after it just doesn't seem possible in all that glowing teal uniformity that a different, more earthy color or even a shape can materialize. It arrives struggling out of a dream. And then the guessing game is over. You know how big the fish is now, too, though for a half a minute at least you were inhabiting a space where you were suddenly tactilely connected to something wild and foreign that was not in your range of vision until you brought it there by manipulating, if not violating, a sacred and organic process. Or were you simply playing your role in the primal chase?

Mostly we caught porgies, and some dogfish, too, which at least had in their appearance the threat of being miniature sharks. There were the occasional weakfish ("sea trout"), named because of how easily their lips would tear when hooked, prized because they were alleged by my aunt to be "good eating" (I vomited for two days after being forced to wolf a slab of her infamous weakfish loaf). The boat erupted in a mutual groan when someone hauled in the reviled and freakish sea robin, a Boschian, ichthyological nightmare with insect legs and pectoral fins like bat wings. The most visually fascinating, however, and the only one I'd eat under any circumstances (see *chicken*), was the northern puffer (*Sphoeroides maculatus*), or what we called *blowfish*. Measuring about three to five inches, they inflated cartoonishly as you reeled them to the side of the boat, a defense mechanism against predators. When we lifted them from the water like albino grapefruits and palmed their taut, distended bodies, the glowing bellies felt like our father's cheek after a few days without shaving. Perhaps it was this textural familiarity that endeared them to us subconsciously, but they also did what fish were not supposed to do: emit a sound, a panicked rhythmic sequence of grunts. A website at the University of Massachusetts actually has sound files of fish, including a clip of blowfish "language" from a specimen in Maryland in 1962, about five years before I saw my first one.

I'd received my own US Divers mask and

snorkel for my birthday, and the Cressi paraphernalia had been reclaimed by my father, so one
of my first self-assigned missions was to see a
blowfish underwater, to study one when its eyes
weren't terrified and threatening to explode
from its stressed enlargement. Although I'd
gotten to know them intimately over the years
as they expired slowly in my grandfather's
yellow bucket, poaching in summer heat, or as
he disemboweled them in the kitchen sink, it
was not the same.

My sister Evie and I had nurtured a mild
obsession with blowfish, impersonating them
at the dinner table when the cigarette-propelled
adult conversation enveloped us, trying to make
each other laugh and choke on food by contract-
ing our lips into bloodless white rings. But I still
wanted to be face to face with one in its natural
habitat. The closest we'd come was trapping one
by accident in our minnow net, an eight-foot
rectangle of fine mesh that we dragged ballooning between us like an underwater sail through
the shallows, going after shiners for snapper
bait. Catching this specimen was almost as much
of a surprise as the school of rare baby striped
bass we hauled onto the sand one day, letting
them go in a panic after we realized what they
were. Inflated, this blowfish was no bigger than
a ping-pong ball.

Fighting the onshore chop one hot July
afternoon at Jessup's Neck, I had to purge my
flooded snorkel after every other breath as white-
caps broke over me. I treaded, rotating to make

sure I was not drifting into the vines of jellyfish tentacles. (My sister had been stung almost to the point of being hospitalized once when the engine broke down and she was drifting, sitting listlessly in her water skis off the stern as my father tinkered with the engine.) The rest of the family was sprawled on blankets and towels, reading. My father's book was on his lap, and I could tell by his yawn and stretch and the way he checked his watch, swiveling his head to scan the beach, that he was thinking about pulling anchor. Shriveled and chilled despite the temperature of the water, I was committed to scouring the area around our boat for as long as I could, doing my best to avoid being filleted or impaled by the raised engine's skeg as the stern bucked crazily. Fifty yards beyond the boat was a staked "pound" net. Ubiquitous in the 1960s and '70s, these bleached and lonely corrals of dead saplings draped and festooned with netting were designed to funnel and trap the fish moving along the beach with the current. They were curious structures, hybrids suggesting the haunted ruins of a burial scaffold or aborted piers, their eeriness intensified because I'd never actually seen a bayman tending one from his skiff. Because of their unselective intentions and a new demographic's growing environmental sensitivity (including a movement to bring back the native sea turtles), they're a rare sight these days. How often I'd studied them from shore, wondering whether they had been abandoned in disrepair and what species might be desperately searching for an exit through the mesh walls below the pennants of dried seaweed.

My father rose from his towel, so my measured plunges below the surface accelerated along with my anxiety; I filled my lungs and dove eight feet to the bottom, where the push-and-pull of the swells was not as annoying, and where I could simulate, briefly, the luxury of scuba, skimming close to the bottom. The beach at Jessup's Neck is banked with pale, rounded, wave-worn gravel that you can hear grinding and clicking in the water's action when your ears are below the surface. The skin diver's backdrop close to shore is scrubbed bright by constant motion. Because of this, the floor is not coated with the green slime or *Codium fragile,* a seaweed known as "dead man's fingers" whose colonies prefer a little more depth.

The blowfish appeared when I was admiring the bubbles of my exhalations catching the late afternoon light. Its eyes hooked me in the lime translucence of sun-charged water. Like any normally evolved creature tattooed with defense in a predatory world, his topside was camouflaged with a muted tiger pattern to blend with the colors of the bottom. But the emerald eyes seemed almost iridescent in their greenness, and humanly expressive, too, dark and surprised, the pupils hemmed by golden irises. With its puny tailfin and that unmistakably blunt, bovine profile, a blowfish does not seem built for speed, but they can dart. Even so, this one didn't scoot away; rather, it hovered patiently, almost seemed bored, fluttering its pectorals to get closer, so close I could have petted it. Around the fish, grains of sand rose and settled in vague answer to the turbulence above. I could see its puckered mouth, its little buckteeth working, and thought of my own. The fish was aware of me, if not studying me, which made the experience different from holding him in my hand as I tried to dislodge a hook, or to confront his glazed, accusatory expression staring from the bottom of a pail. Certainly, it hadn't recognized the targeting of a hungry stalker in the fogged lens of my mask. During the slow voyage home, I debated telling the rest of the family about the encounter and ended up keeping it to myself, wedged in the bow seat, content, wrapped in a towel, blue and shivering, returned to my native element, but not entirely.

The following summer, along with a friend, I stole a twelve-foot chunk of industrial foam from a boatyard near the inlet to the bay. To call it a *boatyard* is a stretch. It was just a sandy scrap of a parcel next to the cottage of a grumpy, semi-retired outboard mechanic. The staved carcass of one sad wooden skiff was the only legitimate boat on the grim property. Nailed to the side of his shed was a rain-shriveled poster with the faded image of a Wankel rotary engine, something he had tried and failed to introduce to the local boating community. The new, orange block of foam gleamed. We had ridden past it on our

bikes for weeks, spotted it lashed incongruous-
ly to a stack of old planks. One night, flippers
tucked beneath our arms, we prized the thing
free from the lumber, thrashed through the
bulrushes with it over our heads, then swam
it back across the pond. The next morning, in
the improvised chop shop of my grandfather's
garage, we spray-painted it Kelly green, fastened
a few sheets of plywood to the top, and reinvent-
ed it as our research station, claiming to anyone
who asked that we'd found it washed up on
Pavilion Beach. For almost a week it was moored
in back of our houses with a cinder block,
bobbing shamelessly in plain sight of the entire
community.

Subsequently, we began plundering the
garage for old tools and bits of machinery we
could fashion into equipment for capturing
specimens, taking core samples (a process I'd
seen on another nature show), etc. A rake, a hoe,
an old length of lead pipe, a dented eel trap, a
disastrously asymmetrical grappling hook from
junior high metal shop, even the wringer of my
grandmother's antique washing machine — anything to which a rope could be fastened and
played out to the depths. On inner tubes, we
floated our lunches out to the raft along with
our towels, and even a transistor that we kept
on low volume, imagining the static crackle of
voices to be a ship's radio. Before long, the deck
was littered with arrangements of plants, bits
of shell, various shades of mud that looked
more like piles of excrement, a row of odd

pails, buckets, and jars alive and flickering with imprisoned creatures. Beneath the sun, our collection of small jellyfish evaporated and crusted like snot on the filthy wood. To any of the neighbors laboring behind their mowers, weeding around their flagpoles or tomato plants, or sitting on their small porches at cocktail hour, it must have seemed like a miniature garbage scow, a floating sculpture of detritus in a tangle of rusted metal and clothesline. And it stank too. So badly that finally we had to shovel and dump everything over the side, pull anchor, and swim the hulk and its useless cargo of contraptions back to shore.

Our timing was good. Handwritten signs in black magic marker with a phone number at the bottom began to appear on the bulletin boards and phone booths of the Pavilion, the tennis court, and even the little general store out on Noyack Road: LOST OR STOLEN, LARGE FOAM PONTOON, ORANGE. We dismantled our station the next day, washed the plywood, and heaved it back into the rafters of my grandfather's garage along with his appropriated tools. The defeat would repeat itself about eight years later in college when I toyed with the idea of focusing on science, fantasizing about fieldwork as my academic world imploded and I bombed exam after exam. In either case, the guilt generated by my trying to be someone else was punishment enough. When the workload accumulated and the material convened on its abstract essence and purpose, I abandoned the related courses as frantically as I had that piece of foam. My accomplice and I sawed it in half and released it one night to the outgoing tide at the inlet to the bay.

Though our academic angle was short-lived, it didn't take us too long to redirect that energy into something else. Instead of pretending we were scientists, we refocused on being hunters, finally appreciating that a percentage of our interest in the sea was driven by *having* (pulling, hooking, trapping, netting, and spearing) the things that lived in it.

When my family embarked on our annual canoe camping expedition to the Narrows of Lake George, I took to snorkeling with a baited drop line in hand, a seedy, unsportsmanlike stalking that took the subliminal guesswork out of angling, but that was immensely satisfying. Though I had fooled them from my perch on the surface, I had always striven to picture what the fish were doing in the vicinity of my hook when they weren't impaling their muzzles on it. Now I had my answer.

Kicking out into the deeper waters off our campsite, where the rock piles or weedy cove gave way to smooth, ominously tectonic ledges and boulders, I hovered over my prey, the shadowy outlines of big fish cruising slowly along the distant bottom. The lake was potable, had an almost tropical clarity. The procedure was surgical, or better yet, like trying to manip-ulate those toy cranes at amusement parks, aiming and dropping that little mechanical scoop on whatever impractical plastic toy your juvenile materialist craving had fixated. But these were sizeable, real animals— lake trout and largemouth bass—and when you dropped that voluptuous night crawler down to their cruising silhouettes, timing the delivery a few inches in front of their snouts, it was like watching a vacuum cleaner inhale popcorn. Getting them back to shore was the next trial, where my parents and sisters watched me emerge from the shallows in a haze of tangled monofilament with a four-pound bass like a demented pug in a frenzied orbit at the end of its leash.

We became armed and dangerous, first by screwing the tridents of two-dollar hardware store frog stickers to warped broom sticks, and finally by going to Hampton Bays and sinking our lawn-mowing money into deadly fiberglass and stainless steel beauties—"flounder pounders" with hinged snells, propelled menacingly by black surgical tubing looped around our wrists. We could not afford spearguns, so these were the next best thing: a marine version of the coveted "wrist rocket" sling shot with which we had been plugging the feathered and furred population of the mud flats on the other side of the pond. After he found us in the yard firing our new spears haphazardly at a cedar trunk, my father (the combat veteran) was appalled by their lethal potential, advising us skeptically to please avoid skewering each other. We were old enough to take boats out alone, so our expeditions eventually drew us away from hazing the landscape and sluggish critters of our local lagoon to tracking down blackfish in the cool, clear ocean currents at the Shinnecock Inlet. There, we had to duck the wakes of passing tuna boats and the big lures cast by people on shore as we probed and plied the jetty's granite blocks with our gleaming prongs.

My hometown in Massachusetts still had its rural pockets, so in the summer weeks before and after my encampments on Long Island, I applied my murderousness to the freshwater ponds and lakes in my neighborhood. No private or public body of water was safe. There were the shallow, tannin-permeated bogs like the Mill Pond, so murky that I once found myself stalled over a snapping turtle half my size, my hairless chest grazing the top of its shell. Like a shark's dorsal, my snorkel cut through the film of pollen on the surfaces of green, translucent, spring-fed lakes like Baldpate and Stile's, where I stalked smallmouth bass and perch poised at the grassy clefts where streams dumped minnows into their waiting mouths. Pumpkinseed and sunfish hovered at the center of their dusted-off gravel "nests" like bull's-eyes.

The gulf was widening between who I was becoming and my original inspiration, the environmental activist Cousteau. Thankfully, the blowfish had crossed my path during a less violent phase. Now, my forays were about neither conservation nor hunting, in its pure, sporting, or subsistence-driven legitimacy. With each kill, I would have to envision my coeval blowfish's benign curiosity and dumb trust curled in its last spasm on the tip of my spear. And though this image wore away at my bloodlust, the genetic sap persisted. No matter how many forests are cleared and meadows filled for a better view of the water, the civic harmony promised by developments, cul-de-sacs, and sidewalks will be violated. The human race can always count on the blind rapture that impels — and the red haze that follows — an adolescent boy loosed upon any corner of the natural world with a weapon in his hands.

Sharks hadn't explicitly entered mainstream consciousness until that summer Peter Gimbel's film *Blue Water, White Death: The Search for the Great White Shark* was released. This was almost four years before the waiting lines for *Jaws* would snake down the sidewalk and around the movie theater in Sag Harbor, and the world would change forever. That was around the time my sister did a book report on shark attacks and signed out the school library's entire collection: a single, frayed, re-bound hardcover whose subject was mostly African Zambezi sharks (known as bull sharks in the United States). It featured gruesome black-and-white photos of anonymous, chewed-off human appendages, but the images of Rodney Fox's stitched-up torso provided a bridge to the film. He was the Australian skin diver who had become a celebrity for surviving a great white attack, and who was also invited to accompany Gimbel's expedition when it arrived Down Under.

I went back to see *Blue Water, White Death* four times. Matinee after matinee, I endured with the same (dwindling) group of friends that excruciatingly slow buildup, the stilted dialogue aboard the converted whaling ship off of Durban, the whole spectacle weirdly portentous of the most contrived reality shows airing today. I watched it again recently after a forty-year hiatus and was a little ashamed of myself for having loved it so much, wondering why I'd repeatedly put myself through the interminable, nerdy, and dated banter of these divers and explorers for almost two hours. In the final scenes in South Australia, the stars of the show appear in all their ragged-toothed glory. But after so many square miles of whale-oil slicks, hundreds of gallons of chum and pig blood dumped into clear water, horse torsos and sheep parts knotted to chains or ropes, I was convinced I had the smell on me when I left the theater.

Free of the endearing and poignant voice of Cousteau, *Blue Water, White Death*'s element of wonder was ratcheted to pure, raw adventure with Gimbel, who was also the first diver to explore the *Andrea Doria*. The crew's intention, it seemed, was simply to push the limits of personal safety and, in a sense, to *conquer* with visual contact and proximity. These were not scientists. I was mesmerized by the spectacle of pelagic sharks scything through slicks of blood one hundred miles off the East African coast and, of course, the divers armed with shotgun shell–powered "bang sticks" leaving the safety of their cages to film a cyclone of finned power tools boring through a whale carcass.

Recently, I reread Peter Matthiessen's *Blue Meridian,* an account of Gimbel's expedition, and was smitten again, but this time my worship was inverted, mostly because I didn't have to suffer through folksinger Tom Chapin's wistful (almost falsetto) contemporary shanties in the film's soundtrack. Matthiessen, who died in 2014, is almost invisible in the movie, but his book is guided by a naturalist's exacting and compassionate eye, a philosopher's insight, and a hero's quest for a mythic beast—all of this a warmup to his classic *The Snow Leopard* and its lyrical, confessional investigation of disappointment and redemption. While the film compels the viewer to accept and revere the ensemble's quirks, Matthiessen is not so submissive, focusing his social critic's scrutiny on each character while not being afraid to probe the flaws of the expedition itself. Only time and maturity can help you appreciate that a book about the making of a film is better than the film itself. Being fourteen, however, changes the paradigm; impatience gratified by the moving image (in color) pretty much wins every time.

Sometimes I wonder why it was Gimbel's film that tipped the balance, stoked the final impetus for my foray into scuba when I was fifteen. When you know the ocean is populated with authentic monsters, where's the sense in acquiring the means that will put you in their vicinity? But what literally brought it home was Matthiessen's affiliation with Long Island; he'd lived near Amagansett where he owned and captained a charter fishing boat. By beginning his book with the story of landing a fifteen-foot great white off Montauk, he infused the project with local relevance. I'd seen the pylons of certain docks in my grandparents' neighborhood decorated with fins severed from sand sharks, blue sharks, and makos. True, these were ocean-going fishermen, but their trophies were enough to remind us what was beyond the safety of our inshore nursery.

To convince myself that a great white could never find its way into our maze of bays, coves, and lagoons, I often imagined inhabiting the mind of the animal, the obstacles he'd have to surmount on his commute from the open Atlantic. His passage through the Shinnecock Inlet would be easy enough, but getting through the locks of the canal linking Shinnecock Bay to the Great Peconic would be nearly impossible. Which meant he'd have to approach from the southeast, taking a left after rounding Montauk Point, after which he'd cruise past Gardiner's Island, squeezing his enormous flanks through the strait between Shelter Island and Sag, then slip around the sand spit at the northern end of Jessup's Neck without beaching himself. Then it would be a straight shot south-southwest across the Little Peconic. Maybe, if the tide were in all the way, he might choose as his exit from the bay the red nun at the mouth of Wooley Pond, churning a hard left to pounce on a pod of weakfish that were following something smaller, shrimp perhaps, browsing our tender calves in the shallows.

As a birthday present from my parents, I spent February and March of 1975 sitting in a classroom at New England Divers in Beverly, Massachusetts, along with my friends Tony and Larry. At fifteen, we were the youngest to attend that session of the NAUI (National Association of Underwater Instructors) certification program. Our instructor, Bill, a WWII/Korean War–era Navy frogman, let us know it every session. Whether he was telling us to shut up and behave or trying to illuminate our immaturity by putting us on the spot with dense technical questions, it seemed that he had it in for us (with good reason) from the first night our parents dropped us off, through our training in the facility's pool, all the way to our final exam. "This ain't *Sea Hunt!*" he'd bellow, when we lapsed into arbitrary giggling fits during his lectures. A maverick in the generation that invoked Lloyd Bridges as the TV icon of scuba, Bill assumed a certain dedicated fan base in us, thinking his disdain for that show's cheesy action/adventure parody of the sport would insult us. As if it were Bridges's example that inspired us to sign up in the first place. And yet it was impossible to communicate to Bill that we were actually his allies in our shared hatred of that lame black-and-white serial.

Outside of class we impersonated that balding, gristly Old Salt mercilessly, his Boston accent, the way he called lobsters "bugs." And we were not prepared for and resented the academic torture he visited upon us. Here we were again, calculating the pressure associated with certain depths, rates of ascent, etc., installed in one-piece desk/chair units no different from the ones we had occupied all day, doing the same sort of math we'd hoped to escape. This was not adventure; it was school. But Bill was trying to make us understand as best he could — in his frogman way — that this was not *Sea Hunt* because it was *real*, and that — beneath all of this theory — our lives were at stake. Of course, we refashioned this admonishment, fitted it to any situation where screwing around was frowned upon, like throwing a brownie at the back of someone's head in the school cafeteria or fabricating boogers out of rubber cement in architectural drawing class. We yodeled it on the paths between buildings, screamed it across the student parking lot and over the heads of our hunched peers in the smoking area: "What the fuck are you people doing??? This ain't *Sea Hunt!*"

Despite ourselves, we finished the course in late April at our anticlimactic "open water test" at Mingo Beach in Beverly. Overheated in full gear, yoked with BC (buoyancy compensator) vests, sagging weight belts, heavy-duty inflexible "beavertail" and "farmer John" wetsuit components, not to mention the tanks them-selves, we sat in a morose circle on the boulders, checking, rechecking each other's gear while Bill droned on about conger eels and goose-fish. ("Don't get your arm anywhere near their mouths. You'll be wearing the fish permanent-ly.") His warnings about the sensation of taking our masks off in forty-five-degree water were particularly robust. A calm reaction to this procedure, which literally takes your breath away, was a required hoop for the exam.

That's pretty much all I remember of the day I was given the go-ahead to venture and breathe below the surface on my own: the grueling sweat on the beach, the relief of cold weightlessness as I waded in and water seeped into my suit, and that lung-paralyzing in-suck, the springtime Atlantic like a frozen railroad spike being driven through my forehead when I was ordered to remove the mask. The visibility was awful, too, and we could barely see our mitted hands gesturing, trying to give each other the finger in the gloom. But we passed the course, and each of us embarked on his own trek down the long road to acquisition: the quest for equipment that could only be gotten after the interminable wait for multiple birthdays, Christmases, working through weekends cleaning rotted leaves out from gutters and from beneath shrubs for local, exploitative landscapers.

By the time summer rolled around, I wasn't even close; I'd saved enough to upgrade my mask and snorkel, and to begin pricing regulators, but nowhere near realization of my vivid day-dreams of possessing the validating Tank. My parents let me rent some equipment for a few dives with my friends, which were only slightly more inspiring than our first official dip at Mingo Beach. I was beginning to think the whole thing had been a waste of time, too expensive, too labor-intensive, and became nostalgic for the less complicated, liberating days of minimal encumberment and limited depth guaranteed by a mask and snorkel.

As our ninth-grade year was ending for the summer, Tony, my NAUI colleague, invited me to Bermuda. His father and stepmother lived there, and he had been volunteering at the Bermuda Biological Station during his longer visits. Now called BIOS, or the Bermuda Institute of Ocean Sciences, but founded as the Biological Station in 1903 by a group from Harvard and NYU. Since we were certified, we would be able to do chores there for the summer and as payment be granted access to the station's diving equipment. At that point I was the only member of my family who hadn't been to Bermuda, let alone any place legitimately tropical or even south of New York. My family's five-year residence in California, including visits to San Diego and Tijuana by car, were almost exclusively prememory for me, an infant and toddler, so they didn't count. Because they waited on tables at a Howard Johnson's during the school year, my sisters had been able to afford a trip to Bermuda with some friends one spring; they were out of high school at this point, and I was alone, so my parents felt sorry for me and relented. How could they not? I would be the guest in a house owned by a respectable, professional family, my goal the culmination of a dream that did not include lathering myself in coconut oil, chugging Planter's Punch at hotel bars, then bombing around suicidally on a moped. All I needed was a plane ticket. Once I was installed on Long Island for the summer, I ramped up the neighborhood mowing and weeding and abandoned — temporarily — the investments in diving equipment. Instead, I set my sights on August and crossing the threshold into a world I had discerned (albeit criminally) through the Oppedisano's window.

If you haven't grown up around it, and you've tried for most of your life to imagine what tropical water looks like, magazines, television, movie theaters can't prepare you for the visual baptism. I had only been on a plane once before, as a baby, when we had flown back East for a visit from Los Angeles, so the experience was amplified. Being alone for that ninety-minute jet ride from Boston, white knuckling the arm rests of my window seat, I was not prepared for the sweat and prickle of adrenaline when we suddenly swung down through the clouds and low over the roiling blues and greens of the reefs. I wanted to share my disbelief, but it seemed I was the only person interested in looking down, craning to get a better look, as if I were seeing that water for the last instead of first time.

The exotic facets of the place, its palm-lined streets, pink-and-white houses with pyramidal terraced roofs, and even the talcy pink-and-white sand itself were soon diluted by my having to surrender again to the very sort of labor adolescents were enlisted to do in New England. We mowed the Biological Station's stiff grass, weeded and cleaned its flowerbeds in the sweltering heat for almost a week before Tony was able to secure the diving equipment for a weekend. During lunch breaks in his shed, Fernando, the sun-baked, wiry Azorean chief of the grounds crew, offered us swigs of cold rum ("rohm") from the sweating unlabeled bottle he'd yank from the small refrigerator. Spurred by that and his Portuguese-inflected English, I lapsed into my laborer's attitude of counting the minutes to cleanup, stowing the tools, and quitting time. I had imagined being taught to fill the scuba tanks from a compressor, or to wave from the dock a hearty "Godspeed!" to departing researchers in their tricked-out Whaler, or, upon their triumphant return, to help them tote plastic bags of writhing specimens back to the lab. At the station, however, scrubbing out the hardened scum from the interior of an old aquarium was the closest I got to a whiff of Cousteau's *Undersea World* or Gimbel's *Blue Water, White Death.*

In the meantime, when we got off work early, we snorkeled at Tony's aunt's place on Castle Harbor and spent one afternoon free-diving for calico clams (*Macrocallista maculata*) off of Tony's backyard on Harrington Sound. You'd kick to the bottom as quickly as possible (about fifteen to twenty feet) and begin the determined scouting for a pattern of two round holes spaced less than an inch apart like tiny eye sockets in the luminous sand. Then you'd simply insert your index and middle fingers in the openings, forking the stubborn bivalve out of his burrow. The clams were clean and perfect. They had an orange hue, a pattern of brown checks, and texture like porcelain, not the chalky, mud-stained quahogs and cherrystones we scooped or raked from the black fudge of Wooley Pond. Turning them over in my hand, I almost believed that I could stay at the bottom of Harrington Sound for as long as I wanted. We wore mesh bags at our waists and filled them quickly, the compact radials of the checkerboard shells clicking, weighing us down as we swam. Sputtering at the surface, we handed them to Tony's father and stepmother, who carried them to the patio table and its open bottle of red wine, plate, and a short, blunt knife.

It was fate that the tenth anniversary revival of *Thunderball*, the first Bond film to be permeated exclusively with scuba sequences, was playing in Bermuda. To see it, Tony and I bummed a ride from his parents to Hamilton. Although it took me years to realize that much of it was probably filmed in a swimming pool, at the time it was like adrenaline injected straight into my heart: not just violence but submarine violence. Not men shooting fish with spears but each other, slashing regulator hoses, wrenching off each other's masks as they raced around, clinging to their personal torpedo-like scooters in trails of bubbles, daggers strapped to their calves. To our surprise and demonic glee in diving class, Bill had told us it was a good idea to carry a knife, neither for the purpose of stabbing enemy agents who might be lurking behind a mound of coral nor for savaging marine life, but for cutting oneself or partner free if he became entangled in ropes, a net, lines from an untethered lobster trap, or even kelp. At that age, to think that a knife had anything to do with safety was a better reason not to get one. A few years later I would find a menacing, brand-new blade still in its rubber sheath at the bottom of Rockport Harbor. I couldn't wear that thing without thinking of Sean Connery — not Cousteau — wreaking havoc on the nameless henchmen of Euro-chic, eye-patched world dominators. That night, after seeing *Thunderball,* while studying the lizards scampering along the ceiling of Tony's bedroom, I kicked at the blankets as if they were coils of anchor line.

At the beginning of my second week in Bermuda, we heaved our borrowed scuba gear into the back of Tony's father's car and drove to the sailboat that they kept in a cove near Tucker's Town. Loading that equipment onboard would be the closest I've ever felt to being on a legitimate, untainted expedition; just the manner in which Tony's father helped us secure it in the cockpit, his implicit trust in our ownership of the process, his faith *almost* convinced me of our technical proficiency. If he had been nervous, he didn't let on, which regulated my excitement and dread, kept me functional. After hoisting the sails, we cruised lazily out of Castle Harbor, picking up speed on our way to the open ocean. I was smitten by the flying fish skittering as they stitched the surface ahead of the bow wave like sparrows bursting from and being reabsorbed by the top of a hedge. But I was even more entranced by the water itself, how depth had elbowed the comfort of soft turquoise into something ominous. I couldn't stop staring into it, wondering at the distance that could inject an element that I knew to be clear with such density that it appeared to be solid navy.

Eventually, we anchored off of Nonsuch Island, one nub in the chain of broken molars fencing the mouth of Castle Harbor that yawns toward the open ocean. Because the boat had a sizeable keel, Tony's dad positioned us a hundred yards from the reef we wanted to explore. And then it was up to us. No crusty dive instructor reminding us to smear a wad of spit in the mask lens to prevent fogging, no one looking over our shoulders to see if we had opened the tank valves properly and backed them off a quarter-turn, or if we had screwed fresh CO_2 cartridges into our vests. Tony's father watched us suit up with the polite awe and reluctant curiosity adults reserve for those moments when children are doing something they themselves can't. We sat next to each other, the blond flags of Tony's straight hair sticking out at angles from the strap of his mask, regulator mouth-pieces gripped in our brace-filled mouths. We had always wanted to roll backwards off of the gunwale, which Tony now did without warning. But I opted to take the other route we'd been taught: to stand and leap, legs locked in a splayed stride, á la Navy frogman, gripping the mask and regulator to my face with my hands. Tony was wearing a compass and set it on the reef, which seemed miles away. As he pointed down and nodded, I thought, *Why can't we just kick over there on the surface, snorkeling to conserve air?* But after all, why had we trained for this? Not descending would have defeated the purpose. I nodded back and we flipped ass-up together. Then, with a dramatic splash, kicked straight down like the veterans we pretended to be.

It was hard to tell how deep we were; we didn't have gauges, but we relieved the pressure in our ears a few times, so it must have been around twenty feet. I couldn't see the bottom, just sterile, pale blue space in every direction, empty, unpopulated. We were side by side, so given the blinder effect of the mask I had to keep swiveling in order to see Tony and follow him to the destination, intentionally falling slightly behind if I lost him in my periphery. He kept glancing down at the instrument on his wrist, and I hoped he knew what he was doing. What if we just kept chugging right on out into the abyss in the opposite direction (Senegal?), his father distracted, lost in a paperback while our telltale eruptions of bubbles were erased by the wind? The swim over to the reef was interminable because there was nothing to see.

William Beebe, the American naturalist, had used Nonsuch Island as his base for the historic launching of his bathysphere in the early 1930s. He died in 1962, breathing his last in Trinidad while I was a toddler tripping around a backyard in L.A., but I'd always relegated his brand of adventure to the boyhood of my father, who would have been around fourteen when Beebe's expedition was in the public eye. Perhaps it was for this reason that I'd gravitated so fiercely to Cousteau and dismissed the important link of Beebe's example. It was Helen DeWitt's densely playful novel *The Last Samurai* (absolutely no relation to an unremarkable film with Tom Cruise) that powerfully reacquainted me with the explorer. I owe DeWitt a debt of thanks for reintroducing me to Beebe's memoir *Half Mile Down,* which is an obsession of her narrator, Ludo, a child genius who balances his literary interests between dated adventure narratives and translating ancient epics. Ludo is on the mythic quest for a father, and Watkins, one of the paternal candidates, is an artist who says, "I paint not things in the world but colour. How can I paint colour if I don't know what it should look like? Is blue paint merely to represent blue?" Ludo is drawn to the artist because he believes he must have read Beebe's memoir. For his experiential research on the color blue, Watkins himself weasels a descent in a bathysphere-like contraption while the scientists who use it are away at a conference. In his profile of Watkins, Ludo cites a small excerpt of a paragraph from Beebe's narrative account of being at a depth of seven hundred feet, but the entire chunk from *Half Mile Down* is worth reading:

> Ever since the beginnings of human history, when first the Phoenicians dared to sail the open sea, thousands upon thousands of human beings had reached the depth at which we were now suspended, and had passed on to lower levels. But all of these were dead, drowned victims of war, tempest, or other Acts of God. We were the first living men to look out at the strange illumination: and it was stranger than any imagination could have conceived. It was of an indefinable translucent blue quite unlike anything I have ever seen in the upper world, and it excited our optic nerves in a most confusing manner. We kept thinking and calling it brilliant, and again and again I picked up a book to read the type, only to find that I could not tell the difference between a blank page and a colored plate. I brought all my logic to bear, I put out of mind the excitement of our position in watery space and tried to think sanely of comparative color, and I failed utterly.

Many of my memories of doing exciting things or being in inspiring places when I was an adolescent are polluted by a more intense memory of the angst that gripped me while I was in the very situation I had craved, shamefully longing for it to be over before it had barely begun. The meager depth of twenty or thirty feet at which Tony and I had leveled on our swim to the reef might as well have been seven hundred. Would I have reacted any differently, felt less duplicitous and nervous if I had been inside a steel globe at Beebe's perch instead? How would a fifteen-year-old react if he were gawking through those protruding, cannon-like windows of fused quartz instead of pushing through the water with his face a thin disc of tempered glass fixed in rubber? So much of Beebe's book cycles back to the difficulty of describing color, and reading his memoir recently I felt a little envious, not only of his eloquence and excitement, but the absence of fear, obliterated by his willingness to accept that blue as its own reward.

A few days before our foray on the sailboat, an old friend of Tony's family, Austin Talbot, had taken us out fishing along the fringe of reefs on the island's southeastern shore on his stripped-down wooden lobster boat. If you look at satellite photos of Bermuda, you'll see that the northern rim of the island is characterized by shallow bays and basins, ancient features of the island, perhaps evidence of peninsulas, coves, and headlands that used to be above sea level. From the air, all that visible texture underwater makes the island look bigger, instead of the whippy, scorpion-shaped sliver it really is, with a gradual, comprehendible inshore demise.

The south-facing shore, however, is different. It plunges without excuse or visual warning from the protective necklace of wave-flecked reefs to three hundred feet and *blackness.* And this is the precipice we straddled with Austin, who knew the reefs by heart, weaving nonchalantly through the nasty spurs and knobs of coral as if he were pulling into the parking lot to which he had been commuting his whole life.

A celebrity and native, Austin had been a member of an island institution, the Talbot Brothers, a calypso/barber shop quartet that had recorded and performed from the 1940s through the early '60s. My parents actually had a few of the group's 78s buried in their stacks of vinyl, souvenirs from their honeymoon. Austin had recently turned eighty when he picked us up at the dock in Tucker's Town. Barefooted, in ragged shorts and a faded red polo shirt, rumpled captain's cap sitting loosely on his closely cropped salt-and-pepper hair, he seemed a Black version of my own grandfather, right down to the last accessory.

Tony and I used spinning rods while Austin sat on the transom with the business end of a big drop line looped over his finger. Beside him were two buckets: one filled with dead baitfish, tiny silver-sided minnows, the other with damp, powdery Bermuda sand. Once in a while, he'd plunge his dark, calloused hand into one, grab a fistful of bait, then with the other a lump of clotted sand and begin shaping, packing the combined ingredients into what looked like a mauve snowball bristling with the half-embedded tails and heads of small fish. Leaning over the gunwale, he'd gently lower his creation to the surface and release it. It came apart as it sank, but slowly enough to carry some of the bait to the bottom, the cloud of glowing shell and coral particles catching sunlight, attracting the attention of the fish. Chumming was never so beautiful. The ball would leave his palm and spiral into invisibility, a grainy white comet diving slowly against the patchwork of cerulean, turquoise, and the dark, intermittent topographical evidence of the reef below. Even at fifteen, I sensed not only that I was in the presence of an aesthetic event, at the crossroads of art and wildness, but that there was also something powerfully emblematic in my straining to follow the ball of sand. This was memory itself.

Even the vivid image of the amazing fish I caught that day, a rainbow runner (*Elegatis bipinnulata*), with its neon-yellow stripes sandwiched between blue and green, even Austin's reverence at my hauling in this feisty and elusive species of jack, have not endured as persistently as that fading sand coil, its trail of liberated dead minnows dispersed, trailing like a convoy of failed satellites.

Having pushed away from his father's yawl and all its earthly steel, brightwork, teak, and fiberglass, Tony and I were suspended, boatless, in that very zone just beyond where we'd fished with Austin, where Beebe's abyss begins to rise and, drained of its immensity, is replaced by a quality of reflective light that trembles with the faintest presence of illuminated sand on the bottom. We just kept kicking, propelling ourselves, trying to close the space between blue-green limbo and the reassurance of a coral-hemmed sanctuary we had yet to glimpse, each stroke of our flippers deliberate, rhythmical.

The spotted eagle ray swept into my field of vision out of this emptiness like a monstrous brown kite blown from its wooden frame, terrible in its grace. So focused ahead in my longing for the reef, I had not seen it sweeping in from my right until its wing almost knocked the mask off my face, the long tail that followed whipping like a winch's snapped cable. What were the odds of this intersection? The fish's wingspan was more than six feet, and in its veering it seemed as shocked as I was, two jets vying for the same runway, two pedestrians shaken out of their sidewalk daydreams en route to the same café. As it banked away and resumed its patient flapping, receding to the size of a lone sparrow, I suddenly realized that I hadn't been inhaling or exhaling. The regulator flew out of my mouth involuntarily in an explosion of bubbles. I bolted upwards — exactly the opposite of what I'd been taught to do in the pool at New England Divers that very spring. Five years past the immature spasms of fantasy at the Oppedisano's window, far away from playing in the shallows of Long Island, finally enclosed in the element I'd been craving. And I'd panicked.

Tony's confused head broke the surface next to mine. I'd already torn off my mask, desperate for wind, sunlight, anything but water to touch my face. "What are you *doing*?" he asked, laughing. "It's just an eagle ray. They're harmless!"

I looked back at the boat. We hadn't really swum that far. "I don't know," I said, somewhere between pure humiliation and hyperventilation. "It was just so big." Among my friends at home, I had a reputation for launching into daredevil stunts without hesitation, whether it was scaling gigantic white pines in search of raccoon kittens, being the first to climb through the windows of abandoned houses, skateboarding the steepest roads in our town, or doing flips from the cliffs into Style's Pond. Nearly colliding with the eagle ray, however, sent an electric current through my entire frame, a mindless and immediate fear so shameful in its aftermath that I didn't know what else to say. *It was big.*

"Good thing we weren't that deep!" he yelled. "Your lungs would have exploded out through your nose, or something. 'This ain't *Sea Hunt*!'" Then he stuffed the regulator back into his mouth and flipped back down without me.

We reached the reef. And it was better than I had imagined, throbbing with light, warm and unthreatening. It seemed to house every character we'd pored over in the waterproof field guides purchased in Hamilton the day before. It was like arriving at a convention center where all your favorite comic book superheroes are suddenly milling about, three dimensional, just as colorful as their facsimiles but even more convincing because of the wrinkles in their tights, their masks ajar. Spanish hog fish, three different species of parrot fish, angels, slippery dicks (yes, two adolescent boys got a lot of mileage out of that one), barracuda, pompano, ubiquitous shoals of sergeant majors and grunts — all of them so distracting that I almost forgot to keep looking over my shoulder back out to sea, half-expecting something to emerge from that void again, and knowing that in about thirty-five minutes I'd be heading back out into it.

The reason I don't get too excited about eating lobsters anymore is not because of David Foster Wallace's brilliant and provocative essay on the subject; rather, it's because I spent most of my free time between 1979 and 1983 prizing them out of their granite clefts in the waters off Rockport, Massachusetts. A noncommercial permit to scuba dive for lobsters cost thirty-five dollars (only five dollars more over a quarter-century later). Once a year I'd drive to the Saltonstall Building in Boston and pay for the piece of paper that guaranteed a pot of water would soon be boiling on the stove almost every time I clambered out of the water, up the rocks, and through the backyard, my mesh bag twitching with claws and tails. The lobsters initiated their march shoreward from deeper water in the early summer, and from that point to mid-autumn my tank was always full of air and at the ready.

Rockport, where my parents moved when I was a freshman in college, was the last stop on the commuter rail line from Boston to Cape Ann, and what my father hoped would be his last stop before retirement from the GE plant in Lynn. For me it was the end of excuses having to do with why I couldn't dive more often. The small house was directly on a headland overlooking the North Atlantic, so close to the action that its windows were festooned with seaweed after each big storm. My parents bought the place for $90,000, and because they planned to renovate and winterize it, there was a lot of work to do. The contractor was touted by the architect as a mythic craftsman and purist when it came to colonial or early-nineteenth-century restoration. Because his crew was stretched so thin on other jobs, he was going to do most of the work himself, enlisting his son when he needed an extra pair of hands. And when his son or any of the other guys couldn't make it, he took me on as a lackey to do the safe tasks: muling buckets of demolished horsehair and lath plaster down the stairs and out to the dump truck, or pounding nails mindlessly along plywood chalk lines (before the days of nail guns).

Stocky, with only a thin skirt of white hair left at his temples, the builder was one of the most ornery men I've ever met. Though he flirted with being polite and even a jovial softy, these were fragile states, especially when his craftsman's opinion of how something needed

to be done was in the balance, and boisterous-
ness quickly evolved into earned arrogance.
He had been a helmet diver in the Navy but
didn't talk about it often, though his son
eventually apprised me of his father's near-death
experiences with explosives that steered him
away from the profession.

But his son was another story. Some vestige
of aquatic magnetism in the family had endured
and pulled him to it. He'd graduated from Maine
Maritime that year and came back to Rockport
to start a one-man underwater salvage company,
the small captive fleets of commercial fishing
and lobster boats at Bearskin Neck, Granite Pier,
Pigeon Cove, and Lanesville providing enough
work to keep him busy without having to venture over to the circus in Gloucester harbor.
From what I gathered, he did things that kept
owners from having to dry-dock, like inspect-
ing or cleaning hulls and propellers, repairing
mooring chains and shackles. Barrel-chested and
equipped with the same glasses, he seemed a
miniature version of his father, with hair, albeit
thinning. Once our paths began to cross more
frequently on jobs, I also recognized a trace of
the inherited signature cantankerousness in his
accent, mannerisms, and demeanor. Though the
patriarch loved to tease us about the cop-out of
tanks versus the "real" diver's equipment (iconic
canvas suit/helmet/air hose), I could sense his
satisfaction that his son and I were going to dive
together.

From the beginning, there was no question

that this was the son's turf, and just as I was
doing with his father in matters of carpentry,
I followed him, the timid apprentice. Before
work, we dove Folly Cove one scorching July
morning, tracing the sheer walls of its popular
seventy-five-foot drop in search of sea anemones,
but the visibility was nominal. Then we had a
rare opportunity to dive the inner harbor at
Bearskin Neck to search for some engine parts
dropped from a boat belonging to one of his
clients. This is usually against the law, but the
Harbormaster (a master artisan with pewter
and perhaps the second most ornery man I've
ever met) gave us official clearance because of
"professional" diving status.

Motif #1, the barn-red fishing shed perched
on the Bearskin Neck jetty with panicles of colorful
buoys fixed to its side, is reputed to be among
the most photographed scenes on the American
tourist trail, rivaling Mt. Rushmore, the Golden
Gate Bridge, and the Statue of Liberty. Even my
father, having become a resident of the town,
was an acolyte of its aura, worshipping it with
his telephoto and wide-angle lenses as shamelessly as a vacationing dentist from Ohio. In his
visual obsessions, the only other subjects that
swallowed more film than that quaint scene
were seagulls and my mother, whom my sisters
and I mockingly called Motif #2. As we backed
up the pickup truck along the wharf, parting
the crowds of shoppers, gear rattling in the
bed, I felt that I was passing into a more legitimate echelon of humanity. What cocky nearly

postadolescent wouldn't want to slip into the skin of the gnarled, local tradesman for a day, especially something as adventurous as a salvage diver?

I noticed that my companion had amped up his swagger a notch for the gathering tourists, pretending they were invisible but definitely giving them a show. The way he swung those tanks out over the tailgate to my waiting hands, how he subdued the black octopus of his regulator, pressure and depth gauges swinging wildly about. His shoulders and biceps were accented by the tank-top design of the farmer johns (we hadn't put on our beavertail jackets yet). This was theater, and I caught on fast, feigning gruff small talk as we took our time suiting up, quietly excited murmurs trickling from behind the wharf railing as I released a hissing blast from the valve on my tank.

Descending the rotting ladder into the water fully suited up was more difficult than I imagined, carrying my fins in one hand and alternately letting go and gripping each rung with the other. I misjudged the weight of the tank between these transitions, a stubborn fat child clinging to my back, threatening to pull me backwards with each release. So I was poised to convert any toppling bungle into an acrobatic entry. But we got down without a hitch and were soon gliding among the boats, diving flag in tow, on our way to the vessel in question.

It was a sunny, windless day, a "corker," according to the builder, the taskmaster who'd given us the day off. On top of that, the harbor was shielded by a solid arm of granite blocks, so the water was almost gin-clear save for that cold, clean tint of jade. Most of the boats were already out, at work, and everything beneath the surface was in focus, the depth of field through the forest of weed-bearded buoys and mooring lines unnervingly generous for New England. The floor of the harbor looked more like a movie set or an abandoned warehouse with its giant mushroom anchors and concrete blocks strewn about, rusted buckets, bait barrels, piles of old chain, a rubber boot, the litter of glowing fish skulls and spines, and a few corroded bicycles near the wharf, the chrome rims and handlebars of one recent casualty still gleaming defiantly.

There were derelict lobster traps, too, some containing a few forgotten prisoners, resigned and listless behind the barnacled slats. I wondered what they could possibly be eating to stay alive. My colleague busted the hatch off of one, extracted two healthy three to four pounders, and stuffed them into his bag, then he gave me the thumbs-up. Since the trap was untethered it was no better than trash, so removing its contents was legally permissible, if not an act of mercy. Otherwise, he would have risked being shot. Actually, there seemed to be a lot of lobsters cavorting, almost like the fairy-tale deer who slip into the hunters' cabin and play a hand of poker while their human pursuers are out in the forest. The builder's son grabbed several more sizeable bugs along the pier wall, and I wondered what we were supposed to be looking for. After poking around in the silt for a few minutes, he gestured that we were ready to wind up our swim and head back to the ladder. Most of the tourists had dispersed, and we loaded our gear back into the truck without the pressure of performance, a hefty bag of shellfish to boot. He never did tell me what we had been commissioned to salvage, though I remember him mumbling something about a drive shaft.

That same summer of 1981, my sister moved home after teaching on the Central Coast of California for five years, where she'd also learned to dive. So it made sense that we'd take a plunge off the backyard together. Truth be told, I had passed up the opportunity to dive the West Coast during a visit the month before because I'd been spooked. Eavesdropping at a barbeque, I'd caught fragments of anecdotes tossed around by her fishermen and surfer pals.

Once in a while, reading about another shark attack, whether in La Jolla, Montara, Aptos, Avila, or elsewhere, I'll be reminded that my paranoia was not unfounded. But my absolution was delivered pretty quickly that autumn after Evie came back East. She'd received a newspaper clipping from a friend, Cas, a lifeguard at the Cayucos Pier beach. It had a photograph of him holding up his rescue paddleboard, explaining to the reporter the enormous crescent of punctures near the board's nose A great white around fifteen feet long (estimate of marine biologists who'd studied the board) surfaced and chomped down while he and another of my sister's friends were singing Harry Belafonte songs as they paddled during a flat spell around the point at Montaña de Oro State Park. He gave the trophy board to the Cayucos Tavern where it hung for a few years until it was stolen.

The waters off of our backyard in Rockport definitely weren't as stimulating as the kelp beds she was used to, but as Evie was kicking along next to me one August day in her rental gear, she started waving frantically. Eyes wide inside her mask, she grabbed my arm and I followed the determined stabs of her pointing finger. Then I saw it, right below us, laboring like an animated scrap of medieval armature across a bright patch of sand, a behemoth of a lobster, weighing around twelve pounds. We hovered, watching it in awe, its steel cable antennae wagging. Affixed to my tank with a lanyard was a small brass gauge to measure carapaces when you suspected the animals below the legal size limit. This creature could have taken that tool, bent it double, and with its mandibles shoveled it into its maw like a trail snack.

Normally, the game of catching lobsters is a one-handed affair, your free hand only brought into action as a decoy to distract with fluttering fingers while the other reaches around from the back and grabs it by the "shoulders," the broad section of the thorax where the claw joints meet the body. You never want to lunge at a lobster head on, not only because of the claws but the threat of impaling your hand on the rostrum, a sharp spike protruding from between the eye-stalks. I kicked toward it and grabbed its back with both hands, as if I were trying to pick up a big fire extinguisher in the most physically inefficient manner possible. It flailed its claws drunkenly in excruciatingly slow motion. Compared to the artful, jerky one-to-three-pounders with whom I was used to negotiating, this was a layup. I swam slowly to the surface holding it out in front like a dowager aunt with whom I didn't want to dance. Evie surfaced next to me, howling in celebration as I tried to lift it out for a better view. It simply didn't look real underwater, five times bigger than any lobster I'd ever seen, in or out of its element. It was heavy enough that I decided the best course was to inflate my BC vest and kick to shore on my back with the thing lying across my chest. It was more like trying to swim with an idling lawn-mower. The big claws waved in my face, opened and closed looking for purchase in their sluggish desperation. Even its pereopods, the spidery and usually harmless walking legs, had pincers that seemed capable of ripping my cheek open.

According to the Lobster Conservancy web-site, adult lobsters carry fifty percent of their body weight in their two principal claws. This was the sunset of my bug-hunting career; I had learned pretty well over a few seasons what the job of each claw was, having in the base-ment a basket full of discarded odd, shredded, and punctured wetsuit mitts. But this animal, stretched from the tips of its claws to its tail was almost half my size, and though it did not have the Bruce Lee reflexes to rescue itself, it made me imagine what damage it might inflict if one of those steroidal vise grips got a hold of me. From the Lobster Conservancy again:

> The *crusher* claw has large, rounded, molar-like teeth on the outside. Inside, the closer muscle of the crusher is comprised of 100% slow-twitch muscle fiber. Slow-twitch muscles are noted for strength and endurance and are characterized by their ability to sustain long, strong contractions. The fast lobster claw has a variety of names, including *cutter, pincher,* and *seizer.* This claw has a serrated edge with great tufts of sensory hairs lining the sharp, pointed teeth. On the inside, the closer muscle of the seizer is made up of fast-twitch muscle fibers. Fast-twitch muscle is characterized by rapidity, but is less able to sustain contractions for long periods of time.

Low tide had delivered a zone of spongy rocks carpeted with seaweed, and across this littoral fringe I skated and tripped, hammering my elbows and knees in my trek to the dry ledge of the yard. The weight of the equipment out of the water and not being able to balance or break my fall with my occupied arms and hands tainted a triumphant return. Overheated, gasping for air, I flung myself onto the lawn, the lobster sitting in the grass next to me like a glistening, patient robot dog.

The only place that might have a pot big enough to boil it was the Peg Leg restaurant next door, owned by my parents' friends Lillian and Bob Welcome. The chef didn't seem surprised at all when, still in my suit, dripping from the dive, I opened the screen door with my foot and rotated through into his kitchen with the lobster. He looked up calmly from what he was stirring and said that he'd be needing all the pots to get ready for the dinner service, and that I should just "rip off the claws and boil them separately." Apparently, he had faced down animals this size all the time, and I hadn't been the first idiot with this request.

My sister and I retreated back to our parents' small kitchen and did what we were told. After a half hour of our two largest pots spewing lobster foam all over the range and floor, the deed was done. Breaking the claws off at the joints had not been too difficult, but it took the better part an hour to extract everything. Always the efficient engineer, my father couldn't resist advising in the dismemberment and hollowing; we must have employed half the tools on his bench, including a miniature sledgehammer and chisel to bust through the crusher claw, which reacted like granite. We gave up, and I decided to remove the smaller "thumb" of the claw and go in through the cave of the existing opening, where needle-nose pliers turned out to be the most effective device, delivering over two quarts of meat. We hadn't even started on the tail. Each claw was a clown car of protein, the endless stream of white fibers and chunks compressed, spring-loaded, almost self-generating as we kept pulling and drawing the stuff out. After we were finished, the kitchen counter looked and smelled like a grenade had been detonated in the carapace.

We are all familiar with the critics' narrative about what a waste it is to kill such relics, and that because of its age a lobster that size would be inedible. Everyone knows the too-tough myth, perpetuated by the assumption that age and experience have a direct physiological impact on texture. Veal versus geriatric gristle. But ultimately, no one knew the difference. By my guess, we froze hundreds of dollars' worth of meat that day, and when my sister was married that following October, we put out a salad for the reception that easily satisfied more than a hundred guests and probably would have received the same compliments if we had raided a lobster orphanage as our source.

I'm also glad I didn't destroy that crusher claw, because in our excitement we never took any pictures of its original brandisher. Other than a profoundly dwindled taste for lobster, it's all I have to remind myself of that afternoon and to keep myself honest, because the size of the crustacean fluctuates, grows and shrinks, and grows in my imagination as the decades pass. Until I glimpse on my dusty classroom bookshelf the girth and lethal potential of that faded tangerine-hued weapon, the two white chisel scars where it deflected my attempts to break it open, to release whatever secrets it might have been storing from its days of *scuttling across the floors of silent seas.*

Any residual guilt abiding that claw is diminished when I look at a photograph of William Beebe as a teenager at his home in East Orange, New Jersey (taken around 1895, the year my father's father was born). It seems to be straddling a life caught in action and curated portraiture. There's formality and posture in the knickers and patterned stockings, the dim cater-pillar of a youthful moustache, staged concen-tration on his face as he sits reading in a wicker chair. Once your eyes start wandering, however, you notice the density of the things arranged around him, all of which reveal who he was more than thirty years before the voyage of his bathysphere. A guitar is leaning against the wall within arm's reach. I hadn't known that the origins of this icon of rebellion and musical portability, this essential teenage bedroom accessory reached back into the nineteenth century. A collection of pistols is mounted verti-cally in a space between door frames.

His taxidermic menagerie are not props but supporting characters in the photograph's implicit narrative. Hung or positioned like an audience near Beebe's crossed legs or eaves-dropping at his shoulders, animals are the true celebrities of the photograph. A great blue heron seems as if it could be listening to his lecture or asking him, like a kindly butler, if he wants a cup of tea. A flock of songbirds and quail are marching across the bureau, while a squirrel prays atop a filling cabinet in front of mounted butterflies. The torso of a swan, wings stretched dramatically across a dark panel, looms where a crucifix might hang in a Catholic household. Some might interpret young Beebe's surrounding himself with the body parts and mummified carcasses of animals as morbidly macho, but to me it is the church of the classifier. Even at that age, Beebe was a collector bent not on the pursuit of trophies but on freezing the animated elusiveness of nature for public scrutiny and enjoyment, to preserve and display and share in three dimensions something they might never see. I also like to think that each relic kept a story within easy reach, like my lobster claw.

In Key Largo, my college friends and I pooled our money to charter a boat for a single day, hoping to do two dives: one in fifteen to thirty feet of water over a shallow reef, and the other in about one hundred-and-twenty-five feet over a lone dome of rock and coral that according to the outfitter was thriving with marine life. As in Bermuda, anxiety surged along with the invisible weight of irreversible commitment pressing in; diving was the reason I had come, so there was no way out.

When our hired boat circled a lonely and battered fluorescent orange buoy in the middle of nowhere, we knew we had arrived at the deep part of our excursion. The wind was stiff and hot, the surface confused, choppy. Sizeable swells had us lurching about, knocking into each other with our gear lashed to our backs, cinched to our waists, strapped to our faces. As I've said, there is nothing more clumsy than dealing with this predive physical awkwardness, which is almost a sort of test, an experience that I imagine must drive a lot of aspiring divers away from the sport before they even plunge, especially if they're sweating in tropical sun on a pitching deck.

It is not so different from the discouraging limbo through which neophyte surfers must pass when they attempt to paddle a board out through the inside break. When you're learning, standing on a beach looking out at the waves with a board tucked under an arm is cool for a few, brief seconds. In sizeable surf, preparation is often accompanied by frustration, however, a situation that seems to have no relation to the potential euphoria of wave riding. By the time you've punched through and ducked under all that disorienting mayhem bent on sweeping you right back to shore and two hundred yards down the beach, you've had enough. If you do make it "outside" after repeatedly being hammered by guillotining garage doors of water or being chewed by gaping maws of foam, you're too exhausted to even think about turning around and paddling into a wave, stroking that cumbersome plank lashed to your leg back toward the direction you've tried so hard to escape.

Soon we were off the boat, bobbing next to each other and trying to forget we were miles at sea. We gave the customary nod, somersaulted like ducks, and began kicking down and over toward the boat's anchor chain, the only vivid object in that space, reaching down mercifully toward us from the undulating light of the turbulent surface. It was not what I had imagined at all, my eyes tricked into believing that the depth of field had been compressed, as if the water were thick and turbid instead of nearly transparent. I might compare this, unfairly, to the state of being with which JFK Jr. probably grappled before he rammed his plane into the waters off Cape Cod, the vertiginous panic of trying to find a horizon while you're navigating a foggy vista with no up or down. I was a long way from the days of safety, from literally feeling my way along the bulkhead near the inlet of Wooley Pond at a depth of four feet, watching the menacing but reassuring mechanics of mating horseshoe crabs. The eyes of the blowfish were as distant as the feeling of the sun on my shoulder blades through a few inches of water.

Given my history, I should have been prepared and not worried about what might swoop, dart, or ooze granularly into my field of vision, should have invested some faith in the possibility of its being beautiful and transforming, instead of harrowing. The eagle ray of six years before had taught me that much. Off Key Largo, there was the return of sickening anxiety, that there might be nothing, that I'd just keep going, putting more and more empty distance between myself and the boat, tethered like a beaked zeppelin above.

Descending, you can't ignore the sound of your own breathing, studied and deliberate. Then a dark spot takes shape in your field of vision. It must be something on the bottom, and you have the comforting orientation of an object, some sense of scale, that this ocean is after all a liquid-filled pocket, a mere indentation on a rocky planet and not outer space. Your target is a lone pebble on the sandy floor, and seeing it has restored your rational, contextually dependent existence. For a moment, you feel that you have to slow your pace because you might drive your face into it if you keep kicking downward. So you reach out, guessing proximity, only to grab an empty fistful of the blue you have been chasing your whole life, understanding that those bacterial spirits zipping like gnats around the rocky protrusion are extremely large fish, almost your size. The reef itself is as big as a three-story house and is still another fifty feet away.

But before the landform came into view that day, some perverse optical illusion convinced my brain I was not liberated and drifting through liquid space but locked in a bluish cube; without being able to focus on anything but my pale hands clutching that interminable strand of anchor line, it seemed like I wasn't getting anywhere and that I was simply in a place I shouldn't have been. Hubris had deposited me, at last, where it had always intended. Some people say they've never felt more alive than when they dive, and I can see why. But being in that middle space was like what I imagine dying to be, a state where the surface begins to lose its definition. The bottom is not yet visible, the dropping temperature begins to leech into your bones, and any promise of connection with other warm forms of life is unlikely. Are you sinking or rising? Even though the scientific part of my brain, the sensible belief in the chemical composition of seawater, its percentage of dissolved salts and gasses, etc., had lit out for more comforting estates, I felt that I was being diffused as dumbly as the other previously reassuring earthly elements swirling invisibly around me.

That same year, I had taken an undergraduate music appreciation course and was drawn to the darker pieces like the opening of Bartok's *Concerto for Orchestra*, physically chilled by the least resolved and more ethereal compositions. But here in the water, there was no trace of the awed and uneasy laughter of my hopelessly stoned roommate when I had put the headphones over his ears and said, "Check this out." Now I was beginning to recognize the featureless cosmic landscape that Charles Ives evoked in *The Unanswered Question* because I was swimming through it.

I was certain that this was the day of reckoning, when something would rear up and visit swift revenge on the boy who had been desecrating and fouling the altar. But it didn't turn out to be a biological life form. It would have neither face nor shape. An eagle ray's presence would have seemed playfully terrestrial, almost goofy, but unquestionably, fluently alive. Now I yearned for fellow pilgrims like that, whose calm determination has a destination. But since I was the first in line to descend, without the reassuring flick of fellow divers' fins in front of me, it felt that each hand-over-hand increment was drawing me closer to something that paradoxically could never be reached, and that I was going there alone.

In his testimony to the U.S. House Committee on Science and Astronautics in January 1971, Cousteau had said, "The sea is the universal sewer." By which he meant it's the place where the population of the world dumps and pours what it doesn't want. And at that moment, the list seemed to include me, meandering like some lost nonnative microbe through a closing vise of color, the ocean, at our middle depth, deliberating in its ascetic trial of blue and green. I'd like to say that I changed the trajectory of my life in the days that followed, that the moment was transformative, victorious in wrenching me out of what was becoming a particularly entrenched, stubborn adolescence. Fear can do many things, but it probably won't make you grow up instantaneously. At that age, the dependable whipsaw action of self-loathing and euphoric indestructibility takes time to cut you free from childhood.

In Shakespeare's *Richard III*, the principal character, while still the Duke of Gloucester, says to his young nephew, the Prince of Wales, "the untainted virtue of your years / Hath not yet dived into the world's deceit" (III.i.8–9). Coming from Richard, it's a wickedly ironic and ominous insight: he will soon murder the boy in his quest for the throne. But what if you're descending into a world of beauty made safe by the conspiratorial scaffolding of pomposity and naïveté, a place *incapable* of premeditated harm to humans, whose sleight of hand and alleged deceit can be nothing but your own? The door opens, you swagger in, but as soon as it shuts, you suspect it might be a big mistake. Imagining at this moment my twenty-year-old self back down there is painful, an exercise that seems voyeuristically sadistic. But it's a card that a late-middle-aged man with a grown family and respectable career plays to shore up his faith in the imperceptible miracle of maturity.

We must have seen other remarkable creatures on the reef when we finally arrived that morning, but I don't remember. What erases their fused, overlapping images as I try to recall the dive is the acuity of my slow progress down the anchor line, neither the giant grouper nor even the lone reef shark we later swore had been orbiting the dark formation of coral, always slipping in and out of that optically confusing perimeter. How badly I wanted the surface to stay in sight as my hands, reluctantly obeying some ancient pact with posterity, ferried me downward. What do you call it, this looking up? Was it cowardice, my straining to follow the silhouettes of schooling juvenile barracuda as they arced through that silver gelatin sky? Now, I

can't be certain about whether I had been cring-
ing beneath those bursting formations of fish
or admiring them, silently praying they'd find
their target. Their waves seemed to me then like
yeomen's arrows on irreversible tracks to some
distant castle rampart.

DOWNSTREAM

Slumped in the raft's bow, my friend Ned was coming to terms with the situation. My dad had made him wear the overturned yellow bucket because he'd seen him shivering. "You lose seventy-five percent of your body heat through the top of your head," he instructed, sitting high on the transom. "Put it on." Paddle locked on his thigh like a tiller, he feathered us around another bend in the black water until we doubled back, watching the same recently navigated segment passing in the opposite direction on the other side of a wooded strip. The rain was steady, cold, and though my father wasn't saying it, we were lost.

I was eleven and admired Ned because he was a few years older, but I took perverse interest in my fastidious neighbor reduced to this state. The bucket was like a robot's helmet atop the saturated shoulders of his blue windbreaker, cocked back on his head so he could brood out from under it, metal handle like a chinstrap. This must have hurt, because I believed then that he took pride in his looks, most likely engineered by his mother, who outfitted him and his brothers from an exclusive men's shop in Beverly with corduroys, Shetland sweaters, Oxford shirts. This, in 1971, was a statement, since the world had embraced bell-bottoms and polyester in patterns and colors that seemed designed to offend, to incite outrage. And in some ways to obliterate class. My own wardrobe turned me into a centaur whose torso on one day might sport a navy Lacoste polo shirt, but whose legs would be sheathed in fire-engine-red flairs or another textile disaster, some nontraditional tartan concocted by the MacAcid clan.

My mother was sensitive to my self-esteem, but her tastes were buffeted by the complicated fads wafting through the split-level ranches and Capes in our middle-class Massachusetts town. She'd recently resisted my whining but finally buckled to paying more than twenty dollars for a pair of suede Adidas, now sodden, ankle-deep because our bailer had been repurposed to regulate Ned's temperature. During my senior year in high school, she returned from vacation in Bermuda with a madras jacket from the English Sports Shop that still hangs in my closet, and that I have worn only twice, once as part of a costume. She wanted me to be current but cultivated, to belong to the myth *and* the rebellion. Even Nixon's sideburns were getting longer at the time, inching down his jaw.

My father had borrowed the massive rubber boat from Don, a friend who owned a local landscaping company (and for whom I would work a few years later). He had met us at the riverbank that morning with the thing, army surplus from the Korean War, bulging over the tail of his forest green flatbed like a black tumor. Built for ten heavily armed men, it afforded us the space to whip our spinning rods, sniping Daredevils and Rooster Tails in all directions without snagging each other's scalp or face. The proximity of air-filled gunwales, I sensed, put my father — who had zero interest in fishing — on edge. ← Out of place

An aeronautical engineer, he often worked a half-day on Saturdays, supervising the test of some engine part or squaring away the week's unfinished business. And this excursion was also a rare respite from the usual spring tasks: raking leaves out of gardens, mowing, spreading wood-chips, transplanting shrubs. If he hadn't been at the plant or hadn't gambled with the weather for the sake of this adventure, he would have been building a bookshelf, wiring his workroom with new outlets, or changing our car's oil. But it was early May in New England, and the green fuzz of new leaves and rusty maple buds that had held so much promise in the morning's warmth and cardinal song now seemed to recede, to con-tract as the temperature dropped. We were on our sixth hour of drifting the Ipswich River's looping switchbacks, oxbows, and swamps. The water was high, its explicit course compro-mised, confused, the woods now part of it all. Submerged trunks had swirling wakes. Open stretches like lakes resolved into five possible exit creeks. But I trusted him and knew we'd get somewhere eventually. We had nothing to follow but the current.

Ned and his siblings talked a lot about their father's plans to buy a CAL 25—a slick fiberglass sailboat with a cabin. Because we'd heard about it incessantly at the bus stop, on the kickball field, or waiting beneath the counter of the ice-cream truck, the phrase had become a joke in our household. Leveled at the absurdity of our cravings or inserted into a grocery list, it became code for something that would never come to pass: "Yeah, right. *After* you get that CAL 25." Or "Could you pick up a CAL 25 on your way home from work?" Or "Do you want those colored pencils or a CAL 25?" I'm still stymied by those distant impulses of mine, to impress a peer whose family seemed to expend so much concerted energy pretending to have more money than we did, though our houses pretty much looked the same.

teased
luvs
family

took
richer

At the time I wasn't aware that Ned's parents had any remote interest in boats or the water until my parents took a Power Squadron course and a few sailing lessons in Marblehead, then bought a used Day Sailer from a guy my father worked with. Once this small boat was flipped like a white turtle in our yard with my dad out there stroking copper antifouling paint across its hull, the theoretical CAL 25 and its accompanying narrative shifted into overdrive. Three

only after they
got a boat first

years earlier, we had arrived in our new town from New Jersey in a '66 Volkswagen Beetle, royal blue with a white convertible top. Which was promptly dismissed as a "toy" and derided by the prevailing tribe of big American-made station wagon owners. They'd also mocked as ugly the midsixties Saab one of my father's co-workers (who was from England) had parked in our driveway. When our paths crossed decades later, after most of the families had left the neighborhood, and "foreign" cars had found their slots in the automotive hierarchy—either as badges of means or emblems of a certain lifestyle—my former neighbors of course were driving them. Though the acceptance of the new, the strange, or "funky" was in the DNA of the '70s, it stuttered and tripped when it entered our street. But before that year was up, a red Bug with a black top was glowing behind the lilacs next to Ned's garage. I was not a doubter; I held out for the possibility that one day I would see a yacht being towed majestically up their driveway lashed down like Gulliver, blue keel cradled by the struts of an elegant trailer.

I'd like to think that all of this was less predictable than the passive-aggressive suburban theater of keeping up with the Joneses, that the people around us for some reason had no imagination or were just afraid to take a chance, to go their own way. Status was not in my father's hardwiring; the man had lived through combat and imprisonment. Often, I find myself trying to empathize with what his perspective must have been at the time, how the intensity and breadth of experience set him apart, but without his caring about it. These days, when I run across the formal vocational concept of social media "influencers," I can't help suspecting a certain contrivance of talent, something ironically artificial: if you have to tell people explicitly that this is your title, if you are aware of aspiring to intentionally steer their tastes because you recognize your own gift for identifying what's cool before the herd does, then you've missed the point. There's a fraudulent arrogance behind it, a tragically shallow self-importance. Logically, authentic influencers shouldn't be aware of the social ramifications of what they're doing or wearing, because they've already moved on. Also, my father's profession by its nature demanded an openness to innovation, gadgets, the promise of the future. And this account isn't about socioeconomic revenge, either; comprehension of airs or privilege or snobbery was not quite on my radar yet. I just wanted to be outside, playing, fishing, and *not* to be different or to stand out. And certainly *not* to compete. Though it was not his intention, everything my father initiated seemed to hold us in a different orbit. Which, for a middle schooler, was sometimes humiliating.

It wasn't necessarily his ordeal as a pilot and POW in World War II that dazzled and confounded my friends or their parents; rather, it was the public spectacle of his Eagle Scout self-sufficiency playing out in the reclaimed pockets of our property or atop the ladders and paint pails laying siege to our clap-boards. Rock walls, terraces, split-rail fences, an ornate mailbox post, a dog pen sturdy enough to contain a herd of Appaloosas, a cedar dragged from the woods, honed and sunk in a pool of concrete to hold a backboard. There was also the hockey rink Don's bulldozer scraped into the yard behind our Dwarf Macintosh apple trees, my sisters and I out there on our hands and knees collecting sharp rocks that might puncture the thick plastic my dad was rolling out, after which we uncoiled hundreds of yards of garden hose from every spigot on our house. Were these extravagances? Maybe. We weren't rich, but to some perhaps it might have seemed like we had more, or just did more. There were rarely any tradespeople at our place, because my dad did almost everything himself. — *self sufficient*

But why was my father, the most self-possessed, independent — and perhaps most disconnected — member of the community always the one who ended up mediating and managing the fallout of neighborhood foibles? Our Lab had been shot with a BB gun. I was with him levering fieldstones into place when we heard the dog yelp up in our neighbor's leaching field where she liked to wallow. Two older boys from an adjacent street were laughing at the base of the hill, one pumping the barrel for another go, but she was already tearing down toward home. My father dropped the steel bar, marched across the road, calmly tugged his work gloves off, stuffed them into his back pocket, and grabbed the

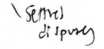

\ *Semi)*
di spray

rifle out of the stunned teenager's hands. Once we were back at the house and he'd thrown it into our kitchen broom closet, he mumbled, "If he wants it, he'll have to come back and ask for it with his parents." About a week later, sure enough, there was the kid apologizing at our door with his squat, muscular, mortified Armenian father behind him, hands folded like a lawyer's or priest's.

In high school a few years later, I was in a car with some older friends, bored, bombing around the dark, deserted streets, chucking our empty beer bottles out the windows. Someone got the idea to grab a tire iron out of the trunk and stave in a few mailboxes. For some reason, it was my dad who had to come and pick us up at the police station, and who sat nodding at the conference table, listening politely to the two officers who'd caught us. It wasn't long before the buddy who owned that car would enlist and after basic training go through Fort Benning's jump school with Army Airborne. It is his reaction that I still recall viscerally, how he spoke to my father the next day in our kitchen after driving over unannounced. To apologize. He told me later in the driveway as we sat on the front bumper of his pickup how much he admired my father, and that the worst part of the ordeal was how angry he was at himself for letting the man down, not his own parents, or himself.

Along with the trickling raindrops, a wet

tag of Ned's dirty blond hair snaked out from under the rim of the yellow bucket. He seemed to be adapting to my father's practical genius, and I was beginning to consider this resourceful triage another seemingly absurd project that would eventually prove visionary. My father was neither being mean nor making an example of the kid; he just wanted to keep someone for whom he was responsible from getting sick. Of course, he hadn't known that Ned was the one who taught me what the word *fuck* really meant one day when we were exploring the frame of a new house rising from its foundation on our street. How I bellowed it operatically among the kegs of nails, mounds of sawdust, and sawed-off ends of two-by-fours while Ned stood back in wonder at the creature he'd unleashed. *humor*

In the afternoon, miles downstream, the skies finally cleared, and the raft's blunt nose butted a steep landing's pine needles beneath Don's waiting truck. We hauled our numbed bodies over the side and, up to our knees in the sepia-tinged water, held the boat while my dad scrambled up the bank to explain why we were so off-schedule. Ned didn't say anything, and by the time his worried parents rolled up, he'd taken the bucket off. We hadn't said much since losing interest in hooking one of the river's stocked trout, surrendering to silence instead for the rest of the bleak, spiraling voyage. I felt responsible for the whole disaster. Perhaps Ned *why?* was disappointed by that long, boring, cold day, or just embarrassed by his chattering teeth. Or maybe he was wondering why he'd been invited on this expedition in the first place after being caught shoplifting lures that same week when he had come along with us to Sears.

My dad had been browsing chisels and block planes while we peeled off to sporting goods and the fishing aisle, then separated for a few minutes. But Ned was crying by the cash register when I found him, his face and ears red, elbow clamped firmly in some strange woman's claw, my dad standing next to them, hand on his shoulder. My heart contracted its hot fist, then nearly rocketed out from between the bars of its cramped cell with embarrassment, fear. It had all happened so fast, I'd barely had time to feel sorry, though I knew my father would reassure him, find a way through that awkward car ride home without humiliation or rage. We talked about the Bruins and Rangers rivalry, then dropped Ned off at the bottom of his driveway, my dad reminding him to tell his parents about it.

At seventeen, I canoed and camped that same region of the river in late March with a bunch of friends. It was still winter really, but my parents for some reason thought it was OK. My father would have blown a gasket if I'd told him that we'd flipped one of the canoes, and two of us—drunk, stoned—had been thrashing, doggie-paddling fully clothed among the sheets and chunks of ice while the rest laughed, gathered their floating gear, and cheered them to the leaf mulch and roots of some miserable island.

When I was in my late thirties and he was at home dying of emphysema and cardiopulmonary disease, I never had that storybook cathartic moment, the tender apology for any of the cruel and stupid shit I'd pulled as a kid, nor did I disown the desire for any of the superfluous crap I'd begged him or my mother to buy for me so I wouldn't feel left out. Always, I'd imagined that my friends' recklessness and shallowness were always more reprehensible than my own. And also that somehow my parents considered my behavior and vanity neither criminal nor narcissistic. Cumulatively, my antics must have seemed volitional and calculated, though I was convinced I could have it both ways, without disappointing my father.

Still, at Sears I had flirted with Ned's same impulse but just didn't have the balls as my fingertips brushed the quivering wall of little packages. Studying those treble hooks, fringed and collared in bright fur and feathers behind their slick plastic capsules, I must have sensed the compromised moral threshold on which I was teetering. In a few moments I would be awash in the warring eddies of Schadenfreude, relief, terror, and camouflaged smugness. Some of the lures were seductive, muted, painstakingly realistic facsimiles of the sleek minnows or hapless frogs they were modeled after, others so fluorescent, so gaudy, I doubted they could fool anyone.

POSSESSION

We were around fourteen or fifteen when we went to see *The Exorcist* by boat, about seven miles away. One of us had convinced his parents that we were responsible enough to take their fifteen-foot outboard such a distance, across a stretch of water as temperamental as Long Island's Great Peconic Bay. We had never been to the North Fork, let alone past Robins Island, on our own. The tidal currents or "races" at both the island's south and north extremities are infamous — the narrow passages between the tines, where the volume of all the adjoined bays flushes in and out.

Deploying a boat for such a transactional, practical vehicular endeavor was also a novelty for us. Until then, boats were rarely about transportation exclusively; rather, they were *for fun* integrated with bay-specific goals, like water-skiing or messing around on another beach for its own sake. The two-mile radius of our Little Peconic neighborhood on the South Fork kept us busy, waterborne, tearing back and forth along its margin of tame pebbled shores, fishing for blues and weakfish at the inlets of coves, digging clams or netting crabs in one of the neighboring lagoons. If we wanted to body-surf on the southern, ocean side of the Fork, we rode our bikes.

Because we hadn't told our parents which movie we were going to see, this amphibious mission felt more like a bank heist or secret incursion across an adjacent country's border. The trip, let alone the movie's content, was a big leap from being installed at the Flanders Drive-In with our families for *The Russians Are Coming, the Russians Are Coming* or the sta-tion/paddy wagon circus of someone's mother carting eight of us to *101 Dalmatians* for a birth-day party. Some of us would have licenses the following summer, when the movie *Jaws* was released, and we'd be driving ourselves to join the interminable line in Sag Harbor. But our parents seemed less tentative about a trans-bay expedition; the water was our native element, after all. The roads were not; they had their own ledger of accompanying dangers, like negotiating at night the gothic Dead Man's Curve on Noyack Road, which we'd heard invoked perennially in hushed tones. Capsizing, drowning, or drifting aimlessly at twilight with a stalled engine didn't seem to be a cause for parental concern.

We pooled our babysitting, car-washing, weed-pulling, and mowing allowances for gas at the Marina in our cove and headed for the matinee in Mattituck without any idea of where we'd anchor once we got there, or if we'd end up having to swim to shore then sit in a cold theater in wet shorts. What made some of us most anxious, however, was whether we would even be allowed entrance, given the movie's R rating. Apparently, being older than sixteen or having a guardian along would have sanded the edges off the concept of demonic possession.

In July, the prevailing afternoon winds out of the southwest can churn three-foot waves on the Peconic in a matter of minutes, but our cruise across the bay was uneventful. A blistering day, the water almost flat, silky. We flew. Our friend was able to open up the throttle; the Glastron, a low, racy thing with an 85-horsepower engine, was a lot of muscle in those days. While he piloted and the boat slapped along to the northwest, the three of us stood around him, steadying ourselves, leaning on the windshield or each other's shoulders, shouting small talk about girls in our neighborhood, one whose brother had come back from Viet Nam nearly blind. Over the engine's steady drone we dissected the rumor concerning the exact coordinates of where an older kid had stashed a six-pack of Michelob, which circuitously delivered us to how extravagantly a certain neighbor, who was a drunk, had paid one of us for the favor of cutting her tiny lawn. We also argued about the lyrics of "Oh Darling," half of us convinced that Paul McCartney's throaty moan was, "Well you know I need a blow job" instead of "Well you know I nearly broke down." In the snarl of these competing conversations, we found Mattituck (with eyes and a road atlas), then the channel markers for James Creek, and we slipped into the marsh. Since the tide was incoming, we snugged the hull up onto the grass as far as we could, threw anchors out the stern and bow, waded in, then scrambled onto the spongy turf, relieved that there would be no one-armed swimming, flailing to keep our balled-up T-shirts and sneakers above the surface.

no
(upsiz)

Despite our ages, we were admitted to the cinema without interrogation by a ghostly, dismal boy with shoulder-length red hair, not much older than ourselves. In the air-conditioned darkness, after the salt water had stopped trickling down our legs, we squirmed and twitched through our shared observations of priests as we'd never seen them before, through the persuasive bucking of Linda Blair's bed, her pea-soup hydrant and antics with the crucifix dildo. We were especially perplexed, reluctantly moved perhaps, by the main charac-ter's guilt of abandoning his elderly mother to a nursing home, who implores with her heavy Greek accent, "Dimi, *why* you do this to me?" There was also his recurring nightmare of her slow descent into a subway stairwell. These were scenes that seemed to have little to do with how the villain, an Assyrian spirit named Pazuzu, would be evicted from Regan's (Blair's) body. One of us had actually read the book, a disintegrating paperback stolen from an older sibling, but he still had no convincing answers.

Then we were released back into the day. The sun bursting from between thunderheads found and seared us as we stood on the theater's curb shading our eyes. That summer we'd already had the theme melody of Mike Oldfield's "Tubular Bells" pounded into our heads by AM radio, but now we hummed and whistled it with confidence in our disparate keys, walking back to our waiting boat, which was lifted high by this time, the marsh having retreated to a submerged skirty impression of its former self, the tidal creek widened, nearly indistinguishable from the bay. If any of us had been scared or traumatized by the movie, he didn't let on, the light and surroundings rallying against any intrusion of occult darkness.

Our friend whose boat it was volunteered to swim out and retrieve it, though we all secretly wanted to jump in, to resume the life that we'd consciously disrupted, the sons of a mechanical engineer, a pilot, a car dealership owner, and a urologist, whose summers were poised to be taken over by jobs—washing dishes, painting houses, volunteering at the hospital, digging and lining swimming pools—while grandparents vanished left and right, some even before we headed back to school, others before the year was over.

From our shelf of marsh grass, we watched his shining body wriggle over the transom like a pirate assassin, followed by his patient coiling of the anchor lines, his lowering and casual ignition of the engine. At first we were silent, but then as the boat glided wakeless toward us, started laughing, howling, our hair smeared back by the hot afternoon breeze, up to our crotches in the tepid water, swiveling suddenly toward each other to demand melo-dramatically, "Why you do this to me?" while our ferryman, yanking the shifter back to neutral, croaked in response, "Your mother sucks cocks in hell!" *teomc boys*

Why this story?
  nothing happens?

Django:
Elegies and Improvisations
with Small Boats

When a boat dies, you usually have two choices: pay hundreds of dollars to have it hauled away, or let it molder and sink into some secluded corner of the yard. A quick tour of my wife's parents' town on the South Shore of Massachusetts, where I moored my boat, would suggest that the latter is the norm: those husks and dark prows entombed in plain sight beside rotting cordwood, abandoned swing sets. Last year, when I discovered that a section of my sailboat's oaken keel had decomposed irreparably, I embarked on my first experiment with time-lapse photography. I rented for twenty dollars a "reciprocating saw" — the contractor's principal instrument of demolition — known as a Sawzall. After positioning my iPad on a kitchen chair in the driveway of my in-laws' home, then unraveling forty yards of extension cord from the garage, I plugged in the nasty tool — part torpedo, part robotic swordfish—and grimly laid into the carapace of the little boat over which I had worried and fussed for almost ten years.

When we first considered buying the wide, or beamy, 12′ x 6′ Beetlecat—a marriage of whaling dory and gaff-rigged sailboat—the owner, George Blanchard, rowed us out to it in his dinghy. The first thing we noticed was that his Beetle sat lower in the water than the surrounding cousins because the hull had been encased in a heavy shell of fiberglass, a last-resort modification by the boat owner who has no interest in maintaining the original wooden hull but still wants it to float. For the time being. The day you wrap a wooden boat in glass, however, the clock begins to tick. An evening thunderstorm had loaded George's boat, so rotten splinters, liberated shims, and the staves of ribs floated troublingly around our ankles. As July sun and humidity amped up, we helped George with pump and sponge until a less sluggish, naturally tippy action returned to the boat. "Bailing every day is my exercise," he said, crossing his legs, khakis rolled, canvas sneakers soaked. "Never invested in a cover. Might be a good idea."

George was a small man, but in his blue windbreaker and baseball hat, a fringe of thin, cropped gray hair visible just beneath the band, he reminded me of my father, who had died a couple of years before. They would have been around the same age, both World War II vets: George a chief petty officer in the Navy and my father a lieutenant and copilot in the Army Air Corps. Each man had gravitated toward planes after his stint in the service: George founding Blanchard Aviation at Hyannis Airport in 1950 and my father becoming an aeronautic engineer, first on Long Island and eventually lighting out for the aerospace revolution erupting in Southern California, where I was born. But with the end of the war my father's interest in aviation was confined to the drawings of jet turbines and combustors on his drafting table, to tests in wind tunnels and pitches in boardrooms. As the years went by, he was content to relinquish control of a plane's flaps and instead translate flight into the elegant curve of a ballooning sail.

We went over the rest of the rigging with George, including his homemade boom-crutch and a complicated chain of hardware store gadgets he'd mickey-moused to extend one of the shrouds. The deteriorating state of the brightwork, bump rail, mast, and gaff fork was muted under heavy coats of varnish, especially the oak mast hoops, stacked and glistening like dark, weathered vertebrae above the boom. In spots, the sail was thinned to translucence, crumbling and powdery like a moth's wing at the grommets and fasteners because of "sun rot" from almost forty summers of exposure.

George explained that he'd secured the Beetle three years earlier from the family of the author Sebastian Junger, who had left Provincetown after his popular book *The Perfect Storm* (about the 1991 wreck of a Gloucester swordfishing boat) had been translated to film, computer graphics, and George Clooney's unconvincing, Hollywood-inflected Boston accent. He divulged this as quirky celebrity novelty, but I detected a mischievously ominous smirk when he finished with, "But that's neither here nor there," as if perceiving my tentativeness at acquiring a boat owned by a writer who had immortalized a doomed expedition. We bought it anyway.

Every summer in the 1960s and early '70s, my father, having since moved our family back East, would take his two-week vacation in Southampton, New York. This is where my grandparents owned a small cottage on a salt-water cove developed in the 1930s. Being on the inside of Long Island's South Fork, Wooley Pond is as protected a body of water as you'll find on the Atlantic seaboard, the final spartina-fringed increment in the Russian nesting doll structure of the open Atlantic, Block Island Sound, Gardiners Bay, and Little Peconic Bay.

The Belarusian painter Nicolai Cikovsky seems to have composed *The Inlet at Wooley Pond* from the kitchen window of that bungalow on Southampton Shores. Part of a loosely affiliated group of influential artists on the South Fork of Long Island in the middle of the twentieth century, Cikovsky translates through rough-hewn, frantic strokes, noncommittal perspective, and brash color the bulrushes swaying on the left, peaty marsh bank on the right, a single dark cottage set on pebbled dunes.

Because the windows of my grand-parents' bungalow faced the cove and the house was next to the community dock, I woke up every summer morning in the loft to the sound of boat engines. If it was the gulls on the chimney that roused me first, the boats would follow soon enough, the whining, blue-smoked complaint of outboards being revved too high after ignition, or the mesmerizing, syncopated guttural knocking of the big inboards as they chugged to or from the bay. I knew almost every boat in that little kingdom, but especially the sportfishing boats and big cabin cruisers wedged tightly in the sheaths of their slips at the marina on the far end of the pond. An apostle of gods with names like *Maru, Wahoo,* and the *Black Fin,* I was the first to the binoculars when their rumbling filled the air. Even now, their images are immediate and acute, but back then their regal appearance rounding the bend of the inlet was as punctual a reminder of planetary rhythm as the arrival of the bluefish and blue-claw crabs in August.

My grandfather, a retired New York City fire chief, owned a larger motorboat for his fishing and clamming ventures, but the primary function of his rowboat was for training my sisters and me. I was forced to watch that wooden skiff from the safety of the porch as my sisters were put through their paces: starting the ancient, temperamental maroon-and-white John- son engine, casting off, weaving in and out of the channel markers (in forward and reverse), dropping and securing an anchor, and finally pulling alongside the dock and tying up. My grandfather had left the job of their induction to my father, who like some nautical DMV officer sat in the bow with his arms crossed, uncharacteristically silent, as one of my sisters sweated it out. Watching all of this from the house, I pined and worried, kneeling at the redwood picnic table trying to focus through the porch screens to follow her yellow windbreaker and tangled wake.

Not long after my initiation, my grandfather bought an eleven-and-a-half-foot square-nosed Sears Gamefisher, which was made of aluminum. Because owning a wooden boat is like caring for a sentient, perishable being, the explosion of low-maintenance materials (like fiberglass and aluminum) in the late 1960s and early '70s was probably what kept boats from disappearing altogether from our family. During those next few summers of elementary school and junior high, I lived—and sometimes slept—inside the olive-drab, machine-bent contours of that Sears rowboat, making contact with terra firma only in the direst circumstances (illness, dinner, or bedtime). Back then, when such real estate as my grandparents' was poised or just beginning to drift irrevocably beyond the reach of the middle class, most of my friends still lived near or on the water, in bungalows strung along the warrens of sandy two-tracks, cedar, and beach plum. The labyrinth of connected lagoons and ponds ramifying from the Little

Peconic guaranteed that, in some circumstances, I could be at their houses by boat almost as quickly as I could on my bicycle.

My grandfather had bought an outboard that was oversized for the skiff, a six-horsepower Evinrude that, clamped to the stern, was certainly in violation of marine safety limits. I could easily lift and drag the boat like a sled into the marsh grass, up past the tide line. The engine itself was another matter. My grandfather decreed that it had to be disconnected from the transom and stored in the garage at night, which entailed a grunting struggle up the gangplank to the bulkhead and then a thirty-yard trek across the lacerating spikes of the dried-out backyard lawn, through the cedars, and around to the garage. There's no easy way to carry an outboard. Adults simply grab it by the mounting bracket and heft it with one arm like a stubborn child by the waistband of his jeans, but when the machine is as big as you are, it's like dancing with a drunk, as you hold it out in front trying not to ram your shins into the propeller or paint your chest with grease.

With the engine mounted, the boat was stern heavy, especially since I had to sit back there to steer without a throttle extension. It was difficult enough to see where I was going but also took a thick skin to deflect the descriptive eloquence of my friends, who'd dubbed it "The Flying Boner." I tried positioning a few cinder blocks in the bow, but the only way to make it drop was to open up the engine, and to do that you had to be out in the bay and the bay had to be calm. On those still July or August mornings, before the hot southwest wind would crank up and whip the bay into a white-capped nightmare, my world expanded. With the boat's snout aloft, I would creep around the dredged elbow of the Wooley Pond inlet, poised for the moment when I could round the last red nun buoy to open water, wrist that throttle, and wait for the deck to plane like a battle lance leveling in its downward arc to the target. And when it did, my view of the boat cushions, buckets, gas tank, fishing rods, tackle box, crab net, oars, and everything else I'd packed along sank, replaced by the panorama of the Peconic's oily sparkle. The reassuring features of Robins Island, Jessup's Neck, the inlet at North Sea, and the Saharan oak-dotted bluff of Cow's Neck all seemed projected onto the hazy boundaries. Then the wind became charged with the exhilarating stench of hot salt, the beaches' freshly drying seaweed interlaced with the faintest perfume of other boats' exhaust. Global warming, carbon footprints, and their essential contrition were decades away. Even the memories of the fuel embargo of the '70s and any crisis that it might have visited upon my two-cycle-engine-dependent lifestyle have dispersed and evaporated almost as thoroughly as the rainbows of gasoline trailing the stern whenever I'd flooded the engine.

The development of my marine aesthetic and

experience, spanning the mid-1960s through the '80s, was not only a confusing geographical tug of war between Long Island and New England, but a fundamentally vehicular one of motor and sail. Right up through my late twenties, before my conversion (and the purchase of the Beetle-cat following his death), my father and I sustained a perennial argument about the benefits and drawbacks of sailing. The meditative hush of wind, water, the mewing gulls—the sonic purity of it all; this was his locus. Soon followed by a polemic defending his reverence for the more organic behavior of a boat that is not fighting or trying to master the elements. I just thought it was boring, a waste of time, and asked him if he'd ever tried to cast a fishing rod from beneath a boom, or between stays, spreaders, and sails. He would continue to wax lyrical about the way a sailboat's hull would roll or track with the swells instead of percussively whacking against them.

My very earliest boat-related memory with him was not so Zen-like. Before those years with the aluminum rowboat, I had been a hopeless coward at sea, a condition for which I blame my father partially. It was on Long Island, and I was probably not much older than three when we were on one of his famous drift-wood-gathering missions to Cow's Neck, a headland that separates the Little and Great Peconic Bays. In 1963, my grandfather still had a stubby wooden cruiser with a roof and a white, black, and silver Mercury engine whose shape reminded me of an electric razor.

The water off Cow's Neck was shallow, so my father had to anchor the boat a mile out. At least it seemed that way to me. What I remember best from that hot, windy day, other than contemplating the distance between myself and the deserted beach, was being handed over the gunwale then placed in a small inner tube, told to hold tight, to keep my arms outstretched. When you're that small, choppy water seems Odyssean. My mother and aunt floated me toward land and my father waded behind us with a coil of rope around his shoulder, the red bucksaw lifted over his head. Because of the size of the waves, I was inevitably torn from the group, lost my grip on the tube, and slipped through its center as if flushed down a toilet. This happened a few times, someone's quick hands always yanking me out of the green mayhem back to the surface just before I took a lungful and sputtered my last. When my feet gripped the sand and rounded pebbles of Cow's Neck, I was cried out, exhausted, and already dreading the return expedition. But when the time came, my father skipped the tube, put me on his shoulders, and took me out there himself, breasting the waves like a giant, an oceanic demigod, while I locked my arms around his chin, gazing down at the ineffectual wavelets, wondering how I could have been such a baby.

What my sisters, mother, and I knew but never discussed was how persuasive my father was in getting us to trust him while he himself was still learning to understand the sea and boats. His earliest trials with boats — with the family as his guinea pigs — contradicted his reputation as a famously cautious man. He was good with a canoe, a skill he'd honed as a Boy Scout on Long Island in the 1930s and early '40s. He had flown a B-17 during WWII. (True, he had been shot down, but not until he'd flown a number of missions from North Africa to Italy, then eventually into Eastern Europe.) He had never been in an auto accident (that was my mother's job). He was Mr. Safety First — the gate-keeper to lighting fires, handling power tools, opening jackknives — except in his station at our passage to handling boats. On the water, our family tacked erratically from idyllic leisure to frantic situations that went against every-thing he preached in his pounding, impromptu lectures. The perfectionist tendencies of the aeronautic engineer and preparedness of the Eagle Scout seemed to fly out the window or, more accurately, gush out over the transom.

The stakes were raised when my father decided to import his nascent hobby from Long Island back to our home in Massachusetts. In 1968, he bought a seventeen-foot O'Day *Day Sailer* from a coworker and took the whole family out by himself after *one* lesson with the owner. It was a new game when it came to salt water. A dense and awesome vista of swaying masts, bucking hulls, and cross-hatched wakes, Marblehead's granite-ringed harbor seems to defy the possibility of being navigated by any boat whose captain might actually choose to sail in or out of it. You wonder how all those boats can swing with the tide and wind and not demolish each other. This is where our father chose to moor his Day Sailer, which he had decided to call *Widget* — my mother's nickname at the adult camp where they'd met after the war.

Once aboard, I gazed out through the jungle of spruce and aluminum, confident that we'd deploy the outboard and wouldn't dare any sort of passage under sail among the pitching outboards, the daggers of their exposed skegs. Then the sails were hoisted and flapping, thrumming like a motorcade of choppers. One of my sisters, ape-like, was on all fours up on the bow releasing the mooring line. The world suddenly lurched and went diagonal. The nightmare of this first jolt of movement was not assuaged by the sight of my father's white knuckles on the tiller, the main sheet gathered to his chest in the other hand like the reins of a possessed horse. The soundtrack was more operatic, if not apocalyptic. He screamed his panicked orders in what seemed a foreign tongue, each time more impatient, more desperate. The lexicon of our introductory session on the drive over (rearview mirror to back seat) had evaporated, and for the first fifteen minutes he was definitely on his own as the rest of the family tumbled as if trapped in a funhouse barrel. In perverse call-and-response, he barked at us to do something. We shrieked back in terror that we couldn't.

Because I was small, I crawled beneath the

cutty and wedged myself between the boat cushions, army blanket, and anchor line like a trembling rodent. We hadn't capsized. There would be no tragedy, but I stayed there, bitter and fetal, for the rest of the day, vowing never to sail again.

Improving yet discouraged by the intensity and congestion of Marblehead, my father joined the Ipswich Bay Yacht Club the following year—a rustic, understated gem perched on a mowed headland over Plum Island Sound. The annual pulse of dread would surge when I'd see my father wander out to our apple orchard in late spring to peel back the heavy canvas from his boat, but I was encouraged by the paradise its new anchorage offered, the prospect of exploring the maze of Essex marshes or up the Parker River, fishing for flounder off of Grape Island, snorkeling around the jetty at the mouth of the Ipswich River estuary. The relative ease of negotiating the more manageable population of boats in the harbor initiated a slow healing of the anxiety triggered by Marblehead.

The tidal current in Plum Island Sound and Ipswich Bay, however, was fierce, providing the mooring buoys their own audibly riffling wakes at certain times of the day. The volume of water squeezing through that passage made it seem as if all those Styrofoam and plastic floats were engaged in their own crazed regatta, some of them submerged and even oscillating underwater, pulled down by the speed of the current and their short tethers. This rendered my father's obsession with returning to the mooring under sail almost impossible, but it didn't stop him from trying. Either the wind was no match for the current and we were pushed back out to sea regardless of how full our sails were, or the two forces were locked in a stalemate and the boat sat stubborn and motionless on its flowing treadmill. Or we simply careened and spun out of control while one of us, sprawled on *Widget's* bow, flailed with both arms or a boat hook to snag the pickup buoy as the wind and water, working in unison, hurled us past the mooring.

My father was strangely content to let sailing remain in New England for the time being, so it was the glistening, open-bowed Fabuglass tri-hull with its forty-horsepower Evinrude that transformed our family's vacations on Long Island. Our custom after the seven-hour drive from Massachusetts was to head immediately for the backyard, climbing over each other to bypass our smiling and forgiving grandparents for a glimpse of the pond, as if we had to reassure ourselves it had remained intact over the long winter. If we arrived in the middle of the night and the tide was high, my father would take us to the bulkhead and gangplank with my grandfather's big, sealed-beam flashlight to coax the small fish to the surface. But after one particular disembarkation of the littered and stuffy Impala, we arrived at the edge of the bulkhead to see a modern green motorboat bobbing at the end of the pulley system my grandfather had rigged:

a clothesline suspended between a post on the beach and a mooring buoy about fifty feet from shore. There was something indestructible in the blunt shape out there in darkness, its sleek engine scoffing at any reliance on wind. The exhilaration of seeing that boat for the first time; my heart leapt at its chrome railings apprehended in the darkness by the flashlight's shaft. The era of motorboats and dependability was set to elbow the mayhem and folly of sailing from our family once and for all.

We fell into a pattern of beach trips that would endure for the following decade and eventually (nearly) erase from memory my free-form waterboarding at Cow's Neck, not to mention the psychic trauma of Marblehead Harbor. First there was the early-morning grocery run to buy the makings of lunch, then the efficient factory of our sandwich assembly line, my father's mathematical packing of the coolers, the loading of the boat, the trip to the Marina at the end of the pond for gas, the excruciating crawl at idling speed back along the shore to the inlet, then finally the open-throttle burst into the Little Peconic. "Where should we go today?" my father would yell to us when we hit that critical juncture.

One afternoon he did not give us a choice. After weeks of waterskiing, lazy picnics, and reconnaissance to remote beaches, my father took us on an excursion to the Shinnecock Canal. The density of boat traffic there was the urban antithesis of Wooley Pond's forgiving, sleepy

commerce. It was no place for a novice or inter-
mediate pilot like my father, who was used to
acres of water, not to mention the patience and
goodwill of his fellow mariners. Even our Lab-
rador retriever was nervous as the boat slowed
at the menacing locks. She was perched on the
bow, sniffing the air uncertainly, its foreign
traces of fried food, carnage of charter fishing
boats, and tang of the open ocean, that frontier
on the other side. The creosote-soaked piers and
bulkheads were lined with fishermen, the gauntlet of their poles and rods taunting, dipping, and
lifting like the feelers of some living organism.
We churned through slowly, my father dodging
the other boats, our forty-horse engine struggling mightily against the volume of water
surging through that narrow passage when the
locks were finally opened.

In the cooler air of Shinnecock Bay, we
pounded deeper into perspective toward the
inlet, which my father approached as if he were
at the helm of a tuna boat four times the size of
what now seemed an overcrowded tub. Once I
felt the subtle seismic lift of the ocean swells I
knew it was not going to end well. Sleek sportfishing boats speared past the dark boulders of
the jetties on either side, up and over the standing waves in the tidal current, then out into the
open ocean, their privileged wakes fanning out
like ermine cloaks.

I remember him remarking that the waves
weren't as big as they looked, my mother saying
it still *probably* wasn't a good idea. But they

were already upon us, the bow lifting almost vertically as the big silver Coleman cooler skated the length of the deck and slammed into the transom. Then we were down into the next trough. The dog lost her footing, yelped, and was washed along the same path that the cooler had just taken as the wave broke over us. We all screamed, even my father. If he turned us around, we'd surely be swamped or capsized, but that didn't stop us from being swept farther out the inlet alongside the other boats, whose tanned pilots, cigarettes dangling rakishly from their lips, glared down without pathos from the dry security of their flying bridges.

My aunt began bailing futilely with the yellow bucket normally used to hold fish. My sisters and mother were pale and stunned, sea-water and tears streaming down their faces. We were all yelling at my father until we were hoarse, up to our shins in water as plastic bottles of Coppertone, empty soda cans, cookie bags, assorted sneakers, and flip-flops floated around us like trash. But luck, an eddy, or some deep hole deflated the sets rolling through, flattened the current. My father punched the throttle, spun us around, and surfed us back to safety, outrunning a few alarmingly ravenous peaks by what seemed a few feet.

It took me years to forgive him for that experience, but throughout my teens, twenties, and thirties I'd forge a subtle, evolving peace with boats in general. A few short years later, with late-afternoon Peconic windswell breaking over us as we returned from Jessup Neck, my sisters and I would beg to ride in the bow seats, to be the first to receive the full impact of the waves as our father smiled at the helm. How we howled with crazed pleasure as our grandfather's boat drove into a particularly deep trough and the warm bay drenched us. We held tight to the railing, for a few more summers anyway, wanting that short, dangerous voyage to last forever.

One of *Widget*'s last voyages, before my parents gave it — their first sailboat — to my sister (who soon surrendered to its slow implosion and donated it to charity), was with the cockpit full of my nieces and nephews. I was ferrying the gang home to Ryder's Cove, where my parents finally settled on Cape Cod, in Chatham. We had spent the day on Nauset Beach, my father back at the house, too ill at that time and past his ability to sail, my mother taking care of him. Halfway across Chatham Harbor the wind picked up and clouds darkened. Before we knew it, a summer squall had dropped over the bluffs and was marching grimly across Pleasant Bay. Because I knew the fuel tank was close to empty, I decided to keep sailing, saving those last precious drops for an emergency. I left the sails up, stayed as close to the wind as possible — almost directly into it — and inched toward the cove. "Reaching" is when wind is pouring directly over the gunwale, into the sail from a ninety-degree angle. This creates the most dramatic moments in sailing, what we recognize in those iconic shots of boats leaning — or heeling — so the mast seems as if it might graze the surface of the water. Which is what I tried not to do on that blustery, unpredictable day, when the margin of error was so unforgiving.

Chatham had yet to vindicate me since my parents had moved there, delivering instead its own series of naval mishaps. I'd almost gotten lost fishing with my son in the famous fogbank that can bury the harbor in a matter of seconds. For almost a half-hour, I was forced to watch the back of his little head staring into white limbo from the prow, listening carefully for the sudden roar of a trawler's engine or bow wave. Once, I'd hit a rock with the propeller, cruising along the northern tip of Strong Island, catapulting my mother and a friend from their seats to the deck.

Sailing through that squall, I noticed that the faces of nieces, nephews, son, daughters, sister, and wife seemed vaguely conscious of the black, vaporous clouds and howling wind, but they kept on chatting, laughing, pausing briefly when a gust would hit us and I'd release the singing main sheet. The hull would right itself, then I'd bring it a little closer to the wind to keep us from being knocked over as decisively as a squarely struck tin bear in a shooting gallery. The wind sat down as we approached the cove. It was suddenly a summer afternoon again. We dropped the sails routinely, stuffed them into their bags, started the engine, and idled around the last point to spot my parents leaning on the deck railing in the emerging sun, waving enthusiastically to us, as if they'd been waiting for hours.

At the very beginning of summer, I used to drag my vinyl-cocooned Beetlecat from the woods on its trailer and wheel it into my in-laws' old garage in Duxbury, Massachusetts, where I commenced the annual task of bringing it back to life. This is, of course, after undoing the web of clothesline, peeling off the tarp, washing the hull, applying the antifouling paint, and hosing out the cockpit. You'd put it to sleep knowing exactly what would need attention in the spring, but then at the unveiling you see what looks to be an enormous bite out of the mast, a crack that needs glassing on the centerboard, a previous-ly stout hackle worn as thin as a wedding ring. The deck tattooed black with mildew and new psychedelic paisleys of brownish orange despite the care you put into wrapping. How did it all happen? What was responsible for the damage wrought mysteriously upon components of a boat that seemed perfectly fine when it went into mothballs in early autumn? Then there was the theatrical debarking of the mice; the rank smell of their eight-month static voyage almost knocked me over when I removed the tarp and plywood cover one May. I was expecting a warm wave of cedar but got instead the ammoniac chemical musk of rodent feces belonging to the dozen stowaways who sprang over my shoul-ders and onto the lawn when sun flooded their dank quarters. Once, ramming a vacuum nozzle under the gunwale, I sucked up a generation of pencil-eraser-size pink babies before I realized what they were.

It was always a dismal mess. Mouse occupation aside, my son predicted that one day the boat would just fly apart in a shower of wood, fiberglass, and bronze fittings, surrendering in one final gasp to its decrepitude and marginal captaincy. My youngest daughter had nothing but disdain for my creaky, smelly, temperamental catboat ever since we had enrolled her in the local sailing school. She had been seduced by the sturdy feng shui minimalism of its fleet of fiberglass 420s.

When he'd bought this early '70s Beetlecat, George Blanchard had renamed it the *Carving About*—fusing his hobby of sculpting birds from wood with *coming about*, a sailor's command for an element of tacking—the sailboat's zigzagging process toward its destination if the wind won't accommodate a straight shot. You're more likely to string together a sequence of many lines, some of which don't make any sense. It's frustrating, but if you're going to sail, you need to recalibrate your expectations about time; adaptability is a quality that separates recreational sailors from recreational motorboat operators. In some ways, George's name for his boat captured perfectly the sailor's sporadic decisions behind all those increments and angles. The paradox of sailing is that you can make progress even if the gale is against you, howling out of the very place you want to go.

One spring, after being at the orbital sanders for two days with my son, our dust masks were frosted bright red with the old color of the boat, our hair and faces too, glowing. I was looking forward to a new era, a new identity for the Beetlecat, so I wasn't prepared to balk when I came buzzing around to the stern and its chipped but persevering name, *Carving About*. It had been harder than I thought it would be to expunge that corny history. When each summer came, I was too impatient to get it in the water, to sail it rather than reinvent it. Earlier that month, I'd come across George's business card in my desk drawer, punched his name into a search engine with hesitation and dread, and sure enough, his obituary appeared on the *Cape Cod Times* page from a year before. He had been eighty-seven. I remember running my fingers over the texture of the words before I switched the paper in the sander to a coarser grade and began erasing, grinding away at the oversized vinyl letters he had painstakingly arranged in a subtle arc below the tiller slot.

The family fought for days over a new name, their pretentious or profane candidates wrangling to accompany the boat's new shade of deeper red: *Interlux Burgundy* (only sixty-five dollars a quart). *Pinot* and *Prostitute* squared off half-heartedly (our children had come of age), but one morning, faithful to my father's creed of Captain's Word = Law, I had the final word — literally — the mildly esoteric *Django*. The iconic Belgian Romani "gypsy jazz" or *jazz manouche* guitarist, Django Reinhardt, seemed to embody everything that I understood about the personality of my boat and my relationship with boats in general. Titles of his melodies — "Chasing Shadows," "Nuages" — seemed apt impressionist anthems for my quest. Definitely, like my father I was no virtuoso on the water, but sailing that Beetlecat had invited one lucky improvisation after another, especially when separate squalls had sheared the original mast and snapped a tiller.

Since we'd never bought a dinghy, I always had to swim out to the boat whenever I wanted to use it. This was a deliberate choice, a commitment that made the exercise pure. But it was also a behavior that marginalized me from the growing culture of skiffs, standup paddleboards, kayaks, and motorboats at Shipyard Beach. How many rides had I turned down on my side-stroking journey out there? My in-laws said I was stubborn (and cheap), but immersion as part of the crossing from marsh grass to Django's gunwale was both spiritual and biological. To hoist myself panting from the water onto the sunlit deck like an iguana was like being reborn and becoming a higher life form simultaneously.

Once we'd had our sail, stowed everything, and buttoned up the cover (we did finally have one made), it was time for the flip side of the process: diving off the bow and thrashing back to shore. Like a trained dolphin with his beach ball, I pushed with my forehead a waterproof bag stuffed with shirt, hat, sunglasses, tools, cell phone, and the remains of lunch. Because few of my crew members ever found this phase of the day appealing (except my wife on hot days), this required dropping off on the beach whomever had come along, and then sailing back out to the mooring alone. Sometimes, I intentionally lengthened that brief solo sail, taking a few extra passes at the mooring, which made it seem—from the family's perspective on the beach—as if I were having trouble, living up to my usual standard of inefficiency, when I was actually just stealing a few more selfish moments on the water.

No matter how cold the bay or the air, how late in the season, or how great the distance to shore, the swimming ritual had become the exhilarating framework to a day well spent. In October a few years ago (our boat was always one of the last in the water), the harbormaster, trussed up in his survival gear, churned up alongside me in the town's high-performance Zodiac as I treaded water a few yards from the Beetlecat. With its headdress of whipping antennae and eye-like spotlights, the official craft approached like some inflatable predatory insect. He idled up alongside to ask me calmly if I was drowning. When I calmly answered no, he asked me if I was nuts, then sped away in a huff.

For *Django*'s last season, the marina installed the mushroom anchor extremely close to shore, which meant the boat was high and dry at low tide. This placement of the mooring sheared off an hour of time on the water, compelling us to beat it back to Shipyard Beach if we didn't want to be stranded in the bay. I had begun to miss the long swim but was careful to contain my relief on those days when I didn't have to strip down and plunge; after the clouds moved in, my lower back began to throb, and my fingers were growing white-numb after three hours of gripping the tiller and absorbing spray from boat wakes and wind chop.

About a mile east across Duxbury Bay from Shipyard Beach is Clark's Island, named after the first mate of the *Mayflower*. It was also proposed as a potential settlement before the Pilgrims decided on the mainland. During *Django*'s last few seasons afloat, taking a lap around Clark's became the goal of our more ambitious expeditions. Given a consistent breeze, the sail usually took about three hours. In the course of lazier circumnavigations, no matter who had come along for the ride (four, maybe five adults maximum), the conversation was rich, the family arguments as discursive as the voyage itself, though you could be just as content staring into the water, its hues changing with the depth, texture, and composition of the bottom.

Passing along the eastern shore of Clark's, we'd study the rustic houses (Had Capote really written *In Cold Blood* in one of them?) and contemplate a life off the grid, sustaining

ourselves on solar power, quahogs, and blue-
berries. When friends from Manhattan visited,
it was a stretch of time dedicated to debating
loudly and profanely the year's best and worst
novels. The face of my brother-in-law, the
pediatric cardiothoracic surgeon, was like a
gauge as we rounded that island late in the
afternoon, the furrows of responsibility melting from his forehead, his jaw slackening. Once,
my father-in-law took what he described as the
finest half-hour nap of his life, on his back in
the cockpit when I thought he was actually
rapt, listening to my anecdote about lunatic
colleagues. Staring up into the rigging and
sail, he'd been mesmerized to sleep by passing
clouds, his occasional bursts of snoring competing with the rudder's hiss.

Having snuck out for a morning sail
without our children early one August, my
wife and I interrupted our Clark's trip to anchor off the southernmost reach of Duxbury
Beach. Swimming just inside the little cape had
become a pit stop on our circuits. That morning
we caught the tide perfectly: the wind had died
a little, the sun was warm, and the flood was
rushing around the point from Plymouth Bay
through the straight between the beach and the
island. The sand deposited inside that hooked
claw was white and fine. And even more irresistible when contemplated through the shimmer
of seven transparent feet of the green incoming
surge. We dove in, shrieked with the jolt of the
cold Atlantic, floated on our backs like otters

until the current carried us too far from the boat, then swam back in a panic, and hauled ourselves over *Django*'s solid transom, revived.

We savored those ethereal blue, eight-to-twelve-knot days aboard the Beetlecat — Duxbury Bay eerily silent, the bigger craft already tied up or dropping their sails, motoring against the draining tide, confined to the narrow channel — while we, sail filled, centerboard half-down, skimmed over oyster pens and cobalt-blue mussel beds in eighteen inches of clear water, getting away with something.

What Cikovsky, the halfhearted cubist, captured perfectly in his painting of Wooley Pond is the optical illusion that the cove does not have an inlet to the Peconic Bay; because everything is in focus, the white sand of the near shore appears fused to the channel's opposite bank, as if the pond in fact were closed. I remember returning boats seeming to slip into visibility as if emerging from another dimension. Their departures were just as beguiling, their outlines swallowed slowly by some undetectable rift in the solid perimeter. But I always knew where they were headed or coming from, that the portal was real. In the painting Cikovsky's lone mariner, like the towering bulrushes toward which he leans, is much too large. His boat stretches surreally across half the channel where it should be a speck. He's sitting in the stern, arms angled outward, elbows resting on knees, meditating on the inlet, almost imploring. The bow is facing the channel we can't see; it's impossible to discern whether he has already come back from the bay or it's where he plans to go.

That hot day when George Blanchard first rowed us out to the Beetlecat, both my wife and I noticed a patient deliberateness in his stroke, which we almost mistook for the frailty of age. His trajectory, aimed generously above the moored boat, guaranteed he would arrive without betraying any suggestion of a fight. Barnstable Harbor is a dynamic little pocket of water, especially when the tide is on the move, so if George had missed the target, he would've had to battle his way back upstream to the tantalizing stern, its gentle wake betraying the current that might have swept us out into Cape Cod Bay. He was almost eighty-three at the time and was hoping to sell to us the last boat he would sail alone. If he had been sad about the implications of this potential transaction, he hadn't shown it, just as his compensatory navigation with the dinghy had delivered us precisely to where he had intended.

It's hard to fathom that after an hour's work with a Sawzall I was able to cart what was left of *Django* to the transfer station with one trip: four trashcans packed into the back of a late-model Volvo wagon. Sometimes, when I'm feeling nostalgic and idealistic, I'll play that time-lapse video in reverse, watch the ribs and gunwales levitating from the lawn into the shape of a hull as cloud shadows speed across the meadow like ghost boats, the surrounding trees convulse and twitch, and my frantic doppelgänger, in a scampering crouch, draws the tool along its flanks, seeming to build rather than obliterate.

PART II

LIVE FREE AND SURF

New Hampshire has been in symbolic identity limbo since the natural landmark known as the Old Man of the Mountain crumbled and plummeted a few years ago. The famous granite outcropping near Franconia Notch that with a little imagination suggested a stern, curmudgeonly male profile. Maybe you've seen it on the state coin, its image chosen for the series of quarters issued in 2000, three years before the visage literally dropped from the mountain. Bad timing. The anthropomorphized cliff was in fact mortal. So much for the state's stoic resilience, also memorialized on those quarters and on our state license plates — "Live Free or Die." Little did John Stark, Revolutionary War general, realize when he uttered those words that he was coining a crutch for all political journalists swarming across our state every four years even if many of the state's residents might find it a bit extreme, if not too abstract. Live Free or Die is a more elusive concept than simply riding your Harley without a helmet or not having to pay any state taxes.

New Hampshire looks small on the nation's map, but the state seems awfully big—again, elusive—when one tries to gauge or sum up its political ethos, let alone in this season when the lawns, still green even though the trees are denuded, are suddenly extroverted, bristling and wagging with campaign signs. Listen to reporters interviewing people on the street and you get the usual NH paradoxes (our identity is that we don't seem to have one) and the dependable Yankee clichés: *fiercely independent, unpredictable, stubborn, ornery,* and so on and so on—cut to license plates. But Arthur and Oscar, the two ninety-year-old guys who bag my groceries at the Market Basket, are among the most polite and personable people I've ever met. There is a strong sense of community and cohesion, as binding as any other I have experienced elsewhere, with people pretty open to newcomers and outsiders. Dour New Englanders? I don't think so. With any state, it's not that easy to tidy or generalize, and, like a good poem, that element of mystery is a source of gravity for public attention.

The minute you try to nail New Hampshire down, its face is going to fall off.

Portsmouth Harbor is home to the nation's first naval shipyard. Though it is officially in Kittery, Maine, on an island in the tidal Piscataqua River, the border between states is slippery, apparently. A friend of mine (an

(margin note: political diversity)

engineer who works on submersibles contracted by the military) says that certain express
delivery services will not bring packages to the
facility if they don't have a New Hampshire
address — something to do with where the
maritime channel is. Even so, there are still New
Englanders who are surprised to learn that
New Hampshire even *has* a coast. Most likely,
it's because our coast is the country's smallest.
I moved to the state in 1995, but it was not
necessarily to be near the ocean, though I admit
after teaching just north of Chicago for a year I
missed the Atlantic. My whole family did. I was
born in California's San Fernando Valley but
grew up on the North Shore of Massachusetts
and South Fork of Long Island, spent most of
my childhood in or on top of their surrounding
waters. When I started my new job at Phillips
Exeter Academy in New Hampshire, my wife
and I assumed that we could rely on neighboring states — the marshy coves and muscular
barrier beaches of Cape Cod or the foggy bays
of Maine — for our aquatic escapades.

adventory
outdoors

New Hampshire in our minds was all about
mountains — the White Mountains, specifically.
Skiing. Covered bridges. Balsams, spruces,
maples in full conflagration along the
Kancamagus Highway. And, yes, lakes that
were comprehensible, like Winnipesaukee and
Squam ("Golden Pond"), not the Midwest's
oceanic, city-fringed freighter graveyards. The
prospect of exploiting all of the state's iconic
environmental elements fueled our lumbering

late-model Volvo's odyssey back East. Some seventeen years on, I'm embarrassed to admit that I've rarely taken my kids up North. When they were younger, we did some hiking and camping in Vermont, but we found our corner of New Hampshire particularly sticky. Only very recently have my wife and I laced up the hiking boots and hammered our meniscuses along the ridges of the Presidential Range, Tuckerman's Ravine, the Carter Dome. Sadly, we haven't ventured very often from where we've been hunkering in the town of Exeter, which sits in the oft-overlooked Seacoast Region, down the road from the idyllic, riverine seaport of Portsmouth, home to tugboats, a massive salt pile, restaurants, music venues, galleries, decent coffee, bakeries, and (randomly) the peace treaty that ended hostilities between the Russians and Japanese more than a century ago. There's enough to keep us busy within a fifteen-minute radius. And plenty to keep us confused, too, which is probably why we're still here.

If New Hampshire has a persona, it is not usually derived from its coast, though our diminutive twelve-mile chain of rocky points and crescent beaches (eighteen miles including the Great Bay and Isles of Shoals) is becoming more popular, more confusing, and more prohibitively exclusive. From where I live, I can walk to at least three substantial trailer parks and a Jaguar dealership. Twenty years ago you could still get away with calling our region part of "Cow Hampshire." There was still open land.

Real estate was cheap. The neighboring towns still had that weary, postindustrial, defunct New England mill-town pall. But a *lot* of people have moved here since 1995; the roads have been widened, traffic lights quadrupled, and the re- furbished shopping centers have exploded with all the predictable strip mall retailers. With the traffic, it's faster to ride my 1973 Raleigh Sprite across town rather than drive. How could any- one appreciate the heart of the seacoast if they're ripping up I-95 in the time it takes to down a Coke en route to the outlet stores in Maine, or some hip restaurant in Portsmouth they've read about in the *Boston Globe*?

One of my first forays into New Hampshire was back in the summer of 1972, when my parents sent me across the border from Massachusetts to hockey school. I was twelve years old and it was the first time I'd spent any significant time away from home, but I was game. Skating was all I wanted to do back then, and I banked on playing hockey 24/7 as a distraction from any domestic longing. The first of two problems: I did become profoundly homesick and spent a good portion of my stay in New Hampshire (when I wasn't slathering Bengay on two pulled groins) with knees tucked under my chin, alone in the corner of an empty squash court. The second (more ironic) problem: I had become profoundly homesick on the very campus that I would eventually make my home and where my own kids would grow up. I knew almost nothing about Phillips Exeter Academy's history, its monolithic importance as one of the country's oldest and—here we go again with clichés—"prestigious" boarding schools. I had no idea that men like Todd Lincoln, Arthur Schlesinger, and John Irving had gone there. I probably didn't know who those people were. Nor would I have known or cared then that the two-century-old school was the setting for the iconic novel *A Separate Peace*. All I knew was that it had two state-of-the-art ice rinks.

In our free time between meals, sessions on the ice, or in the weight room (and when I wasn't pining away for my parents and dog), I'd wander downtown and wade into the current with a broken hockey stick to bludgeon lamprey eels that were making their way up the Exeter River from the tidal Squamscott. This was my true baptism in New Hampshire: martial, bodily, and completely adolescent. So it's sort of a miracle—or maybe fate—that I am here today writing this not only two hundred yards away from where that shameful estuarine massacre transpired forty years ago, but also in the epicenter of the last place I would have called home.

My father had wanted us to embrace New England's hearty brand of athleticism, and I did my part by losing myself to hockey. But if he were still alive, how would he react to my return to surfing as a result of living in New Hampshire?

Because it's just out of the shadow of Cape Cod, New Hampshire receives decent swells rolling in from the storm incubator off the coast of Africa, which launches its wave machines spiraling up the Atlantic seaboard. Between the feisty blitz of nor'easters, hurricanes, and mysterious "pulses" that seem to have no origin, this coast is more dependable than most realize. Some acquaintances become bewildered when I mention surfing in the same sentence as New Hampshire, but they're even more incredulous when I tell them the waves are actually pretty good here. Especially in the fall and winter. One of my surfing partners and mentors, an Exeter student from Costa Rica, was on occasion stunned speechless by the peeling green, head-high perfection that greeted us as we pulled up to The Wall in Hampton.

Surfing has kept me facing east, prevented me from making more forays west or north to get a more responsible grip on this irascible state. Right now, the water temperature is around forty-five degrees, kind of warm for this time of year. In a month, it'll be down somewhere around thirty-eight. This is the time to go. The surf shop (Cinnamon Rainbows) closes at five now, French fades from grocery-line chatter, the Canadian tourists for the most part gone. The favored breaks are noticeably unpopulated, except for a few familiar faces. Sometimes, a big gray Stratotanker from the National Guard Refueling Squadron at Pease Air Force Base (between Newington and Portsmouth) swings in low and impossibly slow from the ocean, its distinct nozzle protruding like a blunt stinger, a stunted tail. Another of my surfing buddies flies one, and when I haven't seen him for a few weeks, I always wonder if that's him, back from deployment in Qatar or Spain. I usually get a text from him in a few hours after I get out of the water, when I'm able to taunt him, tell him what he's been missing. Or sometimes he's way ahead of me, already paddling out, on it at another break.

In the fall, there's something sublime about viewing the sparks of foliage as you bob in the lineup, glancing back to shore before the next set reveals its texture on the titanium horizon. Giant vees of Canada geese undulate south, and I am lost in their melancholy off-key honking before it's drowned by the closing of the waves I've ignored. In winter, it's pretty lonely out there, except for the vivid black-and-white plumage of sea ducks arriving from their Arctic migration: buffleheads, goldeneyes, scoters, eiders. And the hapless harbor or gray seal trying desperately to establish eye contact like a tourist who suddenly finds a fellow nonnative in a place where they shouldn't be. All of this scenery is made bearable by a five- or six-millimeter wetsuit with seven-millimeter gloves and booties, if the wind chill isn't too bad. When the air temp drops below thirty, a beard helps, something to supplement the coat of Vaseline, to give the illusion that your cheeks, lips, and chin are protected (here on the coast, we have our own variation of faces falling off).

Notwithstanding General Stark, New

Hampshire hasn't always lived free or died. That motto only replaced the previous one, the generic and shamelessly unimaginative "Scenic" in 1971. Not that *scenic* was inaccurate (almost any state would want to claim that label), but because it was something any state worth its salt (if you will) could claim and didn't evoke a specific attitude. *Scenic* captures my drive through Seabrook on Route 1A on my way to surf with Matt, a colleague and friend whose family has a house there. Like the Central Mosque in Regent's Park in London, the great burnished dome of the nuclear power plant looms over the frozen marshes and flats, over the few remaining lobster boats moored in the harbor. It's a complicated beauty. I want to savor it, but I'm itching to get into my suit. That's New Hampshire. The country keeps wondering what this state's role will be in the election this year. What will those obstinate Yankees, do *this* time? they'll be asking. Some of us will be surfing, of course.

[handwritten marginal notes: "(intrusby", "polibly", "rok", "vs", "nawm /", "pursuny", "role", "haha"]

[handwritten note at bottom: "- humor?", "- thread?"]

SHADE OF THOUGHT, GRIEVING ARROW:
ON PATIENCE, PAIN, AND THE
MYSTERY OF FISHING

My father hated to fish. So his rare submissions to joining me when I was younger, often spurred by my mother's good-natured badgering, were for the sake of companionship, the chance of doing something with his son. Not because he had any interest in the hunt or the gear. He was being a good sport. Though he loved being on the water and actually owned two boats, being anchored in the middle of the bay, sitting there with a spinning rod in his hand was torture, I'm pretty sure. His bored, bewildered expression was probably no different from the one I wore when he excitedly enlisted my help for some woodworking project. The spring in his step as we descended the stairs to the basement workshop was unmistakable, and I knew the two of us would soon be stooped over the bench for some quick, terrifying math, followed by his snugging a square against a plank's edge then running his pencil along it, a map for the infernal table saw

[handwritten margin note: only fished for his son]

215

to rip its nonnegotiable borders.

The very last time I went fishing with him, he broke two ribs. It was my fault.

We were drifting that day, riding the incoming tide along the backside of a barrier beach on the elbow of Cape Cod. It was August, overcast, a little foggy, and the water was dark, clean, and cool. Surveying the shore, I could gauge the boat's speed, impressive against the passing cabins and dunes. The current was brisk, and staring into the water, trying to follow a lure, was confusing because you'd be fooled into thinking the boat was static.

Once in a while, however, we'd glide over a mussel bed, its dark mass rearing up and receding so quickly it seemed that the bed itself was a mobile, prowling entity. To understand the situation, you needed to appreciate the interplay of perspectives, the dance between the surrounding land, the water's surface, and what was beneath. Not to mention what I imagined was down there.

Despite what would happen next, we ended up having a pretty good day, plenty of tenacious striped bass just below the size limit and a few bluefish who snipped off our lures until we wised up and tied on wire leaders. My dad, however, was frustrated because I wasn't keeping anything. Always the practical engineer, he couldn't understand the purpose of going through all of this ritual and technical preparation without an identifiable end, even though he wasn't really

nature

without something physical to take away

a fish eater. All of this was surprising to me, considering that he sailed, spent hours at a time on the water doing nothing but sailing, no destination in mind. He betrayed a calm, bemused excitement when he muscled a fish into the boat, but I could tell he still didn't get it and perhaps was missing that transcendent boost of connection with the sentient wild, the voltage of which could sustain me for days after an experience.

not as [0 nnd with nnn?]

Starting at the gap that a recent nor'easter had ripped through the beach, I cut the engine and let the current carry us through Chatham Harbor toward Pleasant Bay. It seemed that most of the North Atlantic was squeezing through that waterway, and I was certain the fish commuting along the ocean side would be funneled mercilessly to this new exit right to the glitter and snells of our waiting plugs. At the end of the drift, just before we would ram into the sandbar off Strong Island, I'd start the engine again, whip the boat around, and head back to the breach for another cycle. The throttle was sticky, had no transition between idling and significant forward motion, so I mistakenly gunned it without warning him. He fell and slammed into the engine cover, bellowing in pain. I had never seen him react so audibly to bodily injury. How many times had I watched him jog calmly up the stairs with a blood-soaked towel wrapped around his hand as a result of some self-inflicted mishap in his shop? This was different. And it was not only because I had dragged him out there in the

in lot of pain

first place, <u>but because of my impatience and</u> <u>excitement to keep us in the game.</u> It took weeks for him to recover. Laughing and sometimes even breathing were excruciating, but he never blamed me or made me feel guilty. We both knew that his days of being a good sport were probably over, and that we could still love each other without fishing together. *end of fishing*

Just before my mother moves and we pre-pare to sell the house where she and my father retired, I go fishing. She'd sold the boat after he died, then bought another and sold that, too. So now the only way out to the bay is the canoe that my sister and her husband have left lashed tem-porarily to the side of the pier in the marsh grass. I've <u>convinced myself that I need to exploit what</u> <u>will probably be the final seasons</u> of our family's <u>good fortune of owning,</u> inheriting, or having <u>access to any semblance of understated</u> water-front property. *end of water homes*

Summer murk purged, the October water is sunglass green, transparent, with plenty of action swarming in the shallows before winter's sterility scours <u>Ryder's</u> Cove. A month before, this Cape Cod backwater was a tepid stew of detritus and flotsam, clogged with seaweed, rubbery chains of egg casings, and slicks of suspiciously unidentifiable swill. In the sluggish heat, schools of shiners hounded by snappers were just beginning to pock and crenellate the windows between rafts of scum, but the mood was *chill*. Foraging green crabs and blue claws sidestepped diplomatically around each other just beyond the partition of eelgrass. The osprey pumped its wings, rowed itself casually from an aerie in the powerline tower on the other side of the cove, looking as if it were rising from a couch to raid the cold cuts after a miniseries binge rather than setting off to kill something. But in early autumn, the place is fully charged, vibrant, and committed. And it has a tincture of desperation.

In the lee of the eastern shore, there is barely a ripple, and the canoe glides easily along partially submerged spartina bristling at the foot of the bluff's tonsure. The tide is on its way in, about halfway there. Off the boatyard, all moored hulls obey the current, their noses oriented toward the bay. Once I swing around the point and into the wind, the bear cub cry of morning leaf blowers harmonizing with the whine of outboards is muted. The air, though unseasonably warm, is suddenly freighted with Atlantic sharpness. The Cape's high season is over. The harbormaster has yanked out the 5 mph/ NO WAKE signs in the channel, so now it is a free-for-all, and being inshore is almost as dangerous as the open ocean. The dwindling population of active boats has become downright anarchic, if not feral. A few hard-core, late-season fishermen and clammers come ripping in and out of the pond at full throttle. If you're in a small, muscle-propelled craft, it's always safer to skim along shore, keeping alert for the assault of sudden wakes. I dig into the final sprint across a stretch of open water: the deceptive confluence of the

Ryder's Cove and Crowe's Pond inlets intersecting with Pleasant Bay and Chatham Harbor. This is the sweet spot, where Fox Island sits like a resigned, exasperated crossing guard in the determined currents. A great place to fish.

The terns and cormorants are already there, hovering, periscoping, gorging on what must be a dense swarm of juvenile menhaden ("peanut" bunker) or shiners, the principal early-fall diet of stripers. A lone Canadian gray "horsehead" seal, shoulders out of the water, eavesdrops on the frenzy from the outskirts then slips below the surface — *Get Smart*/elevator style — to pick off the bass that are certainly participating in the mayhem. Which is also the reason why I have paddled out here. Tail slaps start to punctuate the channel and, despite the wind's white noise, fill the air with an audible, spastic code. Just before beaching, I begin to pick up on flashes and shadows darting through the shallows where the cobbles of the island's east-facing shore drop into a deep blue-gray trench.

To protect the canoe from the tide's aggressive advance, I drag it from the sand spit and up beyond the dried seaweed line to the gravel at the base of the eroding bluff. The island itself is actually smaller than some of the new, hotelesque mansions brooding self-consciously, chins jutting from their clear-cut perches across the cove. They almost seem embarrassed by their ploy, posing as cottages, bloated architecture cloaked in cedar-shingle dressing gowns, dwarfing the authentic, subdued examples obscured among pitch pines and oaks. Seaward, across the bay, the besieged dunes of the barrier beach hunker under a radiant blue sky. No houses out there, just the forested bluff of Strong Island in the foreground across the strait, melting into a labyrinth of marshes. And not thirty feet from my pile of gear, stripers swatting the surface then pivoting in a swirl to Hoover stunned bait.

Pulling on waders while regarding this sort of activity is as challenging as ramming your legs into a wetsuit while groomed waves build and peel a few hundred strokes away. Especially when there's no one else around, nobody with whom you'll need to share the surf. No one to dilute—if you will—the experience. Waxing a surfboard or engaging a wetsuit zipper, though not as nuanced, requires motor skills that can be just as taxing to summon when you're rigging a fly rod in a situation that promises potential. The odds of taking a shortcut—that your impatience will leave a holiday, a slick, glossy patch of fiberglass—are high in such moments. You plant your foot into the first drop of the day and the ideal conditions are suddenly yanked out from under you by an invisible banana peel on the board's deck. A few paralyzing gallons of nitrogen-cold ocean slosh down your shoulders through a breached, hastily secured wetsuit flap. Or you yank frantically at a halyard, but the sail won't scurry up the mast, jammed because one of the hoops is pinched between twisted lines you rigged carelessly that same morning.

Or more relevantly, on your first cast you try

to load the rod and shoot the line, but it drizzles sluggishly from the tip in a pathetic coil, leader landing in a mess beyond the fly. That's when you notice you've missed threading one of the guides. Or afraid of missing one second of productive fishing, you rush to nail the throttle and knock your father off-balance.

Alone on this October day, there is no need to rush into anything; the ongoing phenomenon doesn't have the feel of transience. Maybe it is the relentless, chaotic behavior of the other predators that ironically makes it reassuring, less ephemeral, and more substantial than the organic flash mob it really is. Experience has taught me again and again that what seems like widespread, enduring excitement tends to evaporate before I ever get a chance to participate in all that raw authenticity. This day, however, being fired up doesn't necessarily equate with being incautious. Any anxiety melts into confident surrender. Missing out doesn't seem possible.

And I am right. An hour later, up to my chest ten yards out, the tendons in my right arm are burning. I have connected with a bass on almost every cast, most of them "schoolies," indiscriminate youngsters between fourteen- and twenty-two inches, who hit the fly close to the surface almost as soon as it touches down. Even with the barb of the streamer's single hook pinched flat, the chore of bringing them alongside for a quick release wears me down, my left hand throbbing from being impaled repeatedly by dorsal spines before I can smooth them down for a better grip to let them go underwater. After *being caught* (the traditionally deflective passive: fisherman exonerated, quarry as escaped criminal or lunatic), most of the fish are liberated with nary a nostril snorting the air. For me, the marvel of the protocol is subsurface, the surge of awe you get reeling them into focus just as sublime as the moment the animal slips from your fingers, suddenly cognizant of its freedom, reabsorbed, gone with one flick. *(unthless then for serin?)*

When I return fish, there is always a predic-*int to vau* tive narrative pulse, a quick musing about where they'll go next. Right back to business, unfazed? A baffled retreat from the school to consider the trauma? It's a similar impulse to Neruda's in his poem "Ode to a Large Tuna in the Market," but in reverse. My fantasies about the immediate future are not elegiac. The poet considers the fish among the earthly piles of vegetables and fruit and, in contrast, is compelled to imagine its previous animated life in a full-throated paean, but with a tremble of heartache:

Only you:
dark bullet
barreled
from the depths,
carrying
only
your
one wound, *(civil)*
but resurgent,
always renewed,
locked into the current,

fins fletched
like wings
in the torrent,
in the coursing
of
the
underwater
dark,
like a grieving arrow . . . .

That night, under the reading lamp in bed, I study the disturbing purple line meandering from a bull's eye puncture on the meat of my palm, whispering to myself, "Serves you right." Poisoning? Infection? No. But my abuse of the fish is undeniable no matter what precautions I take to minimize any suffering in the game. At fifty-six, I am still mired in my addiction to the hunt but also embroiled in the ongoing ethical tug-of-war, the angsty considerations and self-reproach that would seem absurd to the nonfishing person whose admonishment would probably circle back to ideas of immaturity, cruelty. Just *grow up*. I can count the times on two fingers that I've kept and eaten a fish in the past twenty-five years, so justifying my behavior is a challenge. It might be lazy, maybe mislead-ing, to call it spiritual, or on the other hand, completely physical. It's a toss-up. One side compels me to link up with them (the fish) from above with all the relevant paraphernalia, tools, and vehicles, maintaining that human foothold in my own dry province. The other has to do

addicted

with being in their world, imagination submerged and searching in that wet dimension.

But I was already among them before I became aware of the schoolies' presence on this stunning fall day. It began long before I boosted myself over the canoe's stern, before the water poured over the top of my boot and I gripped the shaft of the paddle, smitten by the clarity of the water holding me up. The October expedition obliges me to consider what *connect* means literally in this "sport." And the threat of political understatement, of euphemistic sleaze, looms. You take measures to make the whole thing humane, but the truth is you are deceiving an animal that is programmed to eat, piercing some soft quadrant of its mouth for the purposes of dragging it toward yourself through the water by a tendril of monofilament and PVC-coated Dacron. Why?

Everybody has their own answer. If I could have explained it better to my father, perhaps he would have given it another go. But probably not. His own father was a dedicated angler, and yet I can't remember one conversation between the two about the practice itself, only some dim images of my dad in the exact same posture he had with me: sitting on the gunwale as my grandfather's boat rocked gently, rod in his hand, looking down into . . . empty water.

His discomfort with the mystery of it all now seems to be closer to the truth, how ill-attuned his furniture-building-aeronautic-engineer's brain was with speculating, waiting, wondering if anything would happen at all. He was a visualizer, a planner who dreamed a shape — whether a fuel vaporizer for a gas turbine or a cherry coffee table — and brought it dependably to full, concrete, three-dimensional realization. Also, considering his perspective as a bomber copilot who'd spent almost two years in a stalag, my father might have been adhering to some unspoken internal promise geared toward not engaging in any pastime that might inflict pain on any conscious creature. It might have been something informed by his own suffering and, no doubt, the blind cruelty of it all, including the guilt that endured long after his B-17 had released its payloads on the factories and civilians of European cities. *Guilt from War*

Richard Wilbur in his poem "Trolling for Blues" gets as close as any writer to describing that liminal space, the limbo that's so easily dismissed or diminished by fishing's traditionally ensuing narrative of triumph, defeat, or redemption (see Elizabeth Bishop's hyperanthologized, nay, *bludgeoned* hymn "The Fish"). In Wilbur's description, the distinctions between fish's and fisherman's (and even the poet's) consciousnesses seem intentionally ambiguous:

> Blue in the water's blue, which is the shade
> Of thought, and in that scintillating flux
> Poised weightless, all attention, yet on edge
> To lunge and seize with sure incisiveness,
> He is a type of coolest intellect,

Or is so to the mind's blue eye until
He strikes and runs unseen beneath the rip,
Yanking imagination back and down
Past recognition to the unlit deep . . . .

Whatever I was capable of explaining to my father (when I was young) about the force that drove me to embark on this adventure of apprehending fish has changed, sharpened. Now I'm almost certain that it is stoked by a need to have my imagination "[yanked] back and down." To say, as most of us do, that it's just about "being outside, in nature" feels cursory, like a cop-out at this phase of my life. The psychological, emotional, and creative storm that gathers before anything has even happened is a big part of the thrill, the addictive predicament. And, yes, it does seem more like play, just another way of getting to the element. Like surfing or sailing, fishing is about the promise of experiencing something you've experienced before, that you know you enjoy but that has its attendant unpredictability. It's something you hope will happen again and again, but differently, and that its residual buzz will get you through the times between. You are open to the compelling variations of delight and sublimity, danger and fear. You'll take whatever reward or reproach comes your way. But you never come away with nothing. Every foray is fraught with and sustained by those same old propulsive questions, but they're suddenly in concert with something more profound, the interplay of immediate

227

environmental concerns and the personal.

Will the face of that wave hold up and develop into a barrel? Could those be false albacore zipping along the rim of that sandbar? Will my keel or propeller scrape those mussel beds? Did my father really hate fishing? Were we really that different from each other? The dimpled, turquoise pocket behind that boulder looks fishy; what does it hold?

Is that the point of this piece?

THE LEGIBLE ELEMENT:
ON HOPKINS, SURFERS, AND THE
SELVES OF WAVES

I've driven my wife and children crazy during beach walks <u>because I feel the need to point out the waves</u>. I drift in and out of conversations, distracted by the way a set is wrapping into the lee of a particular point, organizing itself. Pure glee when the outgoing tide suddenly jacks the waves a few feet higher as they roll across an emerging sandbar. Then I begin to <u>brood because I didn't bring a board or a wetsuit</u>. Nothing, I'm told, is more boring than when I do start talking about the waves, harpooning dialogues with a tour guide's gesticulations, effusiveness tinged with longing and frustration, because I just want to surf and can't at that moment. My fellow walkers nod politely, resume their pace, pick up the threads of their sabotaged topics, and leave me ogling seaward as if I've suddenly forgotten where I am.

Surfers spend a lot of time looking at waves, our fixation geared toward the prospects of

[handwritten margin note: — instincts]

[handwritten margin note: humor]

experiential gratification. We want to be out there in it. Even mind surfing, the shore-bound close reading that might not necessarily be a surf check but a fantasy, has the practitioner imagining himself superimposed, spliced into the empty wave's short film. It can be excruciating for surfers to stand back and give the water a chance to be itself, to do what it does without our inhabiting its mutating textures.

So when I ran across the following excerpt from Gerard Manley Hopkins's journals, I leaned forward in my chair with a twinge of caffeine-amped suspicion and envy. Suddenly awake and able to transcend the oppressive spring drizzle gnawing the snowbanks outside in the New Hampshire dawn, I joined the beguilingly contented, nonsurfing poet for a legitimate evocation of surf:

> I was looking at high waves. The breakers always are parallel to the coast and shape themselves to it except where the curve is sharp wherever the wind blows. They are rolled out by the shallowing shore just as a piece of putty between the palms whatever its shape runs into a long roll. The slant ruck or crease one sees in them show[s] the way of the wind. The regularity of the barrels surprised and charmed the eye; the edge behind the comb or crest was as smooth and bright as glass. It may be noticed to be green behind and silver and white in front: the silver marks where the air begins, the pure white is foam, the green/solid water. Then looked at to the right or left they

use of excerpts/poetry

are scrolled over like mouldboards or feathers
or jibsails seen by the edge. It is pretty to see the
hollow of the barrel disappearing as the white
combs on each side run along the wave gaining
ground till the two meet at a pitch and crush
and overlap each other . . . .

I hadn't planned on meeting a more
unnerving kindred spirit in the literary lineup
that morning: a newly minted Jesuit, sexually
repressed in late-nineteenth-century England.
But on August 10, 1872, twenty-eight years old,
he was riding the wave of his recent discovery
of the works of medieval philosopher Duns
Scotus, who, according to Stephen Greenblatt
and colleagues in the *Norton Anthology of English
Literature*, gave Hopkins the idea of *inscape* — the
"distinctive design that constitutes individual
identity":

> This identity is not static but dynamic . . . . And
> the human being, the most highly selved, <u>the
> most individually distinctive being in the uni-
> verse</u>, recognizes the inscape of other beings in
> an act that Hopkins calls *instress,* the apprehen-
> sion of an object in an intense thrust of energy
> toward it that enables one to realize specific
> distinctiveness.

Scotus's belief in "haecceity" or "thisness,"
which defended the uniqueness of individual
things, seems to fuel Hopkins's observations
in this particular journal entry written while

he was on vacation on the Isle of Man. Here the poet strives only to describe, to *possess* by translating perception into an accurate, scientific, and vaguely poetic visual language.

Most poets can't help enlisting waves on their solipsistic quests for meaning or some direction in their forays into the problems of being human. Robinson Jeffers's "smoking mountains bright from the west" ("November Surf") or "white-maned, wide-throated ... heavy shouldered children of / the wind" ("Granite and Cypress") are usually gaining on the rocks they'll pound or cover, where the poet stands contemplating time and erasure, the insignificance and sins of the human race and what the waves suggest rather than what they are. Basil Bunting too, though "agog for foam" (#3, *First Book of Odes*) admits "how much more the sea / trembling with alteration must perfect / our loneliness by its hostility."

Hopkins's exegesis of surf is untainted, almost clinical in its syntactical breakdown of the breaking wave's physical process, its variation of color and architecture. His notes on waves are a field sketch, a quick plein air watercolor with words, but one with a restrained riptide of joy and connection. Suppressing the poet, in some ways, is almost as hard as suppressing the surfer. But Hopkins seems to get it, even though he's asking himself neither, "Where would I be on that wave?" nor, like his poetic counterparts, "What does it mean to me?" He employs the words *hollow* and *barrel* — monolithic descriptors in the contemporary surf lexicon. He gropes into the twentieth century, building phrases around the holes that will be filled by words like *tube, lip,* or *closeout*. There's not a brushstroke of sadness or anxiety in his acuity, however, which would suggest that even though Hopkins had no intention of physically engaging the surf, his charging into the legibility of the animated element was just as satisfying. *(a ensuing the surf through lenses?)*

In some way Hopkins reminds me of the silhouette behind the wheel of a sagging Corolla I see from time to time. Nothing lashed to his roof, no finned tail jutting from his rear window, but there he is, installed on the scrubby promontory of the dim, sandy, dawn-patrol parking lot, staring out, setting up an easel in his imagination rather than crouching beside the vehicle waxing the deck of a beat-up longboard. Is he missing something, or awash in the purest moil of appreciation, apprehending the "true selves" of waves? I'm usually too focused to ask him, too fired up about getting in the water as I jog gingerly past his coffee-steamed windshield across the lot's sharp pebbles. The guy in the Corolla ignores me completely, even seems to understand that the storm conditions are cleaning up, that the protean waves are assuming elegant shapes in their provisional identities. He's dry, warm, and probably in deeper than any of us. *??*

what does this mean?

title of book

FOSTERED ALIKE BY BEAUTY AND BY FEAR: WORDSWORTH, MONTALE, AND THE LANDSCAPES OF CHILDHOOD

When you love a place and lose your foothold in it through self-exile, or the inevitable economics that annihilate real estate across a family's generations, or simply because it has changed, what you write about it risks whiny longing, the tang of sour grapes. A whiff of elegy, however, seems OK, as long as it doesn't idealize. Years ago I wrote a poem about the Little Peconic Bay, and I'm pretty certain the path I took back to it changed my writing for the better.

As a kid, I'd spent a lot of time on the South Fork of Long Island; the setting had been a well-spring in my earlier work, but with the poem "Peconic" arrived a new impulse that seemed governed by memories that were more eerie, their descriptors' tone shaped by desolation, danger, and death. Abandoned fishing nets, the viscera of fish in a kitchen sink, severed deer feet in the dunes, terrifying myths about horseshoe crabs, the competing shame and relief of being land-bound while others embark on a menacing sea. Settling on these particular moments was an important aesthetic juncture; wherever this project seemed to lead, each increment tended to veer from nostalgia into more mysterious, unexplainable realms. As I approached the closure of the sequence (ten seven-line, numbered cantos in trimeter), I realized that I was reclaiming while trying to say goodbye to a beloved and evocative landscape by conjuring its most haunting moments. Beauty was now accompanied by a sketchy sidekick. — *capturing worst moments*

The challenge of writing "Peconic," however, wasn't in deciding over which images to hang spotlights; rather, it was in mustering the faith — as I felt my way along — that they might reveal some unintended cargo in being reconjured. *[faith in memories]* Though a writer's receptiveness to new or dormant emotions that memories might broach sounds pretty boilerplate, shaping their nuanced spiritual freight in ways that are neither saccharine nor too gothic needs mentoring. *[excessively sweet or sentimental]* At certain junctures in my development as a writer, I admired, absorbed, and parroted poems that evoked in the settings of their childhood narratives some proximity to general creepiness, horrors embedded in the everyday.

Poems in Seamus Heaney's *Death of a Naturalist*, Yusef Komunyakaa's *Magic City*, and Dave Smith's *The Roundhouse Voices* provided gritty inspiration propelled by contemporary voices that I could emulate, poets who were neither sentimental nor interested in beating themselves up, wallowing in angst. To be sure, the Peconic Bay in the late 1960s–early '70s was my favorite place on earth. It was paradise, and that was the problem. Especially when it came to writing about it. *too happy?*

During the past decade, however, it was William Wordsworth and Eugenio Montale who nudged me closer to a way of remembering Long Island that was neither unrealistically dark nor selectively euphoric. As an adult trying to dial in the perceptions of a self long gone, my return to mine the aesthetic discord of childhood (via those two poets) also taught me about the roots of aspiration, how these muses — these homes — shape the future.

Wordsworth and Montale shared the blessing of growing up in spectacular natural environments. For Wordsworth, it was the peaks and vales of the Lake District in the northwestern portion of England known as Cumbria; for Montale, the Ligurian coast of Italy's northwest extremity, the string of towns known as the Cinque Terre. Reverberating through the work of both was the echo of that parental binary Wordsworth describes three-hundred lines into his great poem, that he "grew up / Fostered alike by beauty and by fear."

Translator William Arrowsmith said that although Montale's decision to leave his childhood home in Monterosso for the urban literary

bustle and intellectual cafés of Florence was deliberate, the poems in *Ossi di Seppia* (*Cuttlefish Bones*)
prove that "Liguria is not, could not, be abandoned."
Though it wasn't exactly beauty he had exhausted,
Dave Smith says in "Cumberland Station," his poem
about returning to the ancestral railyards in his
native Cumberland County, Virginia, "I hope I never
have to go through this place again." Even though
we are looking over his shoulder as he grimly, com-
pellingly writes his way back there as if in a dream.

Arguably, the anchor of Wordsworth's investigation of memory and one of the most frequently
cited segments of *The Prelude* is the "spots of time"
sequence. What makes it so provocative is its foundational scene of the thirteen-year-old Wordsworth
waiting on a desolate hillside above Hawkshead
for his brothers to bring him home from school for
Christmas vacation. It is a landscape and climate
cinched to his memory by three sensory bolts: a
stonewall, a sheep, and a hawthorn tree, which he
characterizes as "companions." The trinity of images
is explicit enough, but the auditory experience seems
just as formative. The blasted tree "whistles," the wall
has its own "bleak music," and we can only imagine
the implicit bleating of the sheep on the windy fell,
the only other warm-blooded agent in the scene. By
its end we learn that a few days after Wordsworth
arrived home to Cockermouth, his forty-two-year-
old father died, and the three brothers "followed
his body to the grave." The aesthetic miracle of this
memory and its details is that they have become,
despite their origins, a healing force in later years, a
mysterious "beneficent influence."

Montale's and Wordsworth's poems from *Ossi* and sections of *The Prelude* share the plaintive refrains of debt, where any attempt to evoke is buttressed by the poets' doubting their worthiness as the recipients of such gifts, no matter how terrifying some of them should have been (see Wordsworth's narratives about watching the authorities drag a corpse from the lake or his being hounded by the shadow of a mountain after he stole a boat). The persuasive rawness of thought in each convinces me that the poets are deciding within the construction of the line, despite frustration, what they need to do with their art, and what these places have done for it. Montale writes:

> If only I could force
> some fragment of your ecstasy
> into this clumsy music of mine;
> had I the talent to match your voices
> with my stammering speech —
> I who once dreamed of acquiring
> those salt sea words of yours
> where nature fuses with art —
> and with your vast language proclaim the sadness
> of an aging boy who shouldn't have learned how to think.

"Mediterraneo" is a sequence of almost epistolary dramatic monologues, addressed to the paternal sea, the recipient of Montale's churning thoughts and images. Wordsworth turns to the River Derwent, which ran, as the poem explains, in back of his childhood house at Cockermouth. What is unmistakable in the lyric prayers of both poets is a cathartic energy that describes while it addresses; evoking and invoking these bodies of water and their surroundings in memory ultimately bring the poets closer to themselves, their ambitions for their art. In his poem "End of Childhood," Montale seems less satisfied with the ambiguities and acknowledges the chore of remembering (which in *The Prelude* seems so facile, so fluent). Of being a child-denizen of the Ligurian coast, he writes:

> We rarely crossed the nearest ridges
> of those peaks; even now our memory, exhausted,
> lacks the courage to cross them . . . .
>
> But we came back home from those mountain paths.
> For us they became a flickering
> alternation of strange realities,
> but governed by an elusive rhythm.
> Each instant, burning
> into future instants, left no trace.
> Just being alive was adventure, fresh, too fresh,
> hour by hour, and the heart racing, always faster.
> There were no rules,
> no measure, no sure way
> of dividing joy from sadness.

Reconciling or appreciating in our memories the tensions between "beauty and fear" or "joy and sadness" can be as difficult as contending with those skirmishes between confession and complaint, elegy and anthem, or grief and grievance (a paring I steal happily from a conversation I had with Dave Smith). Especially when it comes to physical environments, and even more so when we're thinking about a time when time didn't matter. Montale's longing for oblivion, escape, or passage to another plane of being is more elusive than Wordsworth's faith in the paradoxically restorative value of fear or trauma and how they are transformed in imagination over time (the fulcrum of all of his great works). Though both poets suggest that memories are not immune to the ravages of subsequent experiences, something in their essence — simultaneously melancholic and ecstatic — endures to enhance their aspirations as artists. As I committed myself to "Peconic," I remember being seduced by the glimmer of this redemption in one of Montale's earliest poems, "Seacoasts" ("Riviere"), with which he chose to conclude *Cuttlefish Bones*:

> Today I come home to you
> a stronger man (or I deceive myself), although
> my heart almost melts in memories, happy
> but also bitter. Sad soul of my past,
> and you, fresh purpose summoning me now.

Peconic

The 1935 Thorndike-Century Junior Dictionary, intended for children between the ages of ten and fifteen — the age when children start to relish exploring by themselves — defines land-scape as "a view of the land" and "picture showing a land scene," but is silent about sea-scape, perhaps with good reason.

— *John R. Stilgoe*

I.
Driftwood pylons driven
into bay's floor, with mesh
stretched between. Seaweed
tatters at waterline, rescue
notes ignored, forgotten.
We dreamt of throes, the entangled
collected while we slept.

II.
The word *tentacle* wrapped us
in the thriving water.
Fish with wings and legs,
stilettos, mythic spurs.
We swam with sneakers. Once
you trod the horseshoe crab
you'd never grow again.

III.
Jeans hardened on the line
like garments of the drowned.
Salt corroded zippers
and turned the rivets green.
Pockets bulged with violet
shells, worthless (currency,
we'd heard, before our time).

IV.
Oracle of damp recesses,
the outdoor shower's stubborn,
voyeuristic toad, married
to the leaking copper. Hot
wind across the threshold
from burnt lawn, despite her
auguries of mold and shame.

V.
Poacher's remnants beneath
the red question: poison
ivy wrapping scrub oak.
Like quotations, deer legs
severed in sand. Held,
the hooves replaced the hands
beyond my sleeves. My own.

VI.
Black men, orange rental
boats, their dangerous voyage
through the locks to either
white-capped bay. Marooned
on concrete, we pierced our fingers
on barbs of shrimp, released
bails to punish the bait.

VII.
Wasteland of broken razor
clams when the tide was out,
the lagoon was ruled by blue claws
when water flushed back through.
Reproached by the spit's swollen,
shimmering eye, we waded
behind our nets' shadows.

VIII.
Blowfish in kitchen sink
inside-out. The glistening
bladder, burst with knife-
blade: what, once inflated,
deflected predators' jaws.
Hooked, it rose to surface.
We didn't have to reel.

IX.
Anchored in our inlet,
the dredge a Trojan horse
against the dawn. By noon,
derrick and scoop were clearing
sand, deepening the channel
for bigger keels and wakes,
shark fins nailed to piers.

≋

Memory cups what never
lives again. We knew
our place by necks, enclosing
bluffs, the brittle casings
around the dead; opened,
miniature whelk poured out,
the future washed to shore.

THE RETREATS

O little lost Bohemias of the suburbs!

— *Donald Justice*

Between attention and attention

— *W. H. Auden*

The bewilderment, the despair, arise from fear
that nothing "could e'er be caught" from these new
surroundings.

— *W. Jackson Bate*

CHILMARK

The first time I deliberately traveled to a place to write was more than thirty years ago. I borrowed a friend's outbuilding on Martha's Vineyard. It was an act of desperation, an attempt to claim some sort of writing life just before the birth of my first child. Will, the owner, was a woodworker, an artist whose specialty was building custom mahogany window frames for celebrities in Manhattan (Paul Simon, David Letterman). With its appointments, that intimate vertical space was a gem: integrated bunk and desk, tiny porch, patinaed brass screens. A potential wellspring of productivity, solitude, and silence, interrupted only by Will or his wife, Kathleen, calling me in for drinks or coffee. Kathleen's father had written a definitive work on P.B. Shelley, and I took this as augury, consecration. For the occasion, I had even bought a new computer, a Mac Plus that I unboxed excitedly and learned to use as a cold, light November rain sifted through the oaks. For strolls, Lucy Vincent Beach was my go-to. I bought a copy of Lowry's *Under the Volcano* at the bookstore in Edgartown and read it while reveling in the ceremony of lighting and maintaining a woodstove. On the bookshelf in front of me right now is a flat, black oval stone I pocketed on one of those beach forays. The magazine that published the one poem I wrote that weekend disappeared along with the floppy disk to which it was saved.

PETERBOROUGH

My fellowship at the MacDowell Colony was abbreviated by a horrific storm. Light snow became freezing rain that ravaged the compound and took the town of Peterborough (and a sizeable portion of the state of New Hampshire) off the grid for over a month. One writer's car, windows blown out, roof compressed against its dash, was crimped like a trodden shoebox by a giant oak branch. As the December storm gathered strength throughout the night, I listened to the trees buckle under the weight of accumulating ice, boughs snapping with rifle-shot clarity, trunks bending then exploding like artillery. I didn't sleep at all, certain that my own cottage would be pile-driven. It was apocalyptic. When it turned to rain, I slid off the road trying to drive my own (brand-new) car to higher ground. I sat there paralyzed, watching the water in the culvert climbing above the doorjamb. By the time I leapt out the window, the swollen brook was thigh-deep. After slogging to shore, I went back to my cabin for dry clothes, then spent the day waiting nervously for the overwhelmed grounds crew to rescue the vehicle.

Because I lived within striking distance, in the eastern part of the state, I left three days before my allotted residency was up. Once I got home, I took a hot shower, then instead of returning to my manuscript to work, drove straight back to deliver a case of IPA to the guys who'd winched me out.

San Diego

The place I rented in Ocean Beach, a hip garage apartment, was like a treehouse at the top of a spiral staircase. But this was only after I'd lost three thousand dollars on Craig's List for a fraud in Hillcrest, which actually existed but wasn't for rent. I sat like a bewildered vagrant among the dried leaves on the front porch for more than an hour, trying to call the "realtor." Finally, a young man, the jittery housecleaner, his vacuum stalled in the hallway in back of him, emerged and asked me politely what I was doing there. Back on the sidewalk, pacing, I called my wife in New Hampshire. Though pissed off, she soon secured the funky hovel in OB through her own reliable channels on Airbnb. She felt sorry for me, that a chunk of my sabbatical would be squandered because of impatience, gullibility, and naïveté. Sheepish but conservatively buoyant, I drove through Point Loma over to the new place on Santa Cruz Avenue but decided to check the surf at Sunset Cliffs on the way. The winter swell looked promising: gray and glassy, not many people in, the tide backing out. I had my board and wetsuit in the back of the rental SUV, so I went in for a few hours, snagged some clean, chest-high peelers, and felt much better, my head sluiced of the shame of being swindled. It was a reasonably productive month, but every morning was torture, my four hours of writing invaded by thoughts of waves I might be missing, or the anticipation of pints and a game of pool with my son and his friends at the Catalina Lounge.

BRIDGTON

The main building at Fifth House was a converted early-twentieth-century hunting lodge, And I rented the compound's sole independent cottage a few hundred yards away, perched regally in the upper corner of an overgrown pasture. Far from the other writers, I drank scotch at twilight on the wraparound porch, had nightly staring contests with deer and one swaggering fisher cat. There was a gorgeous spring-fed pond just down the road.

Unlike the classic tannin-steeped, amber waters of many Maine lakes, Adams Pond was luminous, translucent green. It was late June, and soon I was strapping my canoe to the roof of my car, sneaking over in the afternoons of hotter days for a swim out in the deep spot beyond the lily pads. Soon I was driving down there early evenings, too, to fly fish, and discovered that it was loaded with sizeable smallmouth bass. In one shady cove at the southwestern corner, there were a few large maples that had keeled over into the pond the previous winter, visible beneath ten feet of black, spooky water. It was here that the beefier fish hid, lurking beneath submerged trunks or hovering in branches velvety with pondweed, rocketing out like predatory, wingless birds as my olive woolly bugger streamer coaxed them from their dark hangars.

ASHDOD

My in-laws' modest early-nineteenth-century house is like the mothership at anchor on the driveway's canal, while the bunkhouse bobs precariously near the wild currents of the far field, white pines, deer, wild turkey, and coyotes beyond. No one in my wife's family can agree on the shack's origins. Some claim to remember the bunkhouse arriving on a flatbed trailer from the lumberyard, prefab. Others say it was a repurposed chicken coop, already standing when they bought the place in the late '60s. But no one denies that it became a sanctuary for my wife, her sisters, and their neighborhood friends to experiment with booze, cigarettes, and weed. It was the hideout where our own kids famously sequestered themselves for downing a fifth of Grey Goose they'd stolen from the kitchen. One wall socket, no plumbing, it's where my wife and I spend summer when we're not teaching. And it's where I try to get

some writing done. The carpenter who renovated
it took great pains to salvage or leave intact the
ceiling's dark, stained wood, the knots of which
I study like clouds every morning before I get out
of bed, listening to the sirens of male cardinals,
squirrels brawling across the roof. There's an old
drop-leaf table I use as a desk out back to which
I wander with coffee every morning after
breakfast in the main house. Sometimes, I read
in the rotting Adirondack chair I've positioned
carefully in one corner of the meadow, at the foot
of a meandering path my father-in-law
mowed through it. These are the hinterlands
of a town being obliterated by money, the
Duxbury with which people are most familiar
(aka "Deluxe-bury") back across Route 3, exclusive
and smug on the northwestern rim of Cape Cod
Bay.

Pretending I'm not in the suburbs while keeping my elbows out of the bird shit on the arm rests,
I imagine Rilke pacing the parapets of castle Duino.
The Princess, his benefactor, is out of town. No
response from his Angels all day. Hand to his brow,
he surveys the cliffs, the ocean, all that southern
light funneled into the Gulf of Trieste, the Adriatic
searing, accusatory, and luxurious. Is it cocktail
hour yet?

El Dorado

In the final shot of Herzog's *Aguirre, Wrath
of God,* Klaus Kinski, who plays the titular
demented conquistador on a doomed expedition,
is standing on a disintegrating raft as it drifts

down the Amazon. Planted in his iconic slouch as the jungle and wide river spin around him, he is pretty much the sole survivor. A seething knot of squirrel monkeys has boarded the craft, swarming from one edge to the other, a twitching pool of ochre fur and black muzzles around Kinski's legs, some of them abandoning ship, leaping like fleas from a dog's back to swim in a panic for the shore. Once you see it, you never forget it. Embedded in the actor's haunted face are genuine layers of existential torment, ambition thwarted, the wilderness's reflected indifference. I can't decide whether I'm disappointed or intrigued by the anachronistic, postmodern wake of the cinematographer's boat as it circles Aguirre's raft in an effort to capture the character's vortical disorientation. Look carefully, you'll see it: physical evidence, the unintended signature of the maker, a brown wave churned by an outboard engine. I imagine Herzog would have deployed a drone if they'd been around in the early '70s, a tool that would have easily sanitized his directorial intentions, erased his presence. We have to admire the old-school, handcrafted genius. Even more impressive is Kinski's ability to ignore what's happening around him for the sake of his art—those monkeys, that whine of the circling outboard and its anxious camera crew—as he disappears into character, working, just before the wake reaches him.

PART III

BLAENAVON

We thought it was just going to be a tour of the defunct coal mine's above-ground facility, which was already troubling enough. The winding wheels and framework for the conveyor system at the pit head were like the superstructure of an abandoned carnival, like the one I'd read about near Chernobyl. Retired earth-eating equipment had been hauled out to the persistent drizzle of the surface world, strewn in state across the healing landscape, a disfigured Cadillac Ranch radiating from the village-like cluster of grim stone buildings and low white barns. An occasional bird touched down nervously on some rusting apparatus, but there was little evidence of life or sound other than the hum of the raw westerly flowing from the Irish Sea across the Brecon Beacons.

This was Wales, but it felt a little like the preserved battlefields we had recently visited in France, replete with their collapsed bunkers, depressions from artillery explosions softened by a century and grass. But here there were no

prohibitive fences, no signs warning of unex-
ploded ordnance. This was a place where people had worked instead of deliberately murder-
ing each other, after all. Where functional albeit
diabolical metal became a curiosity, a monument, after its operator dismounted and walked
away into a changed world. Out there in the
rocky meadow adjacent to the mine, I could
actually place my palm on the blunt teeth of a
particularly rapacious-looking gang of toothed
circular blades, a gesture akin to petting the
maw of a block-and-tackled trophy shark.
Actually, it reminded me more of the habit
some people have of stroking the rivets of a jet's
fuselage while stepping through the hatchway
into the cabin, before the attendant secures the
door, clamping the lever into place.

It was summer. We were on the last leg of an
aesthetically challenging tour of the World War I
trail, but also the key sites of the Industrial
Revolution. My wife, a history teacher, had
received a grant from her school to do some
research. I was tagging along as chauffeur and
underprepared literary consultant on a gritty
pilgrimage that had begun in the foothills of
Des Vosges near France's border with Germany.
Propelled by a shuddering, tiny Renault across
the superheated agricultural interior (sewing
machine for an engine, no AC), we swung up
to Belgium, to Ypres and Paschendael, then
exited Europe through the labyrinth of temporary chain-link barricades surrounding the
refugee camps in Calais. It was the year when

the ferry workers were in some sort of dispute, and lorries intending to haul freight across to the UK were backed up for hours on the highways outside the port. Every day there was a new story of African immigrants found either clinging to the undercarriage of trucks or apprehended somewhere in the tunnel beneath the English Channel, heroically trying to get there on foot.

We arrived in central Wales having driven across and up from Dover (in a safer rental), hitting Dorset and Hardy Country on the way: the tourist's privilege of trading shell craters, barbed wire, and trenches for literary sentimentality, an agrarian coast, sublime footpaths. For my wife, there was also an aspect of personal responsibility in being here: her people, some of them miners, had left Wales in the nineteenth century for the coal region of Pennsylvania, the Wyoming Valley. It stood to reason that before flying back home to Boston, we were obligated to check out The Big Pit in Blaenavon (pronounced Blye-NAH-von, though I heard BLEN-iffin, too). This was the destination about which I was least excited and had even begun to dread, as the summer tapered down to it. It was that time of year when my happiness depended, more acutely than ever, on my proximity to water, namely, the ocean. We had just driven up from Devon along the coast: a week of long hikes along cliffs, gorging ourselves on the panoramic Atlantic, through landscapes that hadn't been traumatized. Though, I suppose centuries of grazing deliver their own patient violence. Now in the center of Wales, I was on the verge of whining, skeptical about a landlocked, postindustrial site inspiring the same gravitas as Vimy Ridge or Verdun.

We stood at a balcony and gazed out over the empty, echoing locker bays, the showers where I imagined black rivulets snaking down pale bodies toward drains. We were at the Big Pit at a unique historical juncture; some of the men who were giving tours of the place were among its last miners. Initiated in 1880, the colliery thrived through World War I and into the 1920s before spiraling into decline and shutting down permanently in the 1980s, though talk of its becoming a museum had begun in the early 1970s. Some of the mine's surrounding buildings had been refurbished with specific exhibits, others preserved, intact. After browsing photos and plaques in one wing, we found ourselves in a waiting room like a gate at a municipal airport. I assumed it was a hiatus before the next glass-encased display of tools or time-encapsulated chamber. Above, a video display repeated its concise summary of the risks of being in a mine. Then a stocky, boisterously polite older gent appeared in the doorway and with a thick Welsh accent invited us to step through.

They were ready for us now, he said. As our group descended the metal stairs from the slick, modern room into a more austere warehouse-sized space, I noticed the orderly piles of helmets arrayed on a long table with headlamps and web belts. And also, those canteen-like canisters I recognized from the video as *re-breathers*. It was quaintly haunting, I thought, this deliberate re-creation, but then I began to realize what was afoot and wondered how I had missed it. When we were told that no cell phones and cameras would be allowed because of batteries, sparks, and so on, it set in. A bag was passed around; we could retrieve our belongings later. The helmet on my head, its lamp, and the belt I was cinching around my waist were not for dress-up.

I had never been in an elevator without walls; the utilitarian ideal: little more than a floor under the feet. When you're in a cage and not encased in the comfort of a well-lit, brushed-steel, or cherry-paneled cubicle, you can watch the dark, damp walls of the shaft passing by until the light disappears altogether. You notice the rattling, clacking of metal on metal, the throb of tension in the cables that for every other elevator ride of your life had always been muted. The over-powering smell of the earth itself is new, too, a smell of stone, more enigmatic and timeless than the cool, sanitary concrete of a new basement, or a subway tunnel's urban breath. Perhaps I was daydreaming when the claustrophobes had been warned and prudently self-ejected from the expedition, but soon our crew was at the bottom of the shaft, debarking the crude elevator.

At some point, creeping behind our guide along a particularly low tunnel, I realized I was the laggard in our single file. Three hundred feet might not seem such an adventurous depth, but then, isn't the idea of six feet of earth overhead enough to stoke a pulse of anxiety in your temples? People weren't saying much, but from their hushed and unconvincingly relaxed British quips, I figured my wife and I were the only Americans. Told to mind our heads, we walked with knees bent. I passed timbers (yes, *timbers*) with restraint, reluctant to extend a steadying hand for fear of knocking one out of position and bringing the place down.

When I was about nine or ten, a man in our neighborhood on Long Island used to set up a 16mm projector on the beach, its accompanying screen hoisted near the tideline so that the community could watch a film against the backdrop of the bay at night. These were mostly horror movies, made more bearable by the sea. We endured jolts of cheap fear in our army blankets while an outboard with running lights slapped across the waves behind the crazed eyes of Vincent Price or Peter Lorre. It was often hard to concentrate out there, but one movie — without either of those icons — defied the distractions of the moon, gnats, rogue firecrackers, or the orgiastic bonfire party of teenagers over the next dune. *Premature Burial* (1962) was based on Poe's short story of the same title. For years, I couldn't shake the memory of Ray Milland's character Guy Carell waking from his cataleptic state to find he'd been buried alive. It stuck with me through junior high.

Inevitably, my dread mellowed to bemused denial, then disdain for my former self, especially when *Aliens* supplanted woodenly acted, gothic camp with genuine horror. I hadn't thought about *Premature Burial* for decades. Until Blaenavon.

It was a place that chided memory, demanded comparison. Trying to picture the scene of all those people and animals toiling down there over the centuries was a mythologist's exercise: to restore with one's imagination the torture-chamber diorama of a cathedral tympanum come to life. Tolkien had it right, too, his Orcs swarming in Mordor, fabricating their war tools inside a mountain's cavernous bowels. But this coal mine was too cramped for that. I was reaching for anything to explain what I was feeling down there . . . anything except for what was actually happening. Gaining traction was the solipsistic metaphor of my own family situation: the suffocating prison of unrealistic expectation to which my mother and sisters had relegated me after my father died almost two decades ago. It was pathetic. Descents of any sort — personal, historic, and artistic — compel us to swerve from the literal. Although our visit to Wales was during Obama's second term, it now also seems like an oracular vision of our journey into some underworld of national identity just around the bend with Donald Trump.

The personal essay often demands that the writer strive for parallelism, to construct in the ether of the creative process a reliable suspension bridge from the immediate or interior to the universal, or from the cosmic to the intensely human. After sorting through all of my figurative shenanigans, recalling that excursion of a few summers ago can do nothing but underscore its horrible and concrete essence. The intensity of confinement was at once excruciatingly personal and self-obliterating. I was with other people, within a few inches of my wife; we could have held hands. Yet I'd never felt more helplessly isolated, a marooned, living consciousness with memory and emotion intact, but a body that wasn't going to do me any good. We had just obeyed our guide's request for silence and to kill our lights so that we might appreciate the real darkness, the situation that miners endured day after day, year after year. My senses' sleight of hand was working overtime, my brain fighting to transcend what was overhead — the weight that might be space, now that I couldn't see it. It was almost unbearable. I was too aware of what was up there on the other side of that dense, undeniable barrier. As the seconds passed, though, I remembered that indeed I was squatting over a puddle in a tunnel. And, yes, that faint sound of groundwater trickling down the walls I also couldn't see was a message from the surface world, a liquid rope of existential rescue. It had been rain once, plummeting from thousands of feet to make the hills green.

Blaenavon, a World Heritage Site, is the ossified heart of the Industrial Revolution, a principal source of coal for the furnaces that churned out the metal for weapons that would kill nearly twenty million soldiers and civilians in World War I. By 1918, the mine employed about a thousand people, so one can only imagine the undocumented psychological casualties beyond the deaths due to regularly occurring accidents (at least a hundred before the end of the nineteenth century). Children were down here too, of course, hoisted back to starlight after a day of having their wrists tethered to the knobs of tunnel doors so that they couldn't wander off. Their job was simple: to wait in the darkness, anticipating the approach of tool clatter and hooves in the glow of a swinging lantern. Like human valves, their operation of the doors prevented gasses from traveling from chamber to chamber. Explosions could be confined. I imagined them sliding from their chairs, following the string to the door handle, swinging the passage open, watching a horse's flank, the benediction of its black eyes, then yanking it shut, to sit back down and wait again in the wordless dark. As we were at that very moment. All mining tours are exercises in empathy.

I still get emails from the Lion Inn, the "best" hotel in Blaenavon, where we stayed for two nights. Though we were the only guests, the local population seemed well represented in the inn's restaurant: an eightieth birthday party (had the star of the show been a miner?); a rambunctious, loud girls' night out; a young couple not making eye contact, chugging white wine, prodding their shared shepherd's pie; a few smokers cradling pints outside on the sidewalk. Something keeps me from relegating those ads and missives to the spam box, but it's not the announcement for a bangers-and-mash special, the advertised two-for-one cocktails, the men's a cappella group performing on Saturday night, or the promise of a new brewery opening in town. I can't call it nostalgia. I'll probably never go back there again. Perhaps it's the weekly reassurance that normal, modern lives go on despite the dead honeycomb/ant farm a few hundred feet below, where I had hunkered, confused, pretending not to be a terrified tourist for an hour or so.

When I open those emails, I think of the beefy, tattooed guys we bantered with after the mine tour at another pub, the Queen Victoria, across town. One of them—a ubiquitous *Jones,* of course—offered my wife his barstool, which initiated a conversation and the public scanning of her family names: *Evans, Howell.* While their wives and children, familiar with the routine, smirked from a booth in the corner, the men boasted and argued melodramatically, one bellowing, "No! *I'm* the last miner of Blaenavon!" Though he was barely old enough to have been born before the mine shut down. I admired their blasphemy and indiscretion, maintaining the joke as a kindhearted mockery of local folklore as they intermittently checked their phones. Among them: a car mechanic, a builder, a guy who fixed computers, and a website designer.

The day before, out walking, we had asked

a kid where the town's memorial to the Great War was. He said he was pretty sure they didn't have one. They *did,* and we found it by accident after walking on a few blocks. It was a clock tower, a modest cenotaph of stone and bronze about twelve feet high that also listed the men and women killed in the following World War, Korea, and The Troubles. The impassive time-piece, set on a carefully landscaped floral slope behind an iron fence, stood cold as a giant drill parked in a field.

Sometimes I find myself back in the mine when I least expect it. At my desk in the fluctu-ating drudgery and reward of grading papers, revising a syllabus, or just standing at the window looking out at nothing, dreaming of exercise, of getting in the water, of better weather. Of doing something else. Or, even today, reading in the *New York Times* that Wales is considering a ban on the physical punishment of children.

During moments like these, I return to the stables underground, too, which really moved me. Especially after the tour guide told us that some of the pit ponies working in the mine were born, raised, and died there. Why do I feel so sorry for them? How could they crave what they never knew, living and perishing so far down? My headlamp beam had scanned their troughs then jerked up to the names ignited and rearing above the empty stalls, heroic, mythic, human: *Endeavor, Titan, Mike.*

BRIGHT SIZE LIFE

It's about there being no reason why music
can't be all together in one place.

— *Bill Frisell*

J ust south of Encinitas, where I'd been surfing
all day, I pulled off the 101 on to San Elijo
to grab some groceries. When I stepped
out of my car, the unmistakable textures of live
music were riding the punctual onshore, late-
afternoon breath of the Pacific. The tri-tips at this
particular butcher shop are coveted, and I could
already feel my wallet wincing at the pain
around the corner, clenching like a stubborn
mollusk in my back pocket, trying to tell me that
I had no business shopping there. But my appre-
hension abated as soon as I crossed the parking
lot and reached the store's entrance. The source
of the music—a trio of bass, drums, and guitar—
was set up to one side of the front door, the other
flanked by a few smoldering grills. They were
playing something I recognized immediately,
and which took me by surprise: a tune from Pat

Metheny's earliest album as a leader with ECM Records in the mid-'70s: *Bright Size Life.* And the rendition was better than competent. No threadbare, rudimentary "Satin Doll" or "Autumn Leaves" for these guys.

They were kids, couldn't have been out of high school, and were so focused on the music itself that they seemed to transcend the people striding past, who deployed the same polite smiles with which they refused the folks grilling free samples. I wondered if customers were just pretending not to listen, or if they really were that soulless.

Transfixed as I was, I became a little anxious about ruining the vibe, making the musicians too self-conscious, their performance intended to be atmospheric publicity, promotional background, after all, not a concert. Still, I stood there, detained by the restiveness of tangling myself in nostalgia and the fabric of musical interplay while itching for the number to end so I could say something to them. I believed that I had a responsibility to acknowledge their talent, to articulate my astonishment at their choice of cover tune, to celebrate our mutual respect for such an influential and melodic guitarist.

In the waning hour of a dinner party at least three decades ago, I had been chastised by one of my in-laws' friends for naïvely confessing my love for John Coltrane and Miles Davis. "What could you possibly know about the music of my youth?" he sneered, turning from his smudged glass of red wine. Embarrassed, angry, I didn't really engage the asshole, didn't defend myself (all eyes were turned to me), but instead mumbled something half-humorous, vaguely snarky about the absurdity of cordoning music, of certain generations claiming the genres or artists of certain epochs. I was in my early thirties, married with two small children, and had shed, I hope, any of the youthful pretension of my devotion to the genre that had begun while I was an undergraduate at UMass Amherst. My musical education there had been steroidal in its trajectory, fueled by a robust stream of live performances on campus, an established jazz culture in the demographic, and a thriving annual Black Musicians Conference. Max Roach was adjunct faculty. Archie Shepp lived nearby, and his son, Pavel, a percussionist, hung out regularly on my floor in the dorm. Kenny Barron and Buster Williams did a free concert in our dining hall. The school hosted one of Davis's first performances just after he'd returned to the stage at Kix Disco Bar in Boston, which ended his infamous five-year hiatus. I'd seen Metheny perform three times during the year he released *American Garage,* twice with his own group and one unannounced appearance with Sonny Rollins on the stage of the Academy of Music in Northampton just before his album *80/81* came out. I didn't mention any of this to my drunk accuser, who, maybe, wouldn't have known who Metheny was or that his influences actually included Davis, Coltrane,

Jim Hall, Wes Montgomery. But it certainly was a reckoning, an invitation to do some serious thinking that dug to the heart of how I felt about art and ownership — racially, generationally, culturally, tribally, etc. — and my deep belief in the capacity of music to cultivate organic (and sometimes invisible, uncelebrated) alliances among its creators and consumers.

I really can't recall a single throb of possessiveness or outrage in my internal response to that band in the parking lot. Maybe it's because, naïvely, I've always wanted to believe that music, especially jazz, is much bigger, more powerful than all of us, defies the paddocks we're always cordoning it into, the DMZs we try to establish between its provinces and neighboring countries. The pressure to toe the manipulated borders between appreciation and appropriation, entitlement and altruism, reeducation and revolution is puzzling. So often, I hear or read the word *community* slung recklessly about as a catchall and plea, but it's rarely borne out by the factions at whom it's directed. This is when I turn to music to get my bearings, to get to higher ground and closer to understanding that abused word. For me, it's embodied by the purity of humans playing solo in an ensemble while bandmates smile, nod. I confess I sometimes get choked up watching those silent conversations, reveries, reactions. Humans collaborating, regardless of socio-historical context, with a current of rhythm and chords between them, while we listen and watch.

My feeling this way is not for the sake of retreating to some ivory tower, but to get to the essence, to some spiritual ridge above the squabbling, the din. To get some perspective on figurative and nonfigurative harmony before the politics intrude. I'm thinking of John McLaughlin's ongoing journeys with Zakir Hussain and the evolving iterations of Shakti, begun in the '70s, or Ry Cooder's collaborations with Vishwa Mohan Bhatt, and also with Ali Farka Touré on *Talking Timbuktu*.

Certainly, music can be political, powerfully hardwired for protest, emblematic of hardship, deliberately investigating or calling out oppression. Consider Roach's own fusion of civil rights and jazz with *We Insist!: The Freedom Now Suites*. Neither do the narratives of powerful documentaries like *Standing in the Shadows of Motown*, *Fifty Feet from Stardom*, and especially *Summer of Soul* (Nina Simone!) ignore racial, economic, or cultural strife and marginalization; they confront musical events, trends, and phenomena with sociological acuity and poignancy. Like Marvin Gaye's album *What's Going On*, they are nearly inseparable from their times, the intentions (and lyrics) of the musicians; they aren't the music itself. But not all music is activism necessarily, especially instrumental improvisation, though it might seem so by its collaborative interracial or intergenerational example, the dialogue between its cultural and ethnic derivations, its vibrant cross-pollination. In this realm, Rhiannon Giddens's example is the paradigm, her reexamining origins by demolishing flawed conceptions about country or folk music, her diplomatic correction of a nation's prevailing assumptions about genre. We sometimes need somebody to remind or teach us about the journey a particular musical style endured before it even had a name.

Covering and interpreting popular music, reinventing standards, breathing new life into chestnuts, paying homage—all of these approaches and impulses seem to be adrift in the same forces that, thankfully, protect and transform artistic expression. Even so, I imagine it's getting harder for musicians— because they're artists—to dust off the cliché that *there are no rules,* especially in this age of protean mores, overnight demands, potential trigger-finger evisceration on social media. The rule breakers, to me, are the ones who stand out by changing or ignoring the game, the guidelines for borrowing, the trends, prescriptions, and orthodoxies—whether deliberately or unconsciously—and sometimes getting in trouble for doing so. The Next Thing—in any form that it takes—can be as accidental or contrived, as commercially propelled or as ideologically dogmatic as it deems itself to be, but once it's out there in the currents of human creativity and consumption, interpreted or repurposed by the grist of artistic risk and, yes, history (or forgotten completely), it's like an animal returned to the wild, an animal fording a river teeming with piranhas.

Exactly forty years after the release of *Bright Size Life*, here was a new generation deep inside one of Metheny's tunes in a cooling Southern California parking lot with an audience of only a few despondent gulls and preoccupied affluent shoppers bent on their tasks. And here I was, trying to imagine what drove these young musicians to learn and interpret the tune. Was it something they discovered on their own, or had a hip parent or music teacher turned them on to it? An older sibling? How did they really feel about entertaining the entitled, privileged clientele of this meat boutique? Who among them would stay with music, might give himself over to it into adulthood? Did they even care that one patron hesitated because he was rapt, and that their playing had brought one of the chief obsessions of his life briefly into focus in such an unlikely place and moment?

An hour before this parking lot meditation, I had been making tough choices about which waves to paddle for, because I'd lost my leash before launching. The board—a custom, zoomy planing hull—was borrowed. Not the first time I've been undone by impatience. The same reason you don't do a safety check on a jet as its nose is lifting from the runway. I'd done the same sort of thing with my sailboat, figuring out that I hadn't inserted the tiller in the rudder brackets before I'd cast off the mooring line with no way to steer. Just before I'd remembered to secure the leash to my board and ankle, a big set came through, swirled around my knees, and sucked that seven-foot plastic cord right out to sea. Not that a leash is as essential as a rudder, but this put me on edge. At high tide there was no sand on the shore at this reef break, just boulders, an eroded asphalt ramp, so if I lost or dinged the board, there would be damage and reparations to address (humiliatingly, with my son).

What I loved about this spot, which was not the most popular or iconic break in the area, was the accommodating dynamic in the lineup. I wasn't a local, so I tried to be in tune to the five or six other people in the water, to make sure I wasn't dropping in, hogging anything. All of this tempered by being supercautious committing to anything that was going to close out and divorce me from my untethered loaner. I'd seen a few of these surfers here before, especially an older guy in his late seventies, possibly early eighties, whose patient, slow-motion paddling seemed to govern everyone's pace. He could barely arch his back or lift his head, but facedown an inch from the deck he was in the game. Whether he was making his way back out to the lineup, positioning himself, or stroking that aircraft-carrier-of-a-log into a wave, it was always with the same sea turtle–esque delicacy. He got very few waves, but when he did, returned each time with a broad smile, eyes blinking with the sting of the ocean. I imagined we were all secretly rooting for him. Among the other people out there was a thirtysomething stylist on a chubby twin-fin fish, whose precision, speed, and grace were excruciatingly enviable, void of any anxiety or frenetic ambition. All of it reinforced by his *sprezzatura* and the unpretentious encouragement of his presence, authenticity of his good will. He could have had three times the waves, could have owned the place, but instead, between skatey arcs, left us some space as a deft conversationalist might at a dinner table, as someone who listens.

And yet none of us had said anything to each other. We do this all the time: assume we have a certain temporary demographic dialed in, have distinguished insiders from outsiders. It's a reflexive behavior, decoding individuals because we've been observing each other's actions, equipment, age, or *choices*. Like surfing without a leash, which might be either a public declaration of old-school confidence or just plain irresponsible, depending on the conditions and the population density of the session.

In the squinty contentment of postsurf exhaustion, I shifted my weight, my big toe throbbing because I'd banged it on a clumsy, rushed pop-up. I listened for a few minutes, through the band's cycle of solos. Just after the drummer did his thing, and they were returning confidently to the melody for the last time, I turned reluctantly, mopped with a sweatshirt sleeve the released reservoir of seawater draining over my lip, and walked into the store to get my steak. It was not easy climbing back into my silo, to abandon the diminished fizz of the cymbal or the guitarist's evaporating harmonic with neither a head nod, a knowing smirk, ingratiating body language, nor any attempt to tell them explicitly how fiercely I'd been grabbing on to this fragile thing between us, which had possessed and transported us perhaps, in similar but necessarily separate ways.

SANCTUARY

arden Hill is a dead-end road, amputated unapologetically by water or mud, depending on the tide, its demise defined by a haphazard cobble ramp, spartina, a few weedy boulders. You might mistake it for a private road because it cuts through the Sisters of St. Margaret property and past the long driveways of several invisible houses on its way down to Duxbury Bay. The convent, which dominates the north side of the road, is recognizably old-school, unmanicured. At low tide you can saunter out from the landing onto the flats with a rake and have your metal basket brimming with quahogs and/or steamers in less than thirty minutes. If you're approaching by boat, you'll appreciate the inscrutable slope of St. Margaret's as an earthly miracle, an oasis of sorts; there are very few scraggly, sprawling, naturally burnt-out lawns with mature trees overlooking the water in this town. Newer baronial villas with disingenuous accessories of northeast coastal charm are the norm (e.g., the tidy crescent of empty Adirondack chairs), along with sprinkler systems and the attendant subtle green tartan of intentional mowing patterns.

You have to admire the Patriarchy's snagging this gem of a swath. Had their acumen and cynicism extended to the realm of insurance, anticipating a time when they could sell off a parcel to stem the legal hemorrhaging of their brethren's foibles, all that complicit cruelty visited on the flock north of here in Boston and environs? The ensconced Sisters must have some idea that their retreat, this shellfish Shangri-La might be perpetually in the balances, slated for some whittling when the veil — or cassock, rather — is torn asunder again. A few years ago the town acquired a considerable patch of the church's property where the road begins at Washington Street and converted it to a green — a park for events like picnics and music festivals. A sudden boost of cash might explain the impeccable maintenance of the convent's rustic cedar-shingled compound, which looks better than ever. More like an exclusive artists' colony than a nunnery, though the central chapel gives it away. There's tasteful new signage identifying the buildings (St. Marina's, Bertram), just as a well-endowed boarding school might tag its dorms and administrative structures. Before it reaches the convent, the road hooks abruptly and disappears behind that newly anointed public space, which is still a buffer between the nuns and the outside world. So it's difficult to discern whether Harden Hill is a road at all, or if it even continues after the park.

When I owned a smaller sailboat, I used to launch it from the steep ramp at Harden Hill, desperate to escape the traffic, the pressure of impatient queues—all those idling trucks with trailers up around the corner at the paved and maintained municipal landing. Sandwiched between the paternal watchfulness of the harbormaster's shack and the yacht club's putting green–quality grass skirt, not to mention its impenetrable social forcefield (don't be fooled by the Tudor bungalow coziness), Mattakeeset Court is an unforgiving, high-stakes waterfront mainstage. Does its being named after an inland tribe of the Massachuset Nation somehow make its annexation less insidious? At Harden Hill there was always plenty of room and no wristwatch-checking soul to evaluate or add stress to the process of inserting a boat into the bay. It is the same famous body of water traversed by the sanctuary-hungry separatist Calvinists who little by little, along with their followers and military escorts, commandeered the sanctuary of the Wampanoags, whom families across the entire country unintentionally eulogize every November. It's true that my own forbears, Dutchified former Brits who'd similarly bounced from Devon to religious tolerance in Leiden, then to New Amsterdam around the same time, had certainly whipped up their own intrepid wake of destruction that became Manhattan. But here, strangely, I was always alone, a privileged ghost temporarily set apart from the legacy of mayhem, grab, and occupation, the culture of taxpaying citizenship, transfer station and beach stickers, youth lacrosse. After some quick vehicle positioning in the convent's dependably deserted driveways, it was only a matter of moments before the rusty snorkel of the truck's tailpipe would be submerged, farting a few noxious bubbles, and the hull floated free of the trailer's stubborn rollers.

I haven't launched at Harden Hill for years. The boat I own now isn't that much heavier, but just long and wide enough to be too much for this overgrown, shrinking right-of-way. From the water it doesn't look like a landing anymore, and I suspect the residents prefer it this way. There would be very little room to deposit the dripping, empty trailer and temporarily snug my Tacoma without creating a hazard. No neutral sweet spot between Holy Ground and a tragically reduced shoulder on the southern side of the road, where recently arrived settlers have erected an unironic "stockade" fence. I believe the American prototype was invented in this town (see Mr. Standish). The palsied twitching of leftover, sun-bleached Independence Day flags might concur. The building on the other side of the fence is an imposing behemoth, a shit show of angles, bump-outs, dormers, and incongruous windows. Who was this slutty, ingratiating architect? This particular residence, I think, was at the vanguard of the trend that has firmly taken root, its current practitioners on Powder Point and Standish Shores exponentially more extravagant and resort-like as they raze and replace older homes.

If I tried to put my boat in the water now, someone would have to be there to stay with it after I stepped the mast and rigged the spars, so I could park the truck and trailer where they wouldn't be ticketed, towed, or stink-eyed by the ubiquitous, stoic Labradoodle walker. It's a challenge to imagine them ruminating wistfully, repentantly about their routed indigenous progenitors. Perhaps that's too harsh, because scudding up along the shore in my boat recently, I noticed that even the nuns' side of the street is laced with railings—a low, white, understated, almost gestural fence. But the message is the same, which I learned when I drove down there at sunset the other day to investigate (i.e., my staring match with the aforementioned security guard disguised in tights and tank). At intervals along the St. Margaret's fence: NO TRESPASSING signs, along with a direct request to *PLEASE RESPECT* [their] *PRIVACY*. That being said, the convent seems to have preserved for the general public's benefit a carefully measured, charitable space on the sandy shoulder, not quite big enough for two cars. Or maybe it's the stubborn vestige of visitors like myself, a snarky divot, a scar from the old days that scoffs at being absorbed.

On our walks around town, my wife and I chortle, mystified by people's impolite reluctance to acknowledge us. Having grown up here, she remembers a much more cordial place, so she tries to make eye contact as early as possible in our approach, giving fellow strollers a chance to discourage her disappointment, refute her exasperation. At the last possible second, when we're passing each other and they're still locked in tunnel-vision-zombie mode, she hails them, offers a hardy "Good morning!" A stealthy, benevolent assault. Trapped, startled, our counterparts offer obligatory nods or suspicious (not embarrassed) smirks. The pandemic seems to have emboldened them. Striding three abreast, they can hold up traffic on narrow roads, their disdain encompassing automobiles now, too.

The other day, as we were biking past Harden Hill's entrance, there were two nuns marching (hovering!) the sidewalk back from town. A rare and wonderful sighting, which brought to mind the last line of Richard Wilbur's poem "Love Calls Us to the Things of This World" (title derived from Augustine himself) and its tenuous resolution pivoting on an image of walking nuns, "keeping their difficult balance." The sky was clearing after a long stretch of tropical September rain, and summer seemed as if it might keep its traction for a few more fragile weeks. In their gray canvas frocks, amulets, and wimples, the nuns seemed like time-travelers in search of lodgings after a disbanded medieval pilgrimage rather than simple commuters heading back to the ranch from the grocery store. It is probable, however, that we seemed equally otherworldly in our lurid cycling attire: spandex, wraparound mirror sunglasses, neon shirts.

One of them looked up. The other had a cell-phone clamped to her ear. We smiled and waved as we whirred past. They neither acknowledged nor returned our greeting.

Perhaps it's a bold generalization, but recently I've found myself wondering if there's a direct correlation between such encounters and why it's getting harder each year to find an accommodating "public" landing. My favorite portals are being systematically conquered by these pockets of new houses, the concerted determination of their owners to fashion communities into gauntlets-to-be-run, quasi-fortifications that discourage the rest of us from seeing who they actually are. And from finding the water. It's so New England. I can only imagine the town's Dickensian archive of legal briefs, its muffled bickering about property owners' "deeded beach rights."

Heartening news that the local oyster company recently bought — from a scientific research company — a significant stretch in the vicinity. Waterfront that had once seemed off-limits and mysterious is suddenly open, transformed by strings of lights, laughter, tents, food trucks, picnic tables, the smell of woodsmoke. Commercial, yes, but at least more obliging to those who seek entry or are just curious. Paradoxically, the convent, too, in its polite, grudging way seems to offset the privatization of access, cultivating a more porous, unintentionally inclusive or more *secular* environment than most of the current town geography reflects.

It is, after all, a spiritual refuge not a trophy house. Homesick friends of ours who've moved to California often rent one of St. Margaret's vacated outbuildings in the off-season. (That foxy church administration again!) Even so, my worldview and tenure as a lapsed Catholic sabotage any silver lining I might be trying to stitch together here, including the trauma of a friend and former colleague who lost his brother to the church's circus of abuse in Massachusetts. Too much out there thwarting my attempts to whitewash the ravages and inheritances of Christian colonialism (both seventeenth-century and contemporary) in what I have come to understand as one of the sad epicenters of "American" history. Reminders abound, tone deafness rears. There's still a monument to Myles Standish: a massive a 116-ft. granite shaft with a fourteen-foot likeness of the murderous captain balanced at the top (which, I admit, is a handy marker when I'm sailing). A lot of people have plunked Black Lives Matter signs next to their steroidal hydrangeas, but there's still a decorative antique sign above what used to be Sweetser's, the defunct old store in Snug Harbor, that says English & West India Goods.

When my wife was a high schooler here in the '70s, Harden Hill was "Hard-On" Hill. Not just because of the phonetic shenanigans in which all hot-blooded adolescents indulge, but because it really was a popular destination for making out, among other romantic and chemical seductions. And before the near annihilation of native oak and pitch pine for a better view, before the NO PARKING EITHER SIDE signs (are they counterfeit?) proliferated like an invasive species on most of the streets that lead to the bay, before the arc lights of xenophobic embassies washed the shoreline with prison-camp clarity, it was also a place where my wife and I could skinny-dip. She assures me that we were not the first.

After our kids were in bed, and aunts, uncles, or grandparents had been passed the mantle of oversight, we'd head out across town, having triangulated the summer's warmest, clearest night and its highest tide. There was decadent, reliable darkness back then. The ocean-facing "big" beach was out of the question, discouraging our sorties with its built-in owl repellant: the blinding orange security light installed at the guardhouse. And it was "closed" at sunset, too — another traditional strategy for saving teens from themselves. Harden Hill is a public road, as I've said, but out of courtesy we still felt obligated to douse our headlights fifty yards from the target, gliding stealthily to a cereal-crunch stop where gravel and broken shells met the black water. And of course, there was still a subtly energizing vibe of naughtiness presiding over our exploits just below those subservient cottages, where, stripping down, we imagined the nuns turning restlessly in their stiff sheets. The glow of someone's lone reading lamp filtered through a fluttering scrim of low branches. St. Augustine's *Confessions*? *Vanity Fair* magazine?

Once we were immersed, it was only a spatter of stars, the moon's contracted yolk. A coy sky that couldn't compete with the ambient car dealership–like illumination enveloping most of the town these days. But on those nights, we marveled at the luxurious phosphorescent sleeves of dinoflagellates and ctenophores orbiting our limbs like fetal galaxies. We shivered, swam, our laughter low and sinister. I was terrified of being caught, anticipating a good pistol-whipping . . . smug, salty mugshots . . . our teaching careers excoriated on the Internet. My wife, though, was delighted by the prospect of the cops rolling in with a spotlight ("Bring it").

Maybe, in some subconscious fold, while relishing the invisibility of our intrusion and illicit proximity to prescribed Catholic goodness, we were already anxious about the nuns turning more deeply inward, the subsequent waves of usurping hordes, land-devouring sects. How might their behaviors, their evolving totems of ownership and prohibition manifest themselves in the coming decades? Certainly, we couldn't have predicted the swollen paramilitary police force that seems to earmark every pedestrian as a potential terrorist and every beach, parking lot, or intersection — and landing — as a potential Tiananmen or Kent State. One has only to observe the sophistication and diversity of the assault vehicles they pilot around town, sniffing out trouble or poised and predatorial in the shadows of the closed ice cream stand. We just wanted to swim, not to sacrifice goats.

To comfort myself, as we shivered and side-stroked, trod in place, or let our toes flirt with purchase on the oozy bottom, I developed the habit of picturing our sailboat. I knew it was out there somewhere in the night, tantalizingly close, just north in the adjacent nook, its mooring chain taut with the flood, stubby mast worrying like a metronome doing its best to keep up, to stay in time with the final beats and gestures of our furtive, naked dance.

CAT'S-PAW

O bleached mirrors! Oceans of the drowned!
— *Donald Justice*

Meteorological and nautical in essence, *cat's-paw* is a term I learned from my father when he first took me sailing in the late 1960s. Like *whitecap, chop,* or *glass,* it classifies an aspect of the water itself, in this case that velvety patch you might see brushing across the stillness, an indication of a transient breeze on an otherwise calm surface. At their best, cat's-paws can inject the pocket of your sail with a tease, a temporary boost right when you thought there was nothing around to keep you moving.

The lyrical inclinations of mariners have spawned some colorful language, and that terminology is irresistible when you're a child. As with the names of clouds, there's more romance in *mare's tail* and *thunderhead* than *cirrus uncinus* and *cumulonimbus.* Similarly, at sea you are less likely to be charmed by phrases like *Langmuir circulation* (the foamy parallel streaks of wind-driven foam). What's most significant is a cat's-paw's elusiveness, its unpredictable arrival, murky process, and passage. A wave not only has a soundtrack, but multiple, identifiable phases that precede its building and continue after its collapse, including the lingering, rushing, vestigial foam, and the extended commotion of a riptide if it joins forces with another retreating wave. And waves have so many structurally identifiable species. Cat's-paws, however, are not only silent but more like shadowy ophthalmological floaters across your field of vision, not sequenced physical events. They are like ideas in that they often amount to very little.

I watched *The Guns of Navarone* the other night, a 1961 World War II adventure based on a novel by Alistair MacLean. The pandemic has shunted some fresh voltage into my bad habit of watching too much television. Can we call it that anymore, now that once we turn it on we are empowered to make so many choices, not only what we watch, but whether to binge a whole season, to pause, now that the governor of the weekly episode has been removed. The tyrannies have evolved.

Sometimes I justify the indulgence by telling myself I'm screening a *film*, that I am cultivating, feeding my aesthetic. TV is art now, after all. Sometimes, though, I wonder if I'm headed down some dead-end, nostalgic alley watching an old movie like *Navarone*, trapped in a Kerouacian state of paralysis and avoidance. At least I do not live with my mother, I tell myself. *Navarone* was one of my father's favorite movies, so whenever it appeared in the Sunday paper's TV guide, our family's week was organized around it. The protagonists, Gregory Peck, Anthony Quinn, Anthony Quayle, and Irene Pappas (I learned she died last week), had seemed like good-natured bickering uncles and aunt to me. I probably hadn't seen it for at least forty-five years but immediately suspected or identified the details that had transfixed my twelve-year-old imagination: the shipwreck in a raging storm, the hollowed-out labyrinthine promontory with German doomsday cannon, the sado-peroxide Gestapo interrogator, the patriotic saboteurs rappelling down ocean cliff faces, the burly Greek sheepskin-clad partisans with machine guns. What seized me this time around, however, was a cat's-paw. Unmistakable in the foreground of an innocuous, transitional midfilm clip, riffling the lush blues and greens in the lee of a rocky cove. I was not prepared for that short scene to displace the real focus of the narrative: the trope of the heroes' boat embarking in the background.

That it had been filmed on location among the islands of the Aegean Sea had not meant much to me when I was younger. Being mesmerized by the image had little to do with my connection to the encompassing setting. I'd messed around in that part of the world for a few months in the early 1980s like so many other restless, affluent twentysomething nomads with backpacks. Staving off entrance into the inevitable professional maze after college and ricocheting between a few construction, painting, and retail jobs, I was beguiled by that landscape. But in terms of adventure, I was thinking Homer instead of *Navarone*. And truthfully, my companion and I were just as fixated on our quest for the next taverna and its shot of Ouzo or glass of retsina as we were in discovering a deserted headland where we could pitch a tent or score another swimming hole. Then, suddenly, there I was in front of my computer (watching TV), pausing, scrolling back, replaying that cat's-paw from a film released when I was one year old in Los Angeles and wouldn't see for another decade. But I knew I was recognizing something from my childhood that had broken free of its contextual prisons.

This extraneous image from a corny, melo-dramatic war movie got me thinking about art's ability to enshrine some glimpse of nature, to archive phenomena that have been duplicating themselves forever, that should all look the same, are universal to some degree. Poets, writers, photographers, visual artists, and filmmakers are up against absurd odds when it comes to this decision to include something that can deliver a moment from oblivion by isolating it from its anonymous role in a relentless system. Our noticing it is not just a ramification of a viewer's or reader's "personal connection," which can cheapen—if not ignore—the mystery. Although awareness might start by snagging some tendril of our memory or experience, our imagination can turn it into something new.

Clint Eastwood's 1971 psychological thriller *Play Misty for Me* is just as much a paean to the Monterey County coast as it is a suspenseful drama about a stalker and a tribute to lifestyle. Watching it, I never forget for a second that I'm in California. There's an unmistakable hint of seasonal blush and flame in the ice plant carpeting the dunes. Edenic cypress and redwood aren't just props. The aerial shots of churning ocean that inform the film's human discord are indelibly Pacific. All of these locally sourced ingredients meant something to the auteur. They are not a backdrop but instead coalesce into one of the story's most significant characters. Though I am a sucker for this and admire Eastwood's vision, the potential for a cat's-paw moment is diminished.

There's a lot working against the possibility of his images transcending Carmel, Big Sur, Monterey. Everything seems anchored firmly in *place.* And in *time,* too: the West Coast hipness of the early 1970s embedded in fashion, architecture, sex, not to mention Eastwood's braiding in live clips of Cannonball Adderley from the Monterey Jazz Festival—all conspire to limit imagination. The film is seductive, especially if you have a connection to the setting and era. But who knows whose decision it was to seize that moment in *Navarone,* if according lyricism the upper hand in an action movie was a decision at all? Whether it was Oswald Morris, the cinematographer, or the director, J. Lee Thompson, the cat's-paw cameo was probably an accident. But I still owe them a debt.

It's easy to convince ourselves that Odysseus himself, elbows on gunwale, daydreaming in the vicinity of the Sporades and Dodecanese archipelagos (where MacLean placed his fictional island), could have followed a cat's-paw twenty meters off the starboard bow, cruising through his wine-dark world. A fantasy I might have considered while on a ferry with wine-drenched, sunburned Danes on its way to Santorini. Unlike the land, the water is less mutable; even in the paradox of its own restlessness, it is more dedicated to repeating its own behaviors than retaining any evidence of our ever being there. So believing we are part of something (literary or oceanographic) so big, that we are somehow connected to a quasi-historical, mythical character seems like a shortcut. Though my appreciation has matured and deepened, I have always been drawn to Homer. First it was his witty hero, "the strategist." Now it is his characterization of water (in both its figurative and narrative embodiments) that makes my hair stand on end with its familiarity. And not because I am nostalgic for my own farewell party to adolescence in the Mediterranean. In her translation/ remix *Memorial*, poet Alice Oswald inverts the lens to make such descriptive moments the real stars of her treatment of the human dead in *The Iliad*. In the service of figures or images, grief and elegy are powerful engines. Perhaps this is what extends Homer's resonance beyond the confines of the Trojan War or a protagonist's efforts to return home from it. Clichés associated with the sea's vastness always seem to circle back to constant flux and, conversely, stasis, but also to erasure, indifference, inscrutability. Then why am I still inclined now and then to catch some trace of myself in it?

We are all familiar with that yearning for the earth to peel back beneath our feet and the barriers of time to fall away around us when we're standing in a landscape, too. Especially those trafficked by the ghosts of our artistic heroes, where terra firma has its enduring, named, fixed forms, its accumulations. Walcott's Pitons on St. Lucia, Cezanne's Mont Saint Victoire, Wordsworth's Helm Crag. What had we hoped to gain by comparing the rendered versions with reality? And also, when we stand agape in the crucibles of fiction: Penelope Fitzgerald's Suffolk marshes or urban Thames, Sebald's Corsica, East Anglia, and so forth. Why must we hike Hardy's chalky footpaths and not be satisfied with his sentences? The stages of actual historical events, however, seem tempered by damage, violence. Your imagination has a leg up among the shell craters and rebar at Pointe du Hoc, the trenches at Verdun, Vimy Ridge, or at Bolivar Heights near Harper's Ferry. These places are embossed, crackling.

How strange it must have been for production crews to set up in Europe, to film in the rubble in some cases, making movies like *Navarone* about the very war that had ravaged the land barely fifteen years before, whose possibly traumatized survivors might be standing in line at the bakery. Rossellini's *Germany Year Zero* was released in 1947. Watching such films can feel voyeuristic. The audience is caught between the unmistakable residue of horror amidst repair, the callousness of funeral baked meats and wedding tables. Between empathy and amnesia. Exploitation and tribute. The decision to build a dramatic production on that ready-made set is in itself an indication of moving on. Or pretending to. Carolyn Forché, extending Walter Benjamin's and Paul Klee's ideas with her poems in *The Angel of History*, dedicated that entire collection to this theme. Benjamin's and her premise being that time does little to diminish the carnage and destruction, which still find ways to permeate, to "pile up" against the present. Is it banal to ask questions like, "Was this tree here when . . . ?" Or "Did sunset catch the throats of swifts over this meadow in such a fashion back then?" As an audience — as tourists, voyeurs — we come to understand this to be our motivating impulse, our hope. To knock down walls in time, be transported.

Being *in irons* was another nautical description that I understood well as a child. It engaged the Robert Louis Stevenson/Alexander Dumas portion of my brain, the idea of the unjustly shackled hero, or some murderous scoundrel deservedly relegated to the brig. But it made practical, strategic sense, too. I know this better now. When your bow is pointing directly into the wind, the boat is locked in place, especially in a gale. In most circumstances, it's just harder to *fall away* so that you catch the breeze on either face of the sail. It flaps abrasively, hysterically, and never fails to ramp up the emotional tension on a boat, where sounds are usually more nuanced, mesmerizing. Putting yourself in irons deliberately can be a means of slamming on the brakes, pulling over into the breakdown lane to avoid a hazardous situation. It all depends on your desire for forward motion.

Cat's-paws can have a similar duality. What I've come to understand long after my father's death and his explanation of what they were as they appeared before us in real time a half-century ago, and long after I'd adapted his definition to my own experience on the water, is that the phrase can be ominous (a gust that indicates an approaching storm) or welcome. It is the latter toward which I've been leaning recently. Especially on those iconic, muggy July days in southeastern New England. The recognizable doldrums of midsummer with barely a puff, those hours when you're luffing, inching along in the viscous water. From your position in the center of the bay, the shore seems more distant in the haze, the heat inescapable. And you long to see the suggestion of a breeze out ahead because you trust that sooner or later one will nudge you out of being stalled, breathe some life into your slow progress, rescue you.

LOST RIVER

The East Branch of the Middlebury River ran behind the house where we stayed in the Green Mountains for a few summers during the '90s. The narrow, cobble-and-boulder-strewn chute, a violent juggernaut of snowmelt in spring, shrank to a cool, knee-deep stream in July and August. This made it a relatively safe place for our kids to explore or play in the hot-tub size buckets and effervescent pools below the meager falls and sections of faster water. As the fern-lined stream winds its way down the mountain, following, under-mining, and flirting with Route 125 through hemlock, balsam, river birch, and maple toward the Champlain Valley, its volume, depth, and speed increase. But in its higher altitudes closer to the source, where we lived, it is manageable, if not friendly. In it, our kids began to trust their ability to float, to judge the current that carried them to the next gravel bar, to that stand of wild lilies. They waded upstream stalking fingerling brook trout with a fly rod, stretched out with a book on the sun-warmed slabs, flipped rocks for salamanders and nymphs, and on occasion nearly got lost venturing too far from the established footpath along its banks.

We were spending part of our summers in Vermont back then because I was studying and working there. The distances between places a family needs to go dilate in a rural environment, so we did a lot of driving. By necessity, we depended heavily on mixtapes and CDs to get us through not only the three-hour car rides to and from New Hampshire but also our jaunts to town from campus to trailheads, to a restaurant in Burlington, or just to get soft-serve ice cream at the Mobil station in Rochester on the other side of the mountain. When the audio books had exhausted their attention, our son and daughters demanded music; the safety and peace of the vehicle's close quarters were directionally proportional to the choices we could all agree on.

All of them had outgrown Raffi at that point; my wife and I could stop pretending to be enthusiastic joining in on the excruciatingly metronomic "Baby Beluga," degrading even for green-minded children's music. Eliza, our youngest, bypassed the genre altogether. On the accelerated track by necessity, she understood that ballads about wayward infant whales or nursery rhymes set to melodies could never be part of the bargaining. The democracy of the car encouraged them to argue over which songs they wanted to hear, but when tensions seemed irreconcilable, they could at least reach consensus on genre or artist. Motown or bluegrass? Stevie

Wonder or Steely Dan? Beatles or Stones? Aretha or Doc? Being captive in our late-model Volvo wagon had churned them through my wife Gwen's and my own schools of appreciation and taste. They were being conditioned just as I had been when I was their age, dozing in the back seat during our seven-hour rides to Long Island, six to the Jersey Shore, or four to the Adirondacks from Massachusetts, listening to Herb Alpert and the Tijuana Brass, Tommy Dorsey, or the criminally outmoded and cringe-worthy Al Jolson. Strange, the lasting impact of that subtle tyranny. My nostalgia doesn't make sense. I can still dial in so many of those tunes and hum them instantly. Was it surrender, love, or did I really sort of enjoy that music?

As a young father, I was not allowed to listen to my esoteric jazz and fusion unless all other passengers were asleep — a state to which my selections would have led them eventually anyway, if not to outright rebellion. Shove in anything by Ralph Towner, or maybe Weather Report's *Mysterious Traveler*, or Pat Metheny's *First Circle*, or Freddie Hubbard's *Red Clay*, press play, buckle up, hit the road, and wait for the mutiny to simmer. However, the albums that were immune from dispute — from beginning to end — were from the Nitty Gritty Dirt Band's *Will the Circle Be Unbroken* project, volume 1 recorded in 1971. It is a masterpiece of collaborations between the band itself, iconic bluegrass or old-time icons, and contemporary country artists. The roster includes Maybelle Carter and family,

Johnny Cash, Doc Watson, Vassar Clements, Merle Travis, John Prine, and others. The song that elicited the most spirited and concentrated vocal participation from everyone in the car was "Lost River," from volume 2 released in 1989. We loved it because it wasn't Raffi, but also because the subject hooked each of us in a different way. The melody, increments of verses, and the chorus were addictive.

Whether because of the longing embedded in the familiar narrative of love and separation (speaker pining away for his Acadian sweetheart), the swift sensory engagement, the economical and vivid images of nature, or the mysteriousness of it all, the lyrics were appealing. The kids' devotion to the song was so intense that it migrated from our road trips to their bedtimes, when they insisted that one of us sing it after reading to them:

> There's a lost river that flows
> In a valley where no one goes,
> Where the wild water's rush
> Rumbles deep in the hush.
>
> Gone far from there now,
> Lord I'll be back somehow
> To where the lost river winds
> In the shadow of the pines.

Somewhere in that intermixed experience of the car rides, the singing, and our kids' attachment to the place itself, the East Middlebury River became the Lost River. Then it was elongated to the Lost River That Floats, because they had improvised the last word. With this personalized traction in their imaginations, that body of water's place in the family mythology was guaranteed but also imbued, for me, with some wistfulness, even sadness:

> Now everybody knows
> Where that lost river flows
> It's some place he's lost
> Behind bridges that he's crossed
>
> He'd like to return
> But his bridges are all burned
> And he's much too far down
> To return to higher ground

A perennial student of the bigger picture, Gwen had always advised me to enjoy the kids while they were still young, because that window would close before I knew it. And now that time is here, for both of us. She was right: I should have done more instead of making excuses about work and other obligations. Living and teaching at boarding schools, however, tends to draw you away from your family even if they are right there with you living through it all. Recently, I was in California, on sabbatical, visiting my son and his fiancée, reporting back to Gwen on the phone about how they were faring in San Diego. And she brought it up again, but this time both of us were casualties. Though she was happy that one of us, at least, was out there connecting with one of our kids, she ended the conversation by saying, "Is this what it comes down to? You spend a huge portion of your life devoting everything you have to them [your kids] and then they just *disappear*?" I know we're not the first parents who've felt the confusing, bittersweet freedom of the empty nest, and her frustration was also compounded by being home alone, having to work while I gallivanted westward. But the cliché of a postfledged domestic space is sobering once you're in it. The euphoria of having sent off our last college tuition payment was slowly being eroded by a kind of desolation that reminded us how profound the energy of the full tribe had been, how we had depended on it, and, in my case, taken it for granted while it was being borne away.

Through the end of the past century and into the new one, this age of automotive audio progress (a family listening to or singing along with music on a long drive) also became a cliché. The physical act of battling for radio stations graduated to the insertion of some medium into a player, then evolved into whoever's arms were closest to the auxiliary cable and its jack, and now, I imagine, the prevailing DJ is that individual who dominates the Bluetooth queue, battling for wireless connectivity.

Our brand-new 1970 Chevy Impala was a cathedral. My sisters and I knew this when we first climbed through its massive doors and were transported by its quadraphonic speakers. The shoebox rattling with 8-track tapes, however, always stayed in the front seat wedged between our parents. It could hold about five or six, since each was the size of a chunky paperback, so the selection was thin. We didn't get to choose necessarily, but I admire my dad's attempts to make it seem that we did have a say in the matter. "How about some Harry Belafonte?!!" he'd offer contagiously, even if we had already betrayed our desire for the soundtrack to Carol Reed's film version of *Oliver!* My sisters' own library of two tapes, *The Greatest Hits of Blood, Sweat, and Tears* and Iron Butterfly's *In-A-Gadda-Da-Vida,* was nothing more than symbolic luggage and didn't stand a chance. As corny, dated, or just plain awful as some of my parents' music might have been, the snippets rear up even now in moments when I am least prepared. My father's been dead more than twenty years, but I can't separate any of those tunes from the idea of my family being together, the dog, also long gone, snoring away across our laps as we rose and fell over the Throgg's Neck Bridge in the middle of the night on our way toward the Long Island Expressway, the strings of *Mantovani and His Orchestra's* version of "Charmaine" transporting us like a magic galleon on a tide of high-fructose corn syrup.

Like my own kids, my father, too, had a knack for renaming and customizing landmarks and places on our vacations. The islands where we camped in the Narrows of Lake George were originally derived from characters in James Fenimore Cooper's *Leatherstocking Tales,* so they had their own built-in aura of romance and adventure. But we never knew the real name of his favorite island, a chunk of bald rock with one scraggly clump of stunted pines, about an hour's paddle from our campsite on Uncas Island. We ventured there on calmer days to swim, have lunch, and collect firewood on the wilderness mainland across the strait. And similar to my own family's experience with the Lost River, we never had to share it with anyone. My dad was emboldened to claim it for our own and so he called it Loverly Island — appropriated from the *My Fair Lady* soundtrack's cockney paean that had been pummeling us for a few years. I don't really like musicals, and yet a half-century later that melody is insuppressible.

My wife told me a story about taking our kids on a picnic across the Middlebury Gap — on the other side of the Green Mountains — to the Hancock Branch of the White River and its star feature, Texas Falls. I was in classes that day but had been to the spot many times. They were eating lunch and dipping their feet in the tame segment just above the precautionary handrails, fences, and warning signs where the stream is funneled into a steep, narrow gorge that resolves in a dramatic waterfall and pool, then back into a roaring cascade. My son Jake's new sandals — hi-tech, glorified flip-flops, designed for walking on streambeds and rocky beaches — had just appeared on the market. He was proud of them, and, I'm certain, was fantasizing more ambitious forays, deeper explorations up The Lost River That Floats. Gwen remembers being hyperalert about how close the kids ventured out into the stream, which twenty yards from their picnic was a churning, unforgiving torrent. While Jake was dipping his feet into an eddy, one of his Tevas slipped off and was briskly sucked out into the main current. "My sandal!" he screamed. "Mom! Get my sandal! It's getting away!" She and a friend raced along the banks trying to grab it, but it was too late as the little rubber shoe accelerated, the reds and purples of its nylon webbing sailing through the ravine and disappearing over the falls into irrevocability.

Jake was pretty broken up. But Gwen's genius was this: after consoling him, she said, "Well, might as well chuck the other one in, too. It's not going to do you much good!" The scandalous nature of this green light, of actually getting to toss his shoe into a river deliberately—without getting in trouble—seemed to soften the tragedy. "Plus . . . ," she said, "who knows? It might just meet up again someday with its buddy." He carefully undid the Velcro on the remaining sandal and, to his sisters' disbelief, envy, and horror, flung it in with glee but also, I believe, with a sincere belief in a reunion downstream.

WAVE OF THE DAY

I didn't get to say goodbye to Andy because I was surfing. It was one of those October swells we long for in coastal New Hampshire: summer weather, but leaves fully engaged in the chromatic circus, the wind behaving itself. The last session without booties or gloves, gorging on head-high mana from some tropical tantrum on its way to Nova Scotia. Earlier that week I'd learned that Andy was not doing well. His wife Jan's response to our dinner invitation was not encouraging. He was going through a particularly bad patch; the new treatment focused on his brain was throwing him for a loop. She was trying to tell us something, but I was still fighting it, grown comfortable with his pattern of rebounding so many times over the past six years. We had always managed to land in the sweet spots, those pockets of euphoric energy just after he'd climbed from the darkest troughs. Playing guitars, dusting off a big Aussie Shiraz from his basement, cracking a growler of local IPA, checking out some live music in Boston, or heading up to Maine for a friend's gallery opening. It seemed like the ride would go on forever.

When I dragged the piss-steeped neoprene enveloping my trunk from the shallows after four hours, I could tell my left knee was going to pay for it. Worth it, though, because I'd nabbed the caboose of a gorgeous set while the other surfers were hustling back to the lineup or wooing a deserved thumping on the inside trying to milk one more section. It was a fluke. I'd caught the wave too late for my ability but made the drop anyway, then salvaged speed by staying high after a quick turn, which on my 9'0 is behavior that usually guarantees a flamboyant cartwheel over the nose. The wave walled up quickly and maintained its propulsive steepness for the duration. (Fluke #2: it did so against regional odds.) Because I'd gone left, I was able to skim around the bar then straighten out into a gulley where the wave sank like a tent suddenly robbed of its poles. Two strokes after going horizontal, I swung off up to my calves before the fin bit bottom. The entire sequence connected, which almost never happens to me on my final run because I always go past my limit, too burnt to scratch with authority or spring confidently, to put myself where I need to be. Which is the most unsatisfying way to end a session — that exhausted crawl of shame — having to paddle through the zone where you should be perched in regal denouement.

Back in my truck, changed and packed to go, I checked my messages. A few missed calls and a voicemail from Andy's brother Peter. But from Andy's phone.

Surfers, especially, can relate to this moment of reentry and reconnection to the world we've ditched for a few hours of self-gratification. The first thing you do is fire up your device expecting to discover a range of demands: an emergency, maybe an errand as simple as picking up another can of diced tomatoes on your way home. Maybe there's been a change in the evening's plans, or, in my case, a calendar reminder that I've missed another faculty meeting, a conference with a student. There's always an accompanying tinge of adolescent anxiety, some tenacious residue of Catholic guilt. *Am I in trouble?*

In his message, between sighs of exhaustion and authentic surrender, Peter explained that Andy was "winding down" and that if I wanted to say anything to him, now was the time. There was the slim chance he might hear me, even comprehend. He was past the ability to respond, though. Peter had left the message only thirty minutes before. I looked up from my phone with defeated optimism and out through the windshield at the lone McIntosh snugged against my friend Matt's mother's house. It embodies what Keats describes as Autumn's ability "to bend with apples the moss'd cottage-trees." Bizarre to see a thing like this thriving in a seaside suburban development, half a block away from arid dunes, their punished *Rosa rugosa,* beachgrass. I've been parking in this gravel driveway for more than a decade — a gift in a town with very little public parking in back of its mile-long beach — and up until this year, the tree has always been laden.

Salt air must boost its immunities, because I've never seen a tree that hasn't been drenched in pesticide, inoculated, or pampered bear so much fruit. How I savored the postsurf bonus of standing on my truck's bumper to pluck a few shining, perfect specimens before driving back inland to Exeter. They don't even need to be washed, and I imagine I can taste the ocean on their skin while I navigate the antithetical confectionary haze of fried dough, dodging packs of jaywalking pedestrians at Hampton Beach on my way home. On that balmy October afternoon, however, the tree offered nothing but a few sad ornaments twitching in the breeze like scabbed, deformed coin purses. Another fitting emblem of 2020—something else I had taken for granted. I sped out of the driveway in Seabrook and headed up the coast to the parking lot at Little Boar's Head to call Andy and diminish the possibility of interruption. To do it while looking straight at the ocean, a vista that might make the situation more bearable. The enduring contradiction: seeking solace in a panorama of oblivion when existentially it should scare the shit out of us.

Andy was not a surfer. He'd tried it with his son and confessed it wasn't his thing. But he did just about everything else: climbing, telemark skiing, long-distance cross-country skiing, mountain biking, trekking, road cycling, open-water sailing (flirting with circumnavigation more than once). This was all before he was diagnosed, which is to say that he was the sort of person who didn't need a terminal illness to nudge him deeper into a full life. There was an inspiring article written about him in the *New York Times* while he was still undergoing gene therapy for his type of nonsmoker's stage IV lung cancer. The piece spotlighted the break-through therapy at Mass General Hospital, but in the context of Andy's lifestyle, which in this instance involved climbing in Nepal while the symptoms were at bay:

> At the altitude he reached, there's 70 percent less air pressure than at sea level to push air into the lungs. Breathing is hard for the fittest climbers. There was no data on what the high altitude would do to an advanced lung cancer patient: None were found to have tried.... "It's a remarkable achievement," Dr. Neilan said. "My colleagues are flabbergasted."

Flabbergasted — the perfect word to capture the state to which Andy relegated me many times. Especially when his emails with the subject "HOMEWORK" would appear in my inbox with a harrowing chain of PDFs attached — guitar chord melody solos for Steely Dan tunes like "Doctor Wu" and "Deacon Blues," or the complicated, poignant acoustic piece called "40's" from virtuoso Julian Lage's acoustic album *World's Fair*. He was voracious. And a pain in the ass. "I'll see what I can do," I'd respond, while really wanting to say, "Are you fucking kidding me? It's the end of the term! I have papers to grade!" Andy had retired from EBSCO (the pioneering database/archive service), working with libraries, newspapers, and magazines when they were just starting to go digital. However, his demands were never taunts, just earnest invitations to cash in experientially on our shared musical tastes while we were able. I was quick with the excuses.

He was the initiator usually, a charger when it came to managing the logistics of seeing our favorite guitarists live. He set the bar high as the architect of our first foray in the mid-1980s to check out the mythic Chilean band Inti-Illimani, fronted by John Williams and Paco Peña. There were a few times when I really did try to step up, determined not to legitimize my reputation as a lazy sociopath. Once, I'd jumped on snagging tickets to see Bill Frisell in Cambridge months in advance, printed them, watched the weeks peel away from the calendar, gloated. The night before the show, I emailed a reminder and to figure out who was driving, if beers and dinner would happen before or after, etc. He got back to me the next morning saying he was absolutely pumped for the show. But couldn't make it. He was hauled up in Madagascar, getting some repairs done before the next leg of the voyage — sailing around the horn to Argentina.

One afternoon before the illness, after a night of figuring out tunes by Richard Thompson and Quincy Jones while stuffing ourselves with flatbreads from his domed outdoor oven (he was a cook, too), Andy appeared at our door in the full battle array of cycling gear. "Hey, I figured you'd be needing this," he said, reaching around to pull my wallet from one of the sweat-soaked back pouches of his shirt. "Wish I could stay, but I'm losing light." Without even taking off helmet, gloves, or glasses, he strode to the water cooler, refilled his bottles, and was gone. For a biker, it's almost forty serpentine miles — one way — from Ipswich, Massachusetts to Exeter, New Hampshire.

Of course, the phone kept ringing every time I called from the parking lot, watching a few kids skate the short-lived, humpy peak along the tombolo at Plaice Cove. No answer, just a recording of Andy's curt, healthy, upbeat voice. I gave up after fifteen minutes and began to situate myself in the reality I suspected was gaining definition on the other side. If only I had bailed an hour earlier. I'd gotten my fill, but I chose to stay in; I'd deprived both of us of "closure." This is a terrible, corporate, or clinical way of thinking. It flies in the face of the dynamic to which you must surrender when you start down the trail to a river with a rigged fly rod quivering at your side, when you clamber out of the dinghy and swing your foot over a sailboat's gunwale, or when you shove the freshly waxed board ahead into the wash before mounting up. A bargain Andy understood well. And, yes, he died at some point between the last half-hour of my session and when I pulled into that lot, and the tide pushed in, and the cross-shore slowly began to hack away at any promising texture out there.

Recently, I had committed to memorizing James Dickey's poem "At Darien Bridge," and the last stanzas were looping in my head as I played with the truck's emergency brake. The poem is a lyrical origami with narrative aspirations, the speaker conjuring a childhood memory of watching convicts build a bridge then folding its central image into his desire to be liberated from the adult trials of marriage, getting old, mortality. Awash with longing, he wants

> . . . to believe again
> That they worked on the ocean to give it
>
> The unchanging, hopeless look
> Out of which all miracles leap.

Later that same night, Dave Robinson, one of two Daves with me out there in the water that day, texted me:

I saw you get that bomber of a left for your last wave. I had to duck dive on the inside as you dropped in. When I came up you were still going. Possible wave of the day. Nice. Always good surfing with you.

> *Likewise. It was a fun last wave . . . especially since I was almost out of gas. I think that was the last day of summer. End of 3/2 weather. Hope to see you again out there soon.*

I was duck diving with like 5 guys and all were envious of that one. Late last day of summer for sure. You rode it for over 200 yards.

His characterization of the distance travelled might have been a reach, but I was happy to get the message. Old-school validation sans GoPro or drone footage. I already knew Andy was gone at that point but went along, didn't sandbag or argue with his exaggeration. Even so, I could feel the pull of competing demands, the compromised, unintentionally transactional nature of the whole day. Dave hadn't known about Andy, and though his recap of the ride came with a sting, I realized I was miserable because I was ignoring Andy's example. That same evening, in her lucid, generous, no-bullshit way, Andy's wife, Jan, texted me to tell me that she was sorry I'd missed him, but it was exactly what he would have wanted. She was right. I believed her. Though I had to plug it into a different rubric from the one with which I processed his excuse of fixing a rudder somewhere off the coast of East Africa and skipping out on a concert in another hemisphere.

The "miracle" in Dickey's "At Darien Bridge" arrives in the form of a gull that intersects with a convict's raised hammer at the exact instant it catches the sun's reflection. In the child's imagination, it had seemed that the bird was created in that flash. What were the odds of that confluence? I wasn't expecting anything as sublime while staring over the dashboard at the Atlantic listening to Andy's brother's sad message. But it was definitely where I needed to be to sort out my guilt and shock. To ponder the words I never said, what I'd hoped and dreaded to whisper into my phone. Something that would ricochet between a few cellular towers and satellites before seeping from another phone held to a dying person's ear. A few words, which if they were actually heard would have been even more ephemeral because the recipient would be gone forever very soon. It's easier to make it about ourselves and our own shortcomings than to confront the profundity of the loss itself. And by their nature, these moments of goodbye are excruciating and embarrassing because they seem like the verbal equivalent of throwing a handful of dirt onto a casket as it's still being conveyed up the steps into the church.

Late that night in our darkening living room, after my wife and I sat confronting the weight and starkness of Andy's departure, after the kind and unrelated texts from Jan and Dave had rolled in, I kept thinking about what I would have said if I'd gotten through to him. Even though I'd known deep down while brooding in my truck that any occasion for miracles had passed, I decided that it would not have been an apology but, rather, a concise summary of what I'd been doing *instead.* The bald, glorious truth about why I wasn't able to be there while he was still breathing. To whom would I have been speaking? It would have been impossible to discern. Certainly, I would have admitted to being disappointed by the apples' absence but wouldn't have been coy about my exhilaration. I had been surfing, after all. Had crossed paths, connected with a wave everyone else had missed. After taking a chance in a volatile space, I was lucky enough to be borne almost all the way to shore. From the capricious demands of buoyancy and motion to reliable sand, from one season to the next.

CODA

MEMORY AND THE FIRST COAST: CALIFORNIA REVISITED

> Although the ready memory is a great blessing
> to its possessor, the vaguer memory of a subject,
> of having once had to do with it, of its neigh-
> borhood, and of where we may go to recover it
> again, constitutes in most men and women the
> chief fruit of their education.
>
> — *William James*

> Much of the California landscape has tended to
> present itself as metaphor, even as litany.
>
> — *Joan Didion*

1.

Early in the autumn before Obama was elected for his first term, I was asked by a Los Angeles–based magazine to write an article about New Hampshire. The goal, according to the editor, was to offer the readership a personal impression of the state, one that might push beyond the cacophony of the primary season's political circus. I wrote about surfing. At the time, I had been living and teaching in the southeastern corner of the Granite State for more than a decade. The request had come out of the blue, and it compelled a reckoning; though I was born in California, and the first ocean to pool around and retreat from my legs was the Pacific, I had gained proficiency in the waves of New York and New England. I'm pushing sixty now, but it's only in the past twelve years that I've been able to make some progress understanding my relationship with my birth state. The gravity of *Heimat* (home) is nagging, irresistible, especially when surfing is tugging at the compass needle. But I also felt like a fraud in both directions, neither a true Californian nor a craggy New Hampshire-ite, the least qualified person to engineer a bridge between the two states.

Because we moved back East when I was a toddler, the California coast had been obscured by yearning, imagination, and tantalizingly vague memories. It wasn't until long after eating sand during adolescent summers bodysurfing at Flying Point Beach on the South Fork of Long Island, then toying with a board naïvely (suicidally) during my twenties in nor'easter leftovers unspooling around the headlands of Gloucester and Rockport, that I was able to find a way back. Especially after I had settled into my fate with the compressed and fickle bounty of New Hampshire's tiny seacoast twenty-five years ago, which provided the comparative grist to make any pilgrimages to California more meaningful.

As a teen in the mid-'70s on the North Shore

of Massachusetts, I was committed to the fantasy of waves, my adolescent imagination goaded by an absurd subscription to *Surfer* magazine, my own airbrushed idea of it all. All the fits and starts of physical flirtation with the sport—including an undeserved, neglected *Natural Art* thruster on sawhorses in my parents' dirt floor basement—deferred to a teaching career, marriage, family, graduate school, writing. Which is probably why—beyond health insurance and a retirement plan—I have a wife and kids who still like me, a few admirable publications, a job that often kicks my ass. True, I threw away the opportunity to hone wave-riding skills when my body was better inclined, my reflexes and agility at their peak. However, since writing that article—a paean to salt marshes, migrating sea ducks, frozen faces, Quebecois-free mid-February lineups—I've made it my business to reconcile a life in the Northeast with the blurry fluke of occidental origins.

Photos and mementos from the time my family lived in California seem a record of some-one else's past. They've slowly surrendered themselves to open interpretation as those who took or collected them grew older, drifted apart, or died, and the quorum that guaranteed some semblance of contextual meaning dissolved. Natural objects, because of their timelessness, almost seem emancipated from the family narrative: giant pine cones, petrified wood. And abalone shells. My mother dusted around the latter: iridescent *oréjas de mar* cocked attentively at our family's routines and antics from their perches among other souvenirs. New England and Long Island were reinforced throughout my childhood beach walks, their evidence rearing up at every turn in real time: the exposed tangerine hallways of busted whelks, quahogs' lavender tattoos. But California, hidden deep inside its associated mollusk, was always frustratingly just beyond my memory's grasp, the idea of it somewhere in the rose-green, molten-pearl interior and name — *abalone* — which I carried in my imagination like stemware from decade to decade, state to state.

2.

The hinge in the middle of the twentieth century, when my parents moved to Woodland Hills from Stony Brook, seems a time when one group of Americans was grasping desperately at the future and the past simultaneously, trying to become something new without completely abandoning what they imagined their heritage to be. After emerging from two wars they were torn between the Colonial and the Cosmic, the Home Front and the Frontier. Having survived the potential of losing everything, my parents' generation was especially souvenir and knick-knack crazy, dogged perhaps by the ghost of that Depression-era pack-rat impulse to hoard the material proof of experience because the worst might still be around the corner. This tension permeated the living room in each of my childhood houses, but especially my father's study with its matted photos of the helicopter and jet engines he designed, the mounted length of barbed wire he'd clipped after he had been liberated from a German prison camp.

Up on our shelves and mantels, Churchill's *History of World War II* and pewter mugs duked it out with Mexican pottery and a miniature replica of a mission bell. On our walls, Anglophilic prints of thatched Tudor cottages reached an uneasy truce with a series of eight framed Remington portraits of characters on horseback. Like beleaguered boxers in separate corners, a richly colored serape and an off-white Irish knit shawl were draped over the opposing arms of our couch.

My father's experience as a POW from 1944-45 made him less content to return and settle in his hometown of Flushing. Ambition and cultural boundaries seemed entirely mutable. A B-17 copilot, he was one of the lucky who returned relatively healthy from WWII, an experience that made him comfortable with mobility, committed (responsibly) to getting the most out of his life instead of withdrawing from it or spinning his wheels in the memory of it. Imagine the Weimar intellectuals and company—Brecht, Mann, Adorno—in *Los Angeles*, having fled Germany a few years before my father had begun bombing the same regime that had forced them into exile—a regime that would eventually imprison him only so that he could be freed to wind up in Southern California too, refining the very instruments he himself had piloted or dropped. If ever there were proof of the Modern Age's helical crisis, it would have to be European intellectuals seeking refuge in the very city that spawned the military industrial complex during WWII and then the death factories of Cold War deterrence. Where I was born and didn't learn to surf.

It has been said many times in my family that when my father left Grumman on Long Island to take the job at Marquardt Aircraft in Van Nuys, most of my mother's family embarked on a campaign of passive-aggressive marginalization that would last until my family's return East six years later (and beyond, for some of them). The sons and daughters of German and Czech immigrants who had climbed their way to Garfield, New Jersey, out of Manhattan's Lower East Side tenements, these stocky relatives considered any excursion beyond the Passaic River a betrayal.

W. H. Auden's essay "The West from the Air" captures the spirit of that time from a bewildered Old World perspective. One can picture the poet of divided national loyalties, his wrinkled, devastated face pressed against the porthole of a Boeing 707 as he contemplated the mythic American landscape and Americans themselves:

> In a land which is fully settled, most men must accept their local environment or try to change it by political means; only the exceptionally gifted or adventurous can leave to seek his fortune elsewhere. In America, on the other hand, to move on and make a fresh start

somewhere else is still the normal reaction to dissatisfaction or failure. Such social fluidity has important psychological effects. Since movement involves breaking social and personal ties, the habit creates an attitude towards personal relationships in which impermanence is taken for granted.

3.

When my three kids were little, they were perplexed after I told them I had been born in the San Fernando Valley. They had always considered California an exotic place and were incapable of disassociating my family or me from the New England coast. "No, you *weren't!*" they cried, as if I'd told them I'd come from Venus. "It's true," I said. "I thought you knew." This knowledge hurled them through their teens slightly appalled. They'd grown up in Massachusetts and New Hampshire, but the Golden State had been seeping into their imaginations, so their mockery of this biographical quirk was laced with a little jealousy. They wanted to go there badly, and until we finally took them there, their excited confusion generated an evolving stream of abuse; everything I wore or did was viewed through a bright, new lens of my preposterous birth on the West Coast. I was a poser. My flip-flops had never been on their radar, but now my son and daughters looked down at my feet in the kitchen, snorted, and shook their heads. "Dad, those are *sooooo Californiaaaah.*" Even though I had started surfing in my late teens, only to put it on hold for their benefit, they were suddenly crowing things like, "Dad surfs because he thinks he's from California!"

They're adults now, but subtle indignation and doubt endure in the hierarchy, even though two of them have moved there: my daughter, Madeleine, San Francisco to work at the California Academy of Sciences, and my son, Jake, an avid surfer himself, to a PR job in San Diego from Boston five years ago. Barely thirty, he even did a stint as the director of Surfrider San Diego's executive board. Needless to say, he has garnered serious cred in our family, exponentially more than the dude who was born there. Especially because he overturned the platitude on which I've relied for an excuse for most of my life: he's a responsible, happily married charger with lucrative professional ambition — and quiver — intact. Plus, a kid on the way.

On a visit to see Jake and his then-fiancée during their first year on the West Coast, I brought a longboard along to a family outing at Sunset Cliffs. I was the only one interested in getting in the water. They'd spread their towels and started pillaging the cooler's IPAs while I began the paddle out to the sparsely populated lineup, waist-high and crumbly because of the building afternoon onshore. But once in a while a reasonably clean wedge would stand up on the reef and make it pathetically worthwhile. I dicked around for about forty-five minutes until the tide filled in, and the peak deflated to an innocuous whitecapped bump. When I waded out of the shallows toward them, my son came to the water's edge and congratulated me. "Your last drop was great," he said hesitantly. "You almost looked as if you knew what you were doing."

4.

Harmonious shells that whisper
forever in our ears,
The world that you inhabit
has not yet been created.

— Kathleen Raine

Perhaps I was remembering the glorious nacre
Of the home I was introduced to
When first I looked about me

And which protected me in ways
I did not recognize.

— Peter Porter

Almost 160 years ago, William Henry Brewer, a Yale graduate and leader of an expedition for the California Geological Expedition, wrote the following in a letter to his brother back East: "We wandered along the beach and picked up a few shells, some of great beauty." Though he doesn't name them, we can only guess that they were most likely abalones. How abundant they must have been, which is not the case anymore, south of San Francisco anyway. Brewer's frankness, his willingness to veer from his official duties with the assessment of terrain to celebrate this trivial detail, is a great relief. I'm not the only one throughout history seduced by the remnants of these creatures, whether they're glinting from the shelves of my past, from my wife's earlobes, or the headstocks and rosettes of my guitars.

In the summer of 2005, we caved and took our kids to California. In the foothills of Big Sur, we were making our way through sheets of fog past mossy oaks toward the musk of the ocean at San Simeon State Park. Down among the rocks, my daughter Madeleine began her search for shells in earnest before the tide crept in to fill the sandy webs. On that trip she was thirteen and determined to find an abalone, even a splinter of one. The nuanced summer swell was lifting and dropping the kelp beds. When she began to lose interest, I stayed down below the waterline, sidestepping the onrushing wavelets, scouring the meager jetsam with what little time remained. I'd provoked her enthusiasm, reminiscing about my own excitement when I had scrambled to pick up shards on the beach at Cayucos twenty-six years earlier, that summer after my sophomore year in college, which I'd spent with my sister who had moved there to teach. Her boyfriend, a local, had even taken me for a humiliating but memorable flail in the mushburgers at Morro Bay's southern jetty. The loaner was a purple, single-fin swallowtail Lightning Bolt. I couldn't surf, but I could classify the gear.

The Chumash people have a myth, a macabre and beautiful evocation about the journey to the afterlife that features landmarks, genuine geographical references, specific flora and fauna. Point Conception (*Humqaq*) is the gateway to *Similaqsa,* the Land of the Dead, a native Californian version of the Romans' Mount Avernus:

> Once past the clashing rocks the soul comes to a place where there are two gigantic *qaq* (ravens) perched on each side of the trail, who each peck out an eye as the soul goes by. But there are many poppies growing there in the ravine and the soul quickly picks two of these and inserts them in each eye socket and so is able to see again immediately. When the soul finally gets to *Similaqsa* it is given eyes made of blue abalone. (Hicks et al., *The Literature of California*)

When I finally found the shell at San Simeon, I mistook it for the edge of an antique coin or can lid. A delicate tugging of its rim from the gravelly sand revealed an abalone three inches in diameter and intact, the nascent glimmer of color brewing in its immature, silver hollow. I showed it to my daughter, and we stood around it as we might the most fragile ember. It had been gnawed clean, uncharacteristically gently, but whatever its demise, spared in the blender of surf and predation to wind up half-buried in a fragile pocket between two enormous weed-covered boulders. Submerged most of the day, this little eye, staring from the gray sand, misplaced, made available so that it could be picked up by some soul wandering through.

5.

> For an extremely large percentage of the history of the world, there was no California. That is, according to present theory. I don't mean to suggest that California was underwater and has since come up. I mean to say that of the varied terranes and physiographic provinces that we now call California nothing whatever was there. The continent ended far to the east, the continental shelf as well. . . . Then, a piece at a time — according to present theory — parts began to assemble.
>
> — *John McPhee*

> What strange and unlikely things are washed up on the shore of time.
>
> — *William Maxwell*

The torso of my wetsuit is draped across my shoulders, and because the bike is too small, I worry that the flapping legs will be eaten by the spokes. It's 5:30 a.m., but I'm late, pedaling through the dark, deserted streets of Ocean Beach, San Diego, on the rusty vehicle I prized out of the storage closet of my short-term lease. Signs emerge in the mist, tacked to fences and tree trunks: NEIGHBORHOODS ARE FOR NEIGHBORS: STOP VACATION RENTALS.

When I skid into my son's front yard, his neighbors, who had invited me to come along for a butt-crack-of-dawn session, are already out in front of the house, waxing boards, firing up their first cigarettes and Tecates of the day. Having grown up southeast of LA, Adam manages an In-N-Out Burger restaurant east of OB, and his fellow migrant and high school buddy Ryan is a security guard at Target. They tried out college for a little while, moved to the coast, started families, and never looked back. In a way, the intrastate vision quest can be as severe as the transcontinental version.

Cash, the freelance pool cleaner, had been the expedition's most enthusiastic backer at my son's cookout the night before, texted me earlier to apologize for being "way hung over." He is not among us in the hunkering morning damp of the marine layer. Drowsy greetings, groggy banter, cheap shots at the absentee, who a few years later will literally cash in on growing and selling to dispensaries once weed is legal.

Just back from walking his dog, my son puts on a good face. With two months to go before his fourth ACL (N'Gor, Senegal) surgery heals, he regards us wistfully as we slog away up the block toward the cliffs. My frustration at his not being able to join us is distracting. After all, he's the one who hazed me back into surfing again when he was twelve, so it stands to reason that he should preside over this consummation, this partial closing of the loop. It's not until we're making our way along the path, and I'm scrambling to keep up with two guys half my age that I am simultaneously disoriented and grounded by the realization that this is the first birthday I've celebrated in California since the second year of my life, fifty-five years ago.

I try to follow Adam's black buzz cut as he and Ryan scamper like marmots over and between the slick ledges near the tide line. They pivot, pause, then circle back to wait for me, chippy boards snugged under their arms like oversized clipboards. Finally, I arrive at the base of the cliff having scuffed and slid down an adjacent dusty embankment with a nine-and-a-half-foot log wavering above my head. And when I lower the board to them before jumping from the last shelf, they are practically dancing in place, anxious to reach the break before the crowd. Adam is hopping up and down when he hands my longboard back to me. But before I can thank them for their patience with the elderly, they vanish around the next headland, north, toward the pier, which was not the original plan.

I cannot move, cannot wrench my concentration from an advancing, glassy set of head-high waves. I've ventured West from New England more than a few times to surf over the past half-century, but there's something unnerving in the diminishment I feel standing at the cliff base, solitary at this juncture of physical environment, action, and time. Forty yards out, a pod of dolphins emerges in protracted, synchronized arcs, reentering their reflections just as slowly.

It's chilly down here, like being at the bottom of a recently drained well that could refill at any moment. And still too early for the sun to bore a hole through the marine layer. I'm not wearing booties. A godsend. The water back home in New Hampshire this time of year, early spring, is still in the high thirties/low forties. Having been sealed up all winter, my bare feet glow against the dark, wet stone. Below the black wetsuit's shins, they seem severed, independent from the rest of my legs. I am palpably aware of my toes wrapping the solidity of the continent's edge, though there's ominous proof of erosion all around, not to mention the futile schemes above, slapdash sculptural masonry, environmentally friendly sprayed erodible concrete, and incongruous imported rubble netted with chain-link intended for shoring up against the inevitable.

I've told neither Adam nor Ryan about my birthday, this weirdly satisfying but unnerving anniversary. And I understand completely that the graphite-jade walls slapping and exploding below aren't doing so in celebratory response to any sort of homecoming. If bodies of water are like wine, this one, the Pacific, has a strange hue, a different nose. Decay comes to mind, fishiness infused with something darker that emanates from a depth more ancient than that to which I'm accustomed. *This* Pacific is less kind than the ocean I've studied in a particular black-and-white photograph of my six- and eight-year-old sisters holding my hand in the diffuse, sun-injected fog at Zuma Beach. *That* ocean glows behind us, swirls luminously around our ankles.

Isn't the optimism embedded in nostalgia derived from a heightened awareness of mortality? Does it really matter which ocean was the first I touched, or which seems older?

My grandparents' home on Long Island was where I placed my first committed step on my second coast after our move back across the country. I was standing on the front threshold, peering through the house's tunnel at Wooley Pond, the cove glimmering in the opposite door frame. I ran toward it, past everyone who was there to greet the Golden Child. Through the living room, around my grandfather's rolltop desk, into the kitchen, and out the back screen door to take a header off the stoop onto the burnt summer lawn where I lay bawling until someone came out to pick me up, dust me off, and guide me to the water's edge. It must have been like passing from one dimension to another, to scramble ecstatically from the obscurity of my cryptic memories of a half-imagined early childhood on the Pacific to Atlantic clarity and the life that is still going on.

The tide has pushed in almost as far as it can. I time my sprint to higher ground before the whitewater rushes to submerge the path that my companions took, which seemed safe and dry moments before. On my vacations and sabbaticals over the next few years I will surf with this evolving crew more times than I can count. My son will return to the waves and we'll hit more than a dozen breaks between San Onofre and Rosarito. New phone numbers will appear in the mix as the group changes, people move away, pilgrims arrive. Text flurries will consistently debate the perennial agendas of rendezvous, surf checks, the calculus of certain breaks, work schedules, sick babies, hangovers, wind. But they don't give a shit where I'm from, really, and make it pretty easy to slip back into the fold.

For now, I am still thinking about standing in the cliff shadow of a certain street's demise into the Pacific, the quirky go-to local break that the crew calls "Out Front." The ice plant blossoms are like garnets igniting the rim of sagging pavement. Both the weathered natural buttresses and fabricated ramparts converge into something that seems more like an ancient abbey, more compelling in its inscrutable but enduring ruin than the familiar history. The ocean takes another bite, insinuates itself a little farther inland, erasing as it goes. It is as if Adam and Ryan were never here at all, spectral guides who having inserted me deep into foreign territory have abandoned me to my own resources.

ORIGIN STORIES, THANKS

≈

I'm convinced that this is a far better book than it might have been in the hands of any other publisher, so I am indebted and entirely devoted to the crew at EastOver Press (Keith Pilapil Lesmeister, Denton Loving, Kelly March, and designer EK Larken) for bringing another of my projects to fruition, but especially to Walter Robinson, my principal editor whose patience, flexibility, exacting care, and humor helped guide these essays to clarity and concision. Other writers should be so fortunate. Special thanks to copy editor Louisa Castner for being a generous reader beyond her technical obligations (especially appreciating my '60s/'70s cultural references).

Work on this sequence of essays began in 2008, but it happened almost by accident, literally. I was in London, housesitting for a friend in Lewisham, and one morning, riding a bike to the National Maritime Museum in Greenwich, I was almost run over by a bus. The adrenaline was still vibrating through me when I got there, and perhaps being in this disoriented state while studying the museum's images and artifacts was what distracted me enough to convince myself that embarking on a prose project might be a good idea. The towering anchors propped outside the museum's entrance demanded something of everyone passing through, it seemed. Soon I was engrossed in one of the temporary exhibits, *By the Seaside*. I spent the afternoon browsing the permanent collections too: all those follies of explorers, sailors, and soldiers, fishermen in storms, civilians doing what they needed to survive. My imagination kept returning to that particular exhibit, though, and the museum's genius of gathering in its lens a nation's less formal—recreational—relationship to its coasts. I'd seen this sort of curatorial eye before, trained on California, but it turned out that for the sake of spurring my own writing I needed to peruse the cross sections of another country's awareness of its coast as a destination, the evolution of that awareness. Images from *By the Seaside* engendered or became entwined with my own insuppressible memories, a distraction that was so intense it eventually drove me out of the building. Passing the forlorn decorativeness of those sentry anchors on my exit, I knew that I was being nagged by a topic: water. My experiences with the element—in all their amateurish nonmilitary, nonmercantile, nonprofessional adventurism—demanded decoding, form, expression. When I remounted my bike, I knew, if only I could make it there alive, that I was going to start writing these essays as soon as I got back to the house in Lewisham.

I've been working on the book ever since that day at the museum almost fifteen years ago. So I need to thank my friends and colleagues at the American School in London, past and present (Miles Dunmore, Megan McGilchrist, Henry Millman, Stephan Potchatek, Holly vanderMolen, Kim Zeineddine), for what they initiated without knowing.

Thanks also to MacDowell for the residency during which I continued to ride the post-London surge—even though my fellowship there was predicated on poetry and sabotaged by an ice storm. And to the St. Botolph's Club Foundation Emerging Artist

Award for providing the means to bring the Lake District and the Cinque Terre (Cockermouth and Monterosso) into such close experiential proximity, which made all the difference.

I am especially grateful to novelist/story writer/brother-in-arms Paul Yoon for being the first to read these essays, to stoke the fire, but also for introducing me to *The Common* magazine. He had the audacity to nudge my work over the transom to Jen Acker and Liz Witte, whose friendship, support, and editorial grace gave me faith that this endeavor might someday grow to be a collection. It is quite an honor to have so much work in that unique publication—a desired coast, a home port (for my writing and my students) that appeared out of nowhere.

Humble, heartfelt thanks to fellow Exeter writers/musicians/colleagues/brothers-in-arts: Todd Hearon, Matt Miller, Willie Perdomo and Jon Sakata—for their friendship, example, encouragement, and belief.

I would like to thank Phillips Exeter Academy for supporting my sabbatical in California (2008), which after London was the next most important field work for this project. Thanks also to vintage neon photographer and perennial student of the West Coast, Steve Lewis, not only for his inspiring and propulsive imagery but also his guidance on what the school's initially skeptical administration dubbed the "Easy Rider" proposal, and for reintroducing me to the land/cityscape of my birth state (Safari Inn included). For California momentum throughout the years, I am also grateful for the hospitality, enthusiasm, and friendship of Alec

McShane, the Connor family, Andrew Lipsitz, and Kristin Hansen. And to my own children and their families, who, living there at critical junctures during the writing of this book, tolerated my freeloading.

Thanks (once again) to Chris and Deirdre Caldarone for the workspace of Crooked Lane (L'Atelier included), so essential in the final phase of writing this book. And to Arthur and Sarah Evans who generously surrender The Bunkhouse to me every summer.

Gratitude to the editors who believed in some of these essays enough to publish *and* improve them: Sven Birkerts, Bill Pierce, and David Ebenbach at *AGNI*; and Alex Wilson, Scott Hulet, and Whitman Bedwell at *The Surfer's Journal*.

Thanks and apologies to friends in the distant past and unnervingly close present, estranged or otherwise, who might recognize their embellished doppelgängers — named or not — thrashing, stroking through these waters. I hope that my reimagined renditions of our shared experiences come across as an act of love and not sociopathy.

I'd never read a nonfiction book about Long Island, specifically the South Fork, until Peter Matthiessen's *Men's Lives*. His approach to local natural history, to fleshing out a place, and crafting an elegy for the disappearance of a way of life has (since the arrival of the gorgeous hardcover in 1986) been an engine for *The Legible Element* before I was aware of it. Honoring the lives and legacies of commercial fishermen is not the purpose of my book, but Matthiessen's model provided a bearing for how my writing might apprehend — albeit in a less impeccably researched, less journalistic way — the ramifications of shifting demographics and economies, especially the development and destruction of a land-scape and environment that were so formative to me. Likewise, I can't stress enough the importance of Nabokov's spell, cast with his tribute to "unreal estate" — the loss of and exile from his family home, Vyra, in *Speak, Memory*. John Irving said in a recent interview on *CBS Sunday Morning*: "You don't get to choose your obsessions. Your obsessions choose you." The South Fork seems to have pointed its tine at me, coaxed by the implicit permission of Matthiessen's model. My grand-father's retirement from NYFD and migration in the 1950s to Southampton Shores afforded me the childhood that I'm still mining in my work; now I understand deeply that his choice was the start of another era, just another sociological wave whose culture and setting were part of a cycle, and which would also be replaced, devoured in their turn. Almost forty years after reading it for the first time, I now appreciate *Men's Lives* as an act of preservation, a poignant evocation and artistic documentary for some-thing Matthiessen sensed might soon be gone. This is the chance to acknowledge his invaluable, elegiac guide star.

ACKNOWLEDGEMENTS

≋

The Common
"Blaenavon," "Django: Elegies and Improvisations with Small Boats," "Looking for Ice," "Stepping Off: Confessions from the Littoral Zone"

Zócalo Public Square
"Live Free and Surf"

AGNI
"Fostered Alike by Beauty and by Fear: Wordsworth, Montale, and the Landscapes of Childhood," "The Legible Element: On Hopkins, Surfers, and the Selves of Waves," "The Retreats"

The Surfer's Journal
"Memory and the First Coast: California Revisited" and "The Legible Element"

The poem "Peconic" first appeared in *Hayden's Ferry Review* and was included in *Evidence of the Journey* (New York: Harmon Blunt, 2007).

SOURCES

≈≈≈

Wordsworth, William. *The Prelude*, Book IV ("Summer Vacation"), ll. 247–68. New York: Penguin Books, 1995 [1805].

"THE BLUE HOLE: A PREFACE"

Thomas, Edward. "The End of Winter." *The South Country*. Stanbridge, U.K.: Little Toller Books/Dovecote Press, 2009 [1909].

Maxwell, William. *So Long, See You Tomorrow*. Boston: David R. Godine, 1989.

Sebald, W. G. *The Rings of Saturn*. Trans. Michael Hulse. New York: New Directions, 1998.

Borges, Jorge Luis. *The Collected Fictions*. Trans. Andrew Hurley. New York: Penguin Putnam.

"STEPPING OFF: CONFESSIONS FROM THE LITTORAL ZONE"

Williamson, Alan. *Res Publica*. Chicago: University of Chicago Press, 1998.

Dunn, Stephen. *New and Selected Poems: 1974–1994*. New York: Norton, 1994.

"LOOKING FOR ICE"

Wordsworth, William. *The Prelude,* Book I, ll. 433–52. New York: Penguin Books, 1995 [1850].

Heaney, Seamus. *District and Circle*. New York: Farrar, Straus and Giroux, 2006.

Blunden, Edmund. "The Midnight Skaters." *Selected Poems*. Manchester, U.K.: Carcanet Press, 1993.

"Immersion Notes; or 'This Ain't Sea Hunt!'"

Beebe, William. *Half Mile Down*. New York: Harcourt, Brace, 1934.

DeWitt, Helen. *The Last Samurai*. New York: Talk Miramax/Hyperion, 2000.

"Django: Elegies and Improvisations with Small Boats"

Cikovsky, Nicolai. "The Inlet at Wooley Pond." Painting (oil on canvas), 1945. Parrish Art Museum/East End Stories. http://artists.parrishart.org/artwork/1098/

Reinhardt, Jean "Django": Some of the greatest living guitarists (young and old) are still adhering publicly to "gypsy jazz" as the name of this very specific and enduring genre, themselves of Roma or Sinti ancestry (Angelo Debarre, Stochelo Rosenberg, Joscho Stephan, etc.). I am adopting the phrase — as outmoded as it might be in some circles — in quotes in this essay out of respect for these musicians and their artistic community (and as someone who spends a lot of time with their websites, books, instructional and performance videos.)

"Shade of Thought, Grieving Arrow: On Patience, Pain, and the Mystery of Fishing"

Neruda, Pablo. "Ode to a Large Tuna in the Market." Trans. Robin Robertson. *POETRY* magazine, April 2007.

Wilbur, Richard. "Trolling for Blues." *New and Collected Poems*. New York: Harcourt, Brace, Jovanovich, 1988.

"The Legible Element: On Hopkins, Surfers, and the Selves of Waves"

Hopkins, Gerard Manley. *Gerard Manley Hopkins: The Major Works*. Ed. Catherine Phillips. New York: Oxford University Press, 2002.

Greenblatt, Stephen et al., eds. "Gerard Manley Hopkins." *Norton Anthology of English Literature*, 8th ed. Vol. 2. New York: Norton, 2006.

Bunting, Basil. *Complete Poems*. New York: New Directions, 2000.

Jeffers, Robinson. *Rock and Hawk: A Selection of Shorter Poems by Robinson Jeffers*. New York: Random House, 1987.

"Fostered Alike by Beauty and by Fear: Wordsworth, Montale, and the Landscapes of Childhood"

Stilgoe, John R. *A Shallow Water Dictionary*. New York: Princeton Architectural Press, 1996.

Montale, Eugenio. *Cuttlefish Bones*. Trans. William Arrowsmith. New York: Norton, 1994.

Wordsworth, William. *The Prelude*. New York: Penguin Books, 1995 [1850]

Smith, Dave. *The Roundhouse Voices*. New York: Harper and Row, 1985.

"The Retreats"

Justice, Donald. "Dance Lessons of the Thirties." *Collected Poems*. New York: Knopf, 2004.

Auden, W. H. "XXXIV (Between attention and attention)." *The English Auden: Poems, Essays and Dramatic Writings 1927–1939*. London: Faber and Faber, 1986.

Bate, W. Jackson. *John Keats*. Cambridge, Mass.: Harvard/Belknap, 1963.

"Bright Size Life"

Watson, Philip. *Bill Frisell, Beautiful Dreamer: The Guitarist Who Changed the Sound of American Music.* London: Faber & Faber, 2022.

"Lost River"

"Lost River." Nitty Gritty Dirt Band. *Will the Circle Be Unbroken, Vol. 2.* Universal, 1989.

"Wave of the Day"

Dickey, James. *Helmets.* Middletown, Conn.: Wesleyan University Press, 1964.

Balf, Todd. "When the Lung Cancer Patient Climbs Mountains." *New York Times,* January 4, 2018. https://www.nytimes.com/2018/01/04/well/live/when-the-lung-cancer-patient-climbs-mountains.html.

"Memory and the First Coast: California Revisited"

McPhee, John. *Assembling California.* New York: Farrar, Strauss and Giroux, 1993.

Maxwell, William. *So Long, See You Tomorrow.* Boston: David R. Godine, 1989.

James, William. "Talks to Teachers." In *Writings 1878–1899.* New York: Library of America, 1992.

Didion, Joan. *Where I Was From.* New York: Knopf, 2003.

Auden, W. H. *The Complete Works of W. H. Auden: 1949-1955.* Ed. Edward Mendelson. Princeton, N.J.: Princeton University Press, 2008.

Raine, Kathleen. "Shells." *Collected Poems.* Berkeley, Calif.: Counterpoint, 2001.

Porter, Peter. "Hermit Crab." *Times Literary Supplement*, February 10, 2012 (no. 5680).

Brewer, William Henry. *Up and Down California in 1860–1864*, 4th ed. Berkeley and Los Angeles: University of California Press, 2003.

Hicks, Jack et al., eds. *The Literature of California: Native American Beginnings to 1945*. Berkeley: University of California Press, 2000.

ABOUT THE AUTHOR

~~~

RALPH SNEEDEN'S poems and essays have appeared in  a broad range of magazines and literary publications including *AGNI, American Poetry Review, Harvard Review, The Common, Ploughshares, Kenyon Review, New England Review, The New Republic, Southwest Review, Southern Review,* and *The Surfer's Journal.* His work has also been featured multiple times on *Poetry Daily* and is included in *The Second Set,* a jazz poetry anthology edited by Yusef Komunyakaa and Sascha Feinstein. The title poem of his first book, *Evidence of the Journey* (Harmon Blunt Publishers, 2007), received the Friends of Literature Prize from *POETRY* magazine/Poetry Foundation. His most recent book, *Surface Fugue* (EastOver Press, 2021), received the Poetry Society of New Hampshire's Best Book of the Year award. Sneeden is also a recipient of fellowships from MacDowell, Teachers College–Columbia University, and the American School in London. He taught high school English for almost forty years and was most recently the B. Rodney Marriott Chair in the Humanities at Phillips Exeter Academy in New Hampshire, where he retired in 2022. Born in Los Angeles in 1960, Sneeden has spent most of his life in coastal New England, where he lives with his wife, Gwen, surfs year-round, and sails.

Printed in the USA
CPSIA information can be obtained
at www.ICGtesting.com
LVHW010402110823
754876LV00004B/447

9 781958 094280